OXFORD STUDIES IN AFRICAN AFFAIRS

General Editors
JOHN D. HARGREAVES *and* GEORGE SHEPPERSON

THE JAMAA AND
THE CHURCH

THE JAMAA AND THE CHURCH

A Bantu Catholic Movement in Zaïre

by

WILLY De CRAEMER

OXFORD
AT THE CLARENDON PRESS
1977

Oxford University Press, Walton Street, Oxford OX2 6DP

OXFORD LONDON GLASGOW NEW YORK
TORONTO MELBOURNE WELLINGTON CAPE TOWN
IBADAN NAIROBI DAR ES SALAAM LUSAKA ADDIS ABABA
KUALA LUMPUR SINGAPORE JAKARTA HONG KONG TOKYO
DELHI BOMBAY CALCUTTA MADRAS KARACHI

© *Oxford University Press 1977*

British Library Cataloguing in Publication Data
De Craemer, Willy
   The Jamaa and the Church.—(Oxford studies in African
affairs)
   1. Jamaa movement
   I. Title   II. Series
   301.5'8   BL2470.C6
   ISBN 0-19-822708-6

*Printed in Great Britain
at the University Press, Oxford
by Vivian Ridler
Printer to the University*

*To my father, Cyriel De Craemer,
a proud printer, who taught me
reverence for the book*

Acknowledgements

THE study on which this book is based has encompassed ten years of my professional and personal life. Partly for that reason I am indebted to a wide and rich variety of persons who contributed significantly to my training, to this project, or to both. Foremost among those who have taught me whatever sociology I know is Talcott Parsons. He has also directed and encouraged the writing of the doctoral dissertation out of which this book grew. He has become for me the personification not only of a great theorist, but also of an inspiring mentor. Donald P. Warwick, teacher, colleague, and friend went far beyond the duties of an adviser in the unfailing help that he offered me. Ezra F. Vogel took a special interest in my career as a graduate student, and gave generously of his time and energy in commenting on this text. Robert N. Bellah's writings on the sociology of religion, his teaching, and his personal encouragement were a special source of inspiration.

Among the privileges that research for this book opened up to me was the opportunity to come to know the outstanding anthropologist and African historian, Jan Vansina. We have shared the excitement and travail of field work in Zaïre (formerly Congo-Kinshasa). I am grateful to him not only for this special kind of companionship, but also for the role he played in deepening my grasp of Bantu culture.

There is no way I can adequately express what I owe to Renée C. Fox, who shared every phase of this project with me, from its inception to its completion. Her presence and insight helped me gradually to experience, understand, and be able to analyse the essence of the Jamaa.

Joseph Van Wing, S.J., pioneer missionary and renowned ethnographer of the Kongo tribe, was the most decisive influence in my decision to become a social scientist, and provided me with an early model for my future role. Until his death he took an active interest in this study. Guy Mosmans, P.B., had the courage and the vision to establish the Centre de Recherches Sociologiques which provided me with the authority and all the facilities I needed to conduct this investigation and numerous others during 1962 to 1967. It was he who persuaded the Episcopate of the Catholic Church in Zaïre that a social scientific study of the Jamaa was both needed and desirable. Without the collaboration and Franciscan hospitality of Pascal Ceuterick, O.F.M., and Bertien Peeraer, O.F.M., my entrance into and acceptance by the movement would have been impossible. Both men tutored me in the Jamaa ways and provided me with important documents.

While conducting this research I was fortunate to be associated with two groups of colleagues, the members of the Centre de Recherches Sociologiques and of the Centre d'Études pour l'Action Sociale, both in Kinshasa. Their support, involvement, and teamwork were invaluable.

It goes without saying that I am greatly indebted to the baba and mama of the Jamaa, who welcomed me and were willing to share their deepest personal and religious experiences with me. I offer this book to them in the spirit of encounter and union on which their lives are based.

Nellie Miller graciously contributed her administrative wisdom to the final preparation and presentation of this manuscript. And Joan Evis devoted herself to typing it with intelligence and impeccability.

Contents

CHAPTER I

Introduction

'THE Jamaa and the Church' is a study of a religious movement
that originated in the Katanga province of the former Belgian
Congo in 1953 and persists to this day. The Jamaa has many social
and cultural attributes in common with the hundreds of religious
movements known to exist in Central Africa.[1] At the same time,
however, it differs from these movements in a number of important
respects. The most significant difference is that the Jamaa is part of
an Ecclesia. It has emerged, developed, and remained within the
Roman Catholic Church. Partly as a consequence, it has brought
Bantu African, Christian Catholic, and Western European culture
patterns into confrontation with one another. It has also juxtaposed
its own fresh inspiration, the charisma of early Christianity, and the
rational-legal forms of institutionalized Catholicism.

A second distinctive feature of the movement is that its founder
and leader is a Belgian priest, Placied Tempels, a Franciscan missionary of Flemish origin. Most other African movements have as
their leaders indigenous lay men or women endowed with special,
culturally relevant 'gifts of grace'. A third distinguishing trait of the
Jamaa is the participation in the movement of a group of Franciscan
Flemish missionary priests, closely associated with the founder-
leader, who are its charismatic lieutenants. Out of their interaction
with the African membership of the movement, as well as with each
other, a subculture has been created which has influenced the Jamaa's
ideology and its ambience. Another characteristic of the movement
is that its African members have been recruited from the most
highly industrialized and rationalized milieu of the Congo, the
Union Minière mining complex of South Katanga (now Gécamines),
rather than from the rural inland population that makes up the constituency of most African religious movements.

The life history of the movement encompasses the late colonial

[1] David B. Barrett, *Schism and Renewal in Africa* (Nairobi: Oxford University
Press, 1968).

and the early independence eras of the Congo (now Zaïre),[1] as well as both pre- and post-Vatican Council II periods in the Catholic Church. This is the larger social and cultural context within which my study of the Jamaa is set. My intent is to analyse the microdynamics of the movement—its composition and organization, and its beliefs, rites, and symbols—within the framework of the societal and trans-societal changes taking place in the Congo and in the Church. I am particularly interested in what the Jamaa can teach us about social and cultural continuities and discontinuities in the face of these changes. For this reason, in my examination of the Jamaa I shall pay special attention to areas of strain, conflict, congruence, and fusion between the traditional and modern Bantu, Belgian, and Christian components of the movement. Because missionary priests are key figures in the movement, one such area on which I focus is the role and ideology of Catholic missionaries, their gratifications and stresses, before and after Independence and the Council.

Most of the articles written about the Jamaa are cited in the body and the bibliography of this book. By and large, they are impassioned, personal essays, published in relatively obscure church journals and written by missionary priests who express strong positive and negative feelings about the movement. Only an occasional social scientific article on the Jamaa has appeared, always in this same type of journal. Together they present a synoptic account of the Jamaa's early history and summarize some of the published and unpublished reactions of priests and church officials to the movement. In *Schism and Renewal in Africa*, a book-length survey of contemporary African religious movements, David B. Barrett, a sociologist and a Protestant missionary, mentions the Jamaa only in passing.[2]

To my knowledge, apart from my own study, only one major social scientific investigation of the Jamaa has been conducted: by Johannes Fabian for his Ph.D. dissertation in Anthropology at the University of Chicago, which was subsequently published as

[1] In 1971, as part of a planned process of mental and cultural decolonization and of affirmation of African authenticity, Congolese political leaders changed the name of the country to Zaïre. They also gave traditional African names to provinces, cities, towns, rivers, and even the currency. Throughout this book I will use the place-names that existed before this new cultural policy was adopted. My reason for doing so is that these were the names in use during the historical period covered by my study.

[2] In all, Barrett devotes 10 lines and two short footnotes to the Jamaa.

Jamaa: A Charismatic Movement in Katanga.[1] Fabian's book is based
on an analysis of the component parts of a Swahili word-list, derived
largely from the Jamaa's *mafundisho* or religious instructions. On
this linguistic basis and with the aid of his fieldwork on the Jamaa
(1966–7), Fabian presents a carefully circumscribed analysis of the
emergence of the Jamaa's transforming ideology from the 'prophetic
encounter' between the movement's charismatic founder-leader and
his African followers. Fabian's treatment of the Jamaa is not so
much an ethnographic account of the movement as it is a micro-
dynamic, linguistic analysis.[2]

My own inquiry is concerned with the kinds of social and cultural
phenomena that are largely ignored in Fabian's work. From the
outset of my Jamaa research in 1963, my intent has been to make
a sociologically comprehensive study of the movement. Because of
the meeting of Bantu, European, and Christian elements in the
belief and symbol systems of the Jamaa, I decided to look deeply
into its cultural components but, in doing so, not to overlook its
social organizational aspects. I foresaw that one of the more unusual
features of my investigation would be the opportunity to explore the
religious, ethical, and psycho-social dilemmas that such a movement
poses for an Ecclesia. And I planned to study the ways in which the
Church responded to the Jamaa as well as how the movement affected
the relationship of its African members to Catholicism.

My perspective was influenced not only by my sociological
training but also by the circumstances that led to the undertaking
of this study. It was in 1962 that I first became aware of the existence
of the Jamaa. I was then a member of the Centre de Recherches
Sociologiques in Léopoldville, a bureau for sociological research
which had been created by Guy Mosmans, a White Father, who was
Secretary-General of the Episcopate of the Catholic Church in the
Congo. Although directly responsible to Mosmans and the Permanent Committee of the bishops, the Centre had the power to determine what kind of sociological research could and should be carried
out. The major project in which my colleagues and I were engaged
in 1962–3 was a sociological survey of the Catholic dioceses of the
Congo. A phenomenon that repeatedly came to our attention in

[1] Johannes Fabian, *Jamaa: A Charismatic Movement in Katanga* (Evanston,
Ill.: Northwestern University Press, 1971).
[2] For a similar appraisal of the scope of Fabian's book, see Wyatt Mac-
Gaffey, 'Religious Movement in Zaïre', *African Studies Review*, XIV, no. 3
(Dec. 1971), p. 517.

a number of dioceses was the existence within the Church of a religious movement known as the Jamaa. While the movement was hailed by many churchmen as the most significant spiritual event to have occurred in the Congolese Catholic Church, it was regarded by others as a dangerous threat to the orthodoxy of 'the Faith'.

In the summer of 1963 I was asked by Mosmans to find out as much as I could about the Jamaa in the course of the survey that I was scheduled to conduct in Katanga province, where the movement had originated. At this stage, no formal study was envisaged. Mosmans was simply interested in having a personal, sociologically informed discussion about the Jamaa upon my return to Léopoldville.

I arrived in Katanga with two colleagues from the Centre, one a priest, the other a lay woman. In early informal discussion with church contacts, I made it known that the Jamaa figured among my interests. Very quickly thereafter, several Franciscan priests, who could be described as charismatic lieutenants in the movement, made contact with me. To my surprise as well as my satisfaction, they began not only to teach me the rudiments of Jamaa history, doctrine, and ritual, but also to induct me into some of the most private aspects of the movement. Since these confidences entailed revelations of a personal nature and also descriptions of troubling 'deviations' that were occurring in the movement, the willingness of the Jamaa priests to entrust me with this material was not to be taken for granted.

It became apparent that these men were more at ease with me than they were with my priest colleague from the Centre. Both of us were missionaries with a number of years of experience in the Congo; both were sociologists; and both belonged to religious orders other than the Franciscan. (My colleague was a Benedictine, I a Jesuit.) Although we had much in common, from the outset it was easier for me than for him to establish *rapport* with the Jamaa priests. This seemed to be due to our divergent social backgrounds. Whereas he came from an aristocratic French-speaking Belgian family, my origins were Flemish and working class. In this regard, I resembled the Jamaa priests. Furthermore, I was born and raised in West-Flanders, a province of Belgium that has culturally much in common with Limburg province, from which most Jamaa priests came. In ways both manifest and latent these factors contributed to the rapid establishment of positive *rapport* between us. It was not until later that I came to appreciate how critical a role Flemish culture played in the beliefs, symbolism, and interpersonal atmosphere of the Jamaa. The Jamaa priests made it clear that another reason they felt they could talk more freely to me than to my colleague about the movement was that, in their view, I was more 'liberal' in my outlook. By this they meant that they considered me to be more socially and theologically progressive, less puritanical, and, celibacy notwithstanding, receptive to the idea of working as closely with women as with men. As I was to learn later, an indispensable precondition for admission into the Jamaa circle was conversion from conservative, moralistic, and colonialist missionary attitudes. The relationship between my ease and egalitarianism with female colleagues and my admission to the Jamaa group was more immediately revealed by the fact that these priests invited the lay woman from the Centre to participate in all the Jamaa experiences that they opened up to me. There was a certain parallelism between the partnership we were accorded and the initiation of Congolese men and women into the movement as couples. This I did not realize at the time.[1]

The first field contact with the worlds of Katanga, the Union Minière, and the Jamaa lasted for six weeks. In that period I was not only introduced and accepted into the subculture of Jamaa priests, but I also made contact with leading baba and mama, as the African lay members of the Jamaa are called. They, in turn, introduced me to other Jamists whom I had a chance to interview and visit at home. I was granted admission to sessions at which *mafundisho* were taught and attended various kinds of meetings for religious worship.

I returned to Léopoldville at the end of August with the conviction that a social inquiry into the Jamaa would make a fine Ph.D. dissertation. It was already apparent that this would not be just one more study of one more religious movement. Informal discussion with my colleagues and Mosmans about the results of this field trip led to the more immediate decision that the exploratory work on the Jamaa that I had undertaken should be continued with the aim of writing a report on the movement for the bishops. Like most research conducted by the Centre, the purpose of this report was to provide information, present an objective sociological analysis of the data gathered, and make policy recommendations. Although the Jamaa was a religious movement internal to the

[1] This will be more fully discussed in Chapter VII.

Catholic Church, the bishops were uncertain about what it was, how to evaluate it, what to say about it, and how to deal with it. They hoped that the report would be helpful in these respects.

The next phase of my contact with the Jamaa began in early 1964. In my capacity as the new director of the Centre I was commissioned by the episcopate to make a study of the movement. I began this assignment with a three-month field trip to the Katanga and Kasai provinces. In Kasai the movement was not only attracting many adherents, but was also developing some of the most florid examples of the so-called deviations that troubled its founders and church officials. The atmosphere in which I conducted my research was complicated by the growing apprehension about these 'doctrinal errors' and 'unorthodox practices'. This anxiety was reinforced by the fact that many Jamaa priests had heard through informal channels that Tempels and the movement were under investigation at the Vatican. Jamaa leaders were concerned about what impressions I would form of the movement, and about what my report would advocate. They felt that it could have a profound influence on the fate of the Jamaa at that particular juncture: the judicious handling of the deviations, the maintenance of the Jamaa's charismatic inspiration, the integration of Africanicity and Catholicism, and the formal acceptance of the movement by the Church were all at stake. Furthermore, in correspondence with his priestly collaborators Tempels had expressed reservations about the wisdom and the value of an intellectual study of the Jamaa conducted by an outsider, reservations that were not only characteristic of him personally but of the mystical premises on which the movement was based. However, support for my inquiry was equally strong; several of the principal Jamaa priests, including one of the candidates most eligible to succeed Tempels as charismatic leader of the movement, welcomed my study and did everything possible to facilitate it. Not only did they firmly believe that an objective study of the Jamaa would vindicate it in the eyes of the Church and reveal its profound religious implications, but they also earnestly hoped that the analytic perspective of my investigation and its findings would help them to improve the Jamaa both spiritually and socially. Their receptivity encouraged the Jamaa's baba and mama to receive me and to teach me all that they knew and felt about the movement. There was no Jamaa home or meeting from which I was excluded. I was able to carry out participant observation and interviews in all Jamaa milieux. In addition, Jamaa priests and lay members alike provided me with the *mafundisho*, correspondence, church documents, life histories, and dreams that constitute the most important primary data of my study.

My report, entitled *Analyse sociologique de la Jamaa*, was completed and issued by the Centre in June 1964. Its contents and impact will be analysed in some detail in Chapter VIII. Here it is sufficient to state that, in keeping with structural functional theory, the report identified the functional and dysfunctional consequences of the Jamaa for the major institutions of Congolese society, as well as for the goals and activities of the Catholic Church. In balance, I concluded that the functional aspects of the Jamaa outweighed its dysfunctional ones. In certain ways, I said, the movement had surpassed the efforts of Congolese political leaders to transform the attitudes of the population from tribal to national allegiance. It had also effected a deeper conversion of its members to a Bantu-Christian world-view than most organized missionary activities had been able to accomplish. My main policy recommendation was that attempts by the Church rigidly to organize and control the movement would probably have two deleterious results. It would routinize and possibly extinguish the distinctive spirituality of the Jamaa, and it might force those engaging in deviationist practices to go underground and form a separatist sect.

As will be seen in Chapter VIII, although several Jamaa priests made specific criticisms of the report, by and large they were pleased with its conclusions. The bishops' reactions were more diverse, but they informally assented as a group to adopt a beneficent, non-interventionist attitude towards the movement. The fact that the report was well received facilitated my research when I returned to Katanga and Kasai for the third time in early 1965. I was now fully accepted by Jamaa leaders and members as the movement's sociologist. This did not mean that attempts were made to co-opt me; rather, I was granted access to the most disturbing as well as the most uplifting aspects of the movement, and my advise was sought on all these Jamaa matters. My chief methodological problem became that of minimizing observer effect while maintaining the giving of one's self relationship to the Jamaa that the movement expected. The more deeply I entered into the spirit of encounter which was central to the Jamaa, the more evocative were the experiences to which I was exposed. The greatest challenge to my ability to maintain the detached kind of involvement needed for a reasonably objective study was the affective, mystical atmosphere of the movement, entirely antithetic to the austere Jesuit spirituality in which I was trained. The Jamaa ambience exerted a strong emotional pull on me. It both attracted me and made me apprehensive.

In the summer of 1965, an updated version of my Jamaa report was issued by the Centre and circulated to a wider readership than the first. By this time I was also engaged in studying the society-wide rebellion that had swept the Congo in 1964 and 1965.[1] My trip to Katanga and subsequently to Kasai had been planned so that I could pursue both projects. The Jamaa members I met were impressed with the fact that my colleagues and I were willing to subject ourselves to physical danger in order to understand and explain the dynamics of the rebellion. In their piety they saw my status as further enhanced by the attention the bishops paid to the findings in my studies of the rebellion and of the Jamaa.

In these ways, this period constituted the high point of my *rapport* with the Jamaa. It was also the time when I decided to concentrate my study of the movement on the Katanga region. This decision was partly dictated by the sharpening of focus that progressively takes place in fieldwork. As will be seen, an important part of my study is concerned with the origin and development of the Jamaa, its Bantu and Franciscan-Flemish characteristics, its charismatic prophet and leaders, and with the relationship of various attributes of this movement to the setting, at once traditional and urban-industrialized, in which it originated. For these reasons, Katanga had to be the primary site. My fieldwork gradually revealed that the Kasai wing of the movement had developed so many distinctive traits that only a separate study would do it justice. Some of the most significant phenomena that would have to be investigated in Kasai were the social, cultural, and psychological factors that contributed to the extraordinary florescence of deviationist practices in this region. It seemed sensible to forgo this study within a study, for it was doubtful whether the aberrant and secretive deviationist groups would allow themselves to be studied.

From 1966 to 1969 I made two more field trips to Katanga in

---

[1] See my joint article on the first phase of this rebellion: Renée C. Fox, Willy De Craemer, and Jean-Marie Ribeaucourt, ' "The Second Independence": A Case Study of the Kwilu Rebellion in the Congo', *Comparative Studies in Society and History*, 8, no. 1 (Oct. 1965), 78–109.

order to follow the latest developments in the movement and conduct observations and interviews focused on specific Jamaa questions into which I wanted to probe more deeply. I also visited a number of Jamaa priests on leave in Belgium, and paid one long, memorable personal visit to Placied Tempels in Hasselt. In addition, I received a continual flow of letters and documents from Jamaa members. Although my study can be said to have ended in 1970, to this day I maintain contact with prominent Jamists, and continue to receive news about the movement's evolution.

In sum, my study of the Jamaa was carried out by means of field methods during the years 1963–70, principally in Katanga province of the Congo. The subjects of my study included all the European and African leaders of the movement and a representative sample of what will be shown to be its socially homogeneous membership. Of the approximately 1,600 members of the Jamaa in the three major cities of South Katanga, I came to know, directly or indirectly, some two hundred baba and mama.

The seven substantive chapters that make up the body of this book are organized in the following way. Chapters II and III deal with the origin and development of the Jamaa and with the characteristics of its social structure. This section includes materials on the social history and organization of the movement, and on the social backgrounds of its leaders and members. Chapters IV and V focus on the culture; they are concerned with the religious content of the Jamaa, with its doctrine, ritual, and expressive symbolism. Chapters VI, VII, and VIII analyse the major interaction patterns of the Jamaa, and their social and cultural consequences. These chapters examine the effects of the movement on the role-set of its lay and clerical members, the influence that baba, mama, and priests have on each other, the distinctive subculture that has emerged from their interaction, and the informal as well as the formal ways in which the institutional Church has reacted to and affected the Jamaa. Finally, Chapter IX attempts a synthesis of the findings through a discussion of the Jamaa's theoretical implications for the sociology of religion, social movements, affect, and kinship.

CHAPTER II

Social and Historical Origins of the Jamaa

THE first Congolese men and women to call themselves Jamaa (Swahili term for family) were a group of seven married couples, all baptized Catholics and members of the parish of Ruwe, near the city of Kolwezi in South Katanga. These were persons of no more than primary school education, living in a community created by the Belgian copper-mining company, Union Minière du Haut-Katanga (U.M.). The men held positions such as those of industrial worker at Union Minière and primary school teacher and catechist for the Catholic Mission at Ruwe. The women were simple housewives, whose domestic duties included working small plots of land, in addition to caring for their husbands, children, and homes.

The act of conferring the name Jamaa upon themselves was a culmination not only in the couples' relationship to each other but also in their relationship to the priest around whom they had gathered since 1953. The priest was Father Placied Tempels, a Belgian Franciscan missionary of Flemish-Limburg origins. At this time Tempels was religious superior of the Ruwe mission and professor of religion in its teacher-training school. The couples had been drawn to him through their attendance at the unconventional and incandescent sessions on the Christian religion that Tempels conducted in the parish and in the school. One of his Franciscan colleagues described the process by which the couples were pulled towards Tempels in this way:

. . . Father Placied taught the catechism to the children of the parish. His manner of giving religious instruction drew adults and elderly people who came to ask his permission to attend the *mafundisho* [religious lessons] . . . A little later, these same adults asked to receive these *mafundisho* separately from the children. And next, a little later still, when they had come to know each other and to meet regularly for the instructions, they asked him to be allowed to meet among themselves, either at the parish or at one of their own homes, in order to continue to seek and discuss religious things together . . .[1]

[1] Interview with Father Q., Feb. 1964.

According to Tempels, this new way of teaching began on the day that, 'I put aside my catechism, my textbook and I addressed myself in a direct way to [the Blacks]: "What do you think of life, and what do you want from it? What are your thoughts, your aspirations? You are men like me, you do a lot of thinking, day and night, you are searching for something." '[1]

At one such meeting with the seven couples someone asked Tempels what name he thought they ought to give to their little group. They were preoccupied with this question partly because they were frequently asked by others what kind of an association they were, and, above all, how they resembled or differed from the many sorts of Catholic Action groups in the local church. It was not just a nominal identity that the couples were seeking, however; for a name and the act of conferring it have ancient magico-religious significance in Bantu culture. According to Tempels, he was indirectly responsible for the fact that the name Jamaa was conferred on the group:

One day, my people asked me if we were like the Legion of Mary. I answered them: 'No! We are the Church. Christ said to his Apostles: "I have not come to build a Church made of big building stones like the Temple of Jerusalem; I came to build a living Church made of living stones, cemented to me, the cornerstone, to the Virgin, to Peter, John, Veronica, Magdalen, Lazarus, Martha . . ." Now, *that* is our family. That is the Church, in which "all those who do the will of my Father are my father, my mother, my brothers, my sisters. And when I am no longer on earth, you, my Apostles, you will travel all over the world to found this family of living stones who will form my temple." Thus, the Apostles went forth to Greece and after a certain time, the Greeks experienced a new phenomenon. They saw a small community made up of several Roman soldiers, some Greeks, a few Hebrews, Syrians, Lebanese and Asians; men who before were mortal enemies and who now had become brothers. How had that been possible? The fact is that they were a true *ekklesia*, that is a community, a fraternity, a family." And I said to the Blacks: 'That is truly what we are: a fraternity, a family, an ensemble of brothers and sisters; I, the priest, with you; I and you, John, and you, Louis, and you, Mary, and you, Margaret. That is our community. That is the temple of God. That is the Church.' In order not to use the word *ekklesia*, I used the equivalent term in the local dialect and I said: 'We are Jamaa, that is: brothers, family.' Thus it was that people began to refer to the Jamaa, that certain individuals regarded as a new movement in the

[1] Anon., 'Le Père Placide Tempels s'explique', Interview in *La Voix de Saint Antoine*, no. 6 (Sept. 1967), p. 6. (Hereafter referred to as *La Voix*.)

Church, a sort of confraternity . . . Jamaa means nothing other than fraternity, union with others, or, if you prefer: 'Church,' for, the Church is all that, because Christ said: 'It is for that, that I came, in order that you may be one.'[1]

So it was that the couples became identified as the Jamaa and began to address each other as *baba* and *mama*, Swahili terms for father and mother.

Tempels and his disciples began to attract the attention of other Congolese, some of whom became members of the new sort of 'family' that was developing. These recruits were struck by the exemplary husband–wife relationship that the Jamaa couples seemed to enjoy and by the powerfully personal way in which Tempels addressed himself to them. For example, this is how baba Gaston, who was destined to become a leader of the Jamaa, describes his entrance into the movement:

> I was amazed at the life of those seven couples. Ever since I was a little boy, my ideal had been . . . understanding with others. I wanted to establish this ideal understanding with my wife, at the same time that I would remain *bwana* [big boss] and she would remain little. I was amazed by the understanding of those couples, with each other and with Father Placied. So, I went to find Father Placied. I asked him to teach me. He said, 'Bring your wife along.' And so, Father Placied taught us the life of understanding as it was lived in the house of Nazareth.[2]

Placied Tempels had not only travelled a great geographical distance in order to communicate with Congolese men and women in this way, he had also travelled far in religion. He was born in 1906 in the little town of Berlaar, in the Limburg province of Belgium. His father was a local stationmaster. He attended the secondary school in Hasselt run by diocesan clergy, where he specialized in Latin and Greek. He was a *primus perpetuus*, i.e. first in his class throughout the six-year cycle of studies. One of his teachers in particular, Abbé H., had a lifelong impact on him. Abbé H. is described by several of Tempels's classmates as an 'open, progressive, modern' teacher, 'way ahead of his time'. In his discussions with students he emphasized the importance of love for one's neighbour, and told them that their friendship with one another could be an expression of this love. He also broke through some of the puritanical religious norms that dominated the school in this era, by

[1] *La Voix*, pp. 8–9.
[2] From a personal interview with Baba Gaston Feb. 1965.

encouraging his students to learn how to be 'social': how to meet and relate to girls of their own age, how to go out and enjoy a drink with the boys, etc. Tempels was only one of a whole generation of students who felt such admiration for Abbé H. and who became so close to him that, even after their graduation, they still continued to come to him for advice.

There is no record of how Tempels reached the decision to become a priest. However, it seems likely that Abbé H.'s example may have been important in this respect and also that the Franciscan emphasis on love and fellowship had meaning for him, because it was especially compatible with the teaching philosophy of the Abbé. In addition, the Franciscan Order would have been attractive to any religiously inclined Catholic boy in Limburg, where it was particularly appreciated for the warm, humane, popular, mystical, and eloquent way in which it ministered to the lay community.

In 1924, Tempels entered the novitiate of the Franciscan Order. In the course of six years of training for the priesthood, he applied for missionary work in the Belgian Congo, but was turned down by his superiors for health reasons. After his ordination he was assigned to a secondary school for boys in Heusden, where he taught Latin and German. This was a special school created and run by the Franciscans for boys with an 'early vocation', who by the age of twelve felt they were called to the priesthood in the Franciscan Order. According to one of his former pupils, Tempels had 'an enormous influence on his students . . . because of his goodness, gentleness and his special gift for personal contact with them. His ideas on friendship, human love, encounter and freedom created a new spirit in the school . . .' Tempels was interested in music, painting, and literature, and he 'opened these horizons' to the students. He also involved them in his own deepest aspirations. For example, the same student recounted that one day, in the middle of the school year, Tempels entered the classroom and asked the students for their prayers, because he had just reapplied to his superiors for permission to work in the Congo.

There is a striking similarity between Tempels's relationship to his students and the one he experienced and so much admired, ten years earlier, in Abbé H.'s class. Like his mentor, Tempels was non-directive, permissive, artistic, and affective in his teaching, personality, and methods. There were two other young colleagues in the school with the same philosophy of education. Together, they represented what the religious superiors anxiously labelled 'that new trend'. In any case, it was diametrically opposed to the stern, austere, impersonal, formal, disciplining spirit that was characteristic of the school. The disquietude that some staff members felt about Tempels's approach to teaching may have contributed latently to the permission granted him in 1933 to start a missionary career in the Congo.

Tempels arrived in Katanga in November 1933; he began his first missionary assignment at Lukonzolwa in the Lake Moero district. He served as a 'bush Father', constantly on the move from one village to another, instructing, preaching, administering the sacraments, etc. In 1937, he was sent to Kabondo-Dianda, one of the smaller mission posts in the middle of the vast Franciscan vicariate, stretching from Dilolo on the Angolan border in the west to the lakes, the swamps, and the North Rhodesian (now Zambian) border in the east. Here, from 1937 to 1946, he was engaged in essentially the same activities, but this time with the BaLuba of North Katanga.[1] In this connection, it is interesting to note that among the first recruits to the Jamaa in the mid-1950s were members of this ethnic group residing in the mining towns around Kolwezi.

Tempels considers his first decade in the Congo the first of 'three phases' in his missionary life. This was his 'priest phase', the period, he says, when he acted like a 'boss, lord and master of his church, who knows all, says all, while the faithful have only to listen and keep quiet'.[2]

I arrived in the Belgian Congo with a double complex: the complex of the White facing the Black, and the complex of the priest facing his faithful.[3]

. . . Above all, [I believed myself] to be the carrier of a divine message. Nevertheless, I adopted the attitudes of the white, the master, the *Bula Matari*.[4] And the message that God entrusted to me, inspired in me the

---

[1] For detailed ethnological and geographical information and a bibliography on the Luba-Katanga, see Olga Boone, *Carte ethnique du Congo: Quart Sud-Est* (Tervuren: Musée Royal de l'Afrique Centrale, Sciences Humaines, No. 37, 1961), pp. 130–46.   [2] *La Voix*, p. 7.   [3] Ibid., p. 5.

[4] *Bula Matari* is a KiKongo term meaning 'Breaker of rocks'. The name was given by the BaKongo to Stanley in 1879, because of the explorer's use of dynamite in hewing a passage through the rocky hills of the Lower Congo. Later, the Congolese used the name to refer to the Belgian colonial administration and to any of its members. It expresses the awe and fear that Congolese felt in the presence of the White colonizer's display of political, technological, and (to the Africans) magical power.

clerical attitudes of a spiritual master, an authoritarian doctor, a religious bureaucrat, of a chief or a shepherd towards his flock.[1]

In Tempels's words, this is the way that he 'hit the road', that he travelled the circuit in the bush country. 'For ten years . . . my eyes fixed always on my manual, I tried all the methods, all the possible clichés to make the Christian religion understood, accepted, and practised. I scrupulously followed all the directives and, in spite of everything, the engine didn't start up.'[2] Tempels reports that he was 'overcome by despair, because [he] felt that [he] had failed and that nothing had taken root'.[3]

This retrospectively self-denunciatory account of Tempels's first decade in the Congo has to be seen against the larger social and historical background of Belgian colonial policy of the era.[4] The ideology on which it was based hinged on two major conceptions: the idea of 'civilizing' the Congolese and the principle of 'Dominer pour Servir' ('Dominate in order to serve').[5] Its underlying premisses were a blend of paternalistic and moralistic notions. As Thomas Hodgkin has pointed out, Belgian colonial policy assumed that 'the thought and behaviour of the [Congolese] mass is [sic] plastic, and can be refashioned by a benevolent, wise and highly trained élite'.[6] One of its major objectives, 'bringing civilization to the Congolese through both educational and evangelical means', was an expression of this belief. Nowhere was this better epitomized than in the role that the government accorded the Catholic Missions in the Congo. Along with the civil administration, on the one hand, and large business enterprises and concessionary companies, on the other, the Catholic Church formed a trinary colonial power structure in the Congo.[7] In accordance with the 'Dominer pour Servir' tradition of

[1] Pl. Tempels, O.F.M., *Notre Rencontre* (Léopoldville: Centre d'Études Pastorales, 1962), p. 36.   [2] Ibid., pp. 36–7.   [3] Ibid., p. 36.
[4] Based on first-hand experience of colonial policy since 1951, and confirmed by Renée C. Fox, 'The Intelligence Behind the Mask' (1968, unpublished paper), Thomas Hodgkin, *Nationalism in Colonial Africa* (London: F. Muller, 1956), and Crawford Young, *Politics in the Congo* (Princeton, N.J.: Princeton University Press, 1965).
[5] For a classic formulation of this policy, see the works of Governor-General Pierre Ryckmans: *La Politique coloniale* (Brussels: Éditions Rex, 1934), *Étapes et Jalons* (Brussels: Ferdinand Larcier, 1946), and especially, *Dominer pour servir* (Brussels: Édition Universelle, 1948).
[6] Thomas Hodgkin, *Nationalism in Colonial Africa* (5th impression, 1965), p. 52.
[7] The massive presence of Catholic missionaries in the Congo is related to the rather special religious structure of Belgian society. Belgium is a predominantly Catholic country, in which Protestantism is of minor importance, in terms

colonial policy, 'this triple alliance'[1] ramified throughout the entire country. Belgian colonial administration was dense and direct: missionaries, civil servants, and business representatives alike were required to spend a great deal of their time in the interior of the Congo. They were encouraged, and even obliged, as the dictum went, to 'enter into contact with the natives', keep them under close surveillance, and take an active interest in their traditional culture. But this active interest was based on an absolute conviction that European culture was in every way more advanced and superior to African tradition. On these grounds European superordination and African subordination were institutionalized in all domains of Congolese life, and a sharp caste-like dichotomy separated the European from the African world.

Both secular and religious agents of the colonial era felt they had a mission to transmit to the Congolese population the 'unquestioned and unquestionable moral values'[2] of their own society, along with cognitive knowledge and technical skills that they considered essential to the economic development of the country, and to the 'good life' for the Congolese, as well as for themselves. The attitudes and values that Belgians considered hallmarks of 'civilization', and that they were most intent on instilling into the Congolese were those most usually associated with the Protestant Ethic. They included 'thrift, self-help, hard, well-executed work as a duty and a calling, honesty, respectability, domestic decency, civic responsibility, and the achievement of some comfort and success through the exercise of these virtues'.[3]

The colonial regime was convinced that these 'good burgher' attributes should and could be conveyed by what was termed the

of both its small number of adherents and its relative lack of influence. There are significant groups of Jews only in Antwerp and Brussels. On the whole, most Belgians who are not practising Catholics were none the less baptized as Catholics. Some of these define themselves as religiously indifferent, but many such Belgians belong to the religious-philosophical orientation known as Free Thought. Within this category of Free Thought, there is an indeterminate number of persons who are members of the Freemason Lodge, which in Belgium, as in France, was founded as a secret organization, with the primary goal of combating and subverting the doctrine and power of the Catholic Church.

[1] Crawford Young, *Politics in the Congo*, p. 365.
[2] T. Hodgkin, op. cit., p. 52.
[3] Renée C. Fox, 'The Intelligence behind the Mask', p. 83; see also W. De Craemer and Renée C. Fox, *The Emerging Physician* (Stanford: The Hoover Institution, 1967), pp. 24–7, and T. Hodgkin, op. cit., p. 48.

'moral formation' dimension of education. Partly for this reason, the Belgian Catholic Missions were given a quasi-monopoly over the establishment and running of schools for Congolese, which were in turn subsidized by the state. It was maintained that 'only in this way [could] education be given [the] positive moral purpose'[1] that the 'œuvre civilisatrice' ('civilizing endeavour') required. The impact of the Catholic Church extended far beyond its strictly 'teaching and preaching' functions.[2] In addition, 'through . . . their rituals and ceremonial, their pastoral and social work, their network of satellite associations, their range of vernacular periodicals and journals, [its missionaries] exercise[d], or [sought] to exercise, a large measure of control over African minds.'[3] The typical yardstick used by the missions to measure the magnitude of their spiritual, moral, social, and educational influence was the number of Congolese who had received baptism into the Catholic Church. They equated this baptism with conversion to Christianity and 'civilization'. Measured in this way, the Church seemed to have had an effect that was nothing short of spectacular on the souls and minds of the Congolese. During the ten-year period in his missionary life, from 1933 to 1943, about which Tempels wrote, the majority of his church colleagues were inclined to accept this view and to feel 'triumphant' about the progress the Church was making. Their optimism and satisfaction were enhanced by their underlying assumption that the conversions and baptisms meant that they had 'uprooted paganism' from the 'native mentality' of those Congolese who had become Christian. In Katanga, where Tempels was stationed, the prevailing church view of the essence of conversion was epigrammatically stated by Monsignor Jean Félix de Hemptinne,

---

[1] T. Hodgkin, op. cit., p. 50. For a detailed statement on Belgian colonial educational policy, see J. Vanhove, 'L'Œuvre d'éducation au Congo Belge et au Ruanda-Urundi', in *Encyclopédie du Congo Belge*. (Brussels: Éditions Bieleveld, 1953), vol. III, pp. 749–89.

[2] This is not to imply that Protestant missionary presence and activities in the Congo were of no consequence. However, they did have a certain disadvantage in this era with respect to their educational impact. Protestant missionaries were less numerous than Catholic ones, and were largely American, British, or Scandinavian in origin. They were inclined towards fundamentalism and pentecostalism. The foreign status of Protestant missions, their fundamentalist apprehension about the harmful effects that too much book-learning could have on the spirit, as well as the fact that, from the Belgian Catholic point of view, they were minority, 'schismatic' churches, all help to explain why their schools were not as advanced or as well subsidized as were Catholic schools.

[3] T. Hodgkin, op. cit., p. 50.

O.S.B., then Apostolic Vicar of Élisabethville: 'Il faut détruire le païen pour construire le chrétien.' ('The pagan must be destroyed for the Christian to be built.')[1]

As he himself testified, Tempels was infused with the prevailing colonial ideology, even before he arrived in the Congo. In effect, then, his 'priest phase' entailed facile conformity to the general colonial and missionary church 'environment'. It did not involve spontaneous, meaningful interaction with Congolese. Rather, Tempels was the dominant teacher and 'donor', to whom it had not occurred that he might also learn and receive from his 'pupils' and their traditional culture.

From the intensity of the anger and self-castigation with which he described these attitudes, values, and practices, once he had turned against them, it seems fair to assume that he had very deeply internalized them. Tempels's deconversion from a priestly expression of colonial dominance was triggered by his growing awareness of a discrepancy between the large number of Congolese receiving baptism and the small number whose fundamental conceptions, beliefs, and practices were changed by becoming Christians:

. . . I noticed that Christianity taught in this manner had no hold whatsoever or any real influence. We did not have convinced Christians. I saw persons being baptized by the dozens, and they left us by the dozens, also. They were not convinced and they had assimilated nothing.[2]

Tempels contends that the second period of his missionary life, which he terms his 'adaptation phase', began on the day when

for the first time in ten years, I stopped consulting manual, catechism and doctrine, in order to look with astonishment and fascination . . . at that man at whom I had never looked before. I had not been truly interested in him, his thought, his aspirations, but only in the religion of which I was the propagandist. I looked at this man, finally addressing myself to him: What do you have? What do you lack? What sort of man are you? What do you think? What do you desire above all else? Why your magical remedies? What do they mean, how do they work?[3]

Tempels admits that his new attitude was very much influenced by the notions of adaptation that were fashionable in certain segments of Belgian missionary and colonial circles in the early 1940s.

[1] From a personal interview with a missionary priest from Katanga.
[2] *La Voix*, p. 5.
[3] Tempels, *Notre Rencontre*, p. 37.

... I was discouraged and I did not know any longer what to do, when I began to hear people speaking a great deal about 'adaptations'. They said: 'The cause of our failure lies in a lack of adaptation; everything would certainly go better, if we would adapt ourselves more to the mentality of the persons whom we wish to evangelize.'[1]

Among the Belgian groups in the Congo, the strongest advocates of adaptation were certain members of the legal profession. Through the courtrooms in which they handled litigations filed an endless procession of Congolese men and women involved in palavers concerning such matters as marriage, divorce, fecundity, property, illness, sorcery, authority, and solidarity. Belgian lawyers, magistrates, and judges were impressed by the richness, wisdom, and complexity of the system of customary law that applied to these areas of disputation. They were also among the first to recognize that traditional Congolese law, like European law, could not be understood without reference to 'certain general notions about [Congolese] political and social organization'[2] and 'ontology'. Their experience led them to refute the pervasive colonial assumption that the 'Blacks' were 'primitives', inferior to Whites and, as such, had a mode of thought that was immutably 'pre-logical'. Though these jurists were inclined to feel that the evolution of 'black Congolese society' had been mysteriously arrested, they nevertheless affirmed that it had developed far beyond the 'first stage of human society':

... the complexity of their languages, of their institutions, of their beliefs; the richness of their vocabulary and of their oral traditions; their artistic

---

[1] *La Voix*, p. 6.
[2] A. Sohier, *Le Mariage en droit coutumier congolais* (Brussels: Institut Royal Colonial Belge, Mémoires, vol. XI, no. 3, 1943), p. 8. At first glance it may seem paradoxical that although these jurists were more progressive than many of their Belgian colonial contemporaries, the province in which they were concentrated, Katanga, was conservative on these issues. This was partly due to the fact that there were persons more powerful in shaping the social, economic, and political orientation of Katanga than these lawyers. The dominant élite consisted of representatives of big business (Union Minière and Société Générale de Belgique), high authorities of the Catholic Church (most notably Mgr de Hemptinne), and the leadership of the Belgian *colonat* (including such men as J. Sepulchre and O. Defawe, and their professional organization, Fédacol). However, it should also be understood that the group of jurists was not so politically liberal as to envisage a Congo totally independent of Belgium. (But, then, no group of Belgians in the colony did!) Rather, they hoped that the Congolese would join with Belgians to form a federal Belgo-Congolese Community.

development; their knowledge of agriculture, cattle raising, medicine, metallurgy attest to centuries of slow evolution, discoveries, progress.[1]

Their socio-legal outlook was responsible for their characteristic concern about the degree to which Belgian colonial policy had eroded and, in certain respects, uprooted this traditional system. One of the sharpest focuses of confusion and conflict in this area was the recurrent uncertainty as to whether customary, oral, tribal law applied in a particular case, or whether the written law of the colonial administration was more appropriate and authoritative. Belgian jurists were disturbed by what they regarded as the progressive destruction of what was once a mosaic of coherent and viable, ethnically based legal systems. They were aware of the all-embracing importance of kinship in traditional law and realized that it was predominant in Congolese tribal societies, seen as a whole. This insight, together with their appreciation of the interdependence of Congolese law with what they called 'political and social organization', made them apprehensive about the consequences of the deterioration of traditional legal and family structures for all the other pre-Belgian institutions of Congolese society. Belgian lawyers and judges of this persuasion were also inclined to be critical of the ways in which colonial law formalized racial differentiation, making little provision for the 'assimilation' and eventual 'integration' of Africans and Belgians in a unified Congolese society. They also felt the necessity to anticipate and prepare for the time when the 'colonial form of our political organization must give way to another regime'.[2]

Two lawyers from this group who played a significant role in Tempels's own 'adaptation phase', and the period in his missionary career that followed it, were Antoine Rubbens and Ernest Possoz. Rubbens, whom Crawford Young characterizes as a 'liberal Catholic lawyer from Elisabethville',[3] had considerable personal and professional contact with Tempels in the early 1940s. For example, in 1944–5, both contributed articles on colonial policy to a Katanga newspaper, *L'Essor du Congo*. Each seems to have admired the other for his 'great penetration into the native mentality'.[4] Tempels's

[1] Sohier, op. cit., pp. 9–10.
[2] Idem, 'La politique d'intégration', in *Zaïre*, V, no. 9 (Nov. 1951), 909.
[3] C. Young, op. cit., p. 78.
[4] A. Rubbens, ed., *Dettes de guerre* (Élisabethville: Éditions de l'*Essor du Congo*, 1945), p. 17.

relations with Possoz during this period were more indirect, but no less personal. In 1943–4, while Tempels was writing a series of articles on Bantu philosophy, which, as we shall see, were destined to become his major published work, he carried on an intense and voluminous correspondence with Possoz. Possoz was a magistrate in Coquilhatville, Equator Province, and the author of a book, *Éléments du droit coutumier nègre*,[1] that Tempels considered 'remarkable'. In his own published writings, Tempels praised this work because it 'had the great merit to recognize that if the jurist is to systematize a set of customary rules drawn from the practice of native law, he must go back to the ontology of the primitives in order to make them understood'.[2] Both Possoz and Rubbens played even more significant roles in Tempels's life a few years later.

What Tempels terms the 'second lap' of his missionary life thus grew out of prevailing ideas about 'adaptation', as well as personal discouragement with his early missionary efforts. As we saw, Tempels dates the beginning of the second stage of his work in the Congo to the time that he began to approach the Congolese he was teaching with directness, spontaneity, and in a spirit of inquiry. Some time in 1943 he started to 'question the Blacks about their customs, their beliefs, their mentality, their way of thinking'.[3] According to his account, the Congolese at first responded sceptically with incredulity and distrust:

> Their first reaction was: 'So what? How could what we think really interest you? Nobody has ever asked us this.' I pressed them: 'That supremely interests me; I have confidence in you and I want to have confidence in you. What you think is not to be found in my book; thus, you alone can teach me.'[4]

Through this kind of dialogue, Tempels recounts, the Congolese gradually began to open up to him. He was excited and indeed 'overwhelmed' by the 'new world' that these discussions revealed to him and was frankly astonished that 'primitives not (or hardly) knowing either how to read or to write' could express 'a whole universe of profoundly human thoughts and aspirations'.[5] He was

---

[1] E. Possoz, *Éléments de droit coutumier nègre* (Élisabethville: Lovania, 1943).
[2] Tempels, *La Philosophie bantoue* (see below, p. 26 n. 2 for details of publication), p. 96.
[3] *La Voix*, p. 6.
[4] Ibid., p. 6.
[5] Tempels, *Notre Rencontre*, p. 38.

struck by the recurrence of certain themes in the 'man-to-man, being-to-being colloquium'[1] he held with them.

'What we think,' they said to me, 'what we want, what we are looking for is life, full, strong, total life. What we are looking for is fecundity, paternity, maternity, a great fecundity, all the fecundity, an intense fecundity, not only physical, but totally human: to be father, to be mother, to transmit life, to survive one in the other, to communicate our thought to others. Next, after our desire for total life, our desire for fecundity, what we wish is vital union, union with other beings, visible and invisible. We cannot live in isolation, isolation kills us. We want a communion of life, a union of life between all beings. If we are left solitary, we are dead; it is as if we did not exist.'[2]

These three fundamental values that Tempels discovered through his interchanges with the people—life, fecundity, and vital union— became central to all his subsequent missionary activities and constituted the basic premisses of the Jamaa, the movement he helped to found. However, looking back on the quality of his insight in his 'second stage', and on his motives for wishing to come to know 'the Bantu' in this period, Tempels is profoundly self-critical:

... My goal in this search for the Bantu man was ... to feel myself 'Bantu' at least one time. I wanted to think, feel, live like him, to have a Bantu soul. All that with the intention of being able to adapt myself ...[3]

Once having arrived at the level of these Blacks, it seemed to me that then I would finally have learned what I ought to do; I would have learned to teach Christianity to them in an intelligible 'adapted' language. In essence, I would maintain my European personality, but in 'adapted' form.[4]

Tempels's adaptation stage was not static. As he saw it, almost from the inception of this period, it provided him with the momentum to move beyond it and 'do something more or other than adaptation'.[5] From the point of view of the observer, Tempels rapidly evolved from an external to an internal adaptation phase. The 'external transformation' of the missionary, he felt, was relatively easy and fell short of what he came increasingly to consider the ultimate goal that the priest-missionary, the Church, and 'all colonials of good will' ought to realize. In his eyes, simply 'speaking an adapted language' to the people one was teaching and evangelizing was analogous to 'putting on the robe of a mandarin' rather

[1] Tempels, *Notre Rencontre*, p. 37.   [2] *La Voix*, p. 6.
[3] Tempels, *Notre Rencontre*, p. 37.   [4] *La Voix*, p. 6.
[5] Tempels, *Notre Rencontre*, p. 31.

than becoming 'Chinese in your soul'.[1] It resembled the approach of an ethnologist for whom 'foreign people are an object of science', and who does not seek 'communion with the men whom he comes to study'.[2] 'One can build churches in native style, introduce Negro melodies into the liturgy, use the native language, borrow the clothing of Bedouins or mandarins; true adaptation, nevertheless, is to be found only in the adaptation of the spirit.'[3] Through his continuing dialogue with Congolese, Tempels rapidly came to feel that the 'principal, essential integration' that adaptation entailed was 'the priest's interior adaptation and integration with what is the most noble, the most intimate in each people: its soul, its way of thinking and feeling'.[4] It is this 'interior transformation' that the people want, Tempels was now convinced. They want to 'understand not only [the missionary's] spoken message but the man himself and to be able to feel "ONE" with him, to commune with him'. What Tempels was asking of himself and his colleagues was nothing short of a 'mental and spiritual conversion', a becoming 'Bantu in soul . . . not through initiation to Bantu thought, but by *receiving* the thoughts of living people whom one encounters'.[5]

Tempels's conception of true adaptation made him a particularly severe and derisive critic of the efforts made by the most progressive groups in the missionary Church and the colonial administration to create a new class of Congolese *évolués*. In effect, this was to be a modern élite, 'civilized' through the Belgian, Christian attitudes and values, and through Western knowledge and skills transmitted to them by teachers, civil servants, missionaries, and employers. On the one hand, Tempels regarded this programme to assimilate 'rare' and privileged Congolese to 'European civilization' as one that created more 'uprooted and degenerate' persons than 'true *évolués*'.[6] On the other hand, he observed that, outward appearances notwithstanding, the majority of Congolese *évolués* remained Bantu 'under a thin layer of imitation of the white man'. For him, the *évolués* represented a particularly flagrant and bitter demonstration of the fact that

all of us, missionaries, magistrates, administrators, and all those who guide or have to guide Blacks, have not reached their 'soul', at least not as

[1] Ibid., p. 32. [2] Ibid., p. 31.
[3] Tempels, *La Philosophie bantoue*, p. 18.
[4] Tempels, *Notre Rencontre*, p. 32. [5] Ibid., p. 33.
[6] Tempels, *La Philosophie bantoue*, p. 19.

deeply as we should have . . . because we have not grasped the ontology of the Bantu, we have remained incapable of offering them an assimilable spiritual doctrine and a comprehensible intellectual synthesis. Because we have not understood the Bantu 'soul', we have not made a methodical effort for them to have a more pure and intense life. In condemning their so-called 'childish behavior' and 'savage mores' through the judgement 'it is stupid and it is bad', we have shared the responsibility of having killed 'the man' in the Bantu . . . In order to introduce Blacks to true civilization, much more is needed than material well-being, the so much heralded social action, the production of clerks, and something other than the teaching of 'ki-français'.[1]

Although, as we have seen, Tempels's adaptation phase partook of the most progressive Belgian colonial thought of the 1940s, it carried him beyond the experiences, insights, and convictions of most administrators and missionaries of the period. He was willing and able to go so far in his relations with Congolese as to reverse completely one of the primordial assumptions on which any form of colonialism or evangelism is based. This is the idea that one comes as a teacher and benefactor to a people who have not as yet either heard or absorbed the 'superior message' one brings. According to Tempels, in his exchanges with Congolese he told them: 'In unveiling to me the depth of your human being, you have been "fathers" and "mothers" to me, who have helped me to discover for myself the truth of my being. You have given me something. I have drunk and I have eaten your words.'[2]

In insisting on the fact that he was their 'son', rather than their 'father', Tempels remained within the traditional kinship frame of the Catholic Church, which is based on the belief that all its members belong to the same spiritual family. Nevertheless, in one important respect he undercut a basic Catholic premiss about this family: the doctrinal belief that in the economy of salvation the priestly 'dispensers of grace' and all those who have committed themselves to the 'religious state of life' through the vows of poverty, chastity, and obedience have a higher status of spiritual kinship than lay people. Tempels's tendency to express his relationship to Congolese in kinship terms derived from his recognition of the predominance of the kinship system in Congolese society, and of its especially close relationship to two other primary Congolese institutions, religion and magic. Partly deliberately, partly unconsciously, Tempels used this

---

[1] Tempels, *La Philosophie bantoue*, pp. 19–20.   [2] *La Voix*, p. 7.

knowledge of the attributes of traditional Bantu culture and society to 'adapt' himself and his message to the sentiments and values of the men and women with whom he entered into dialogue. As he recounts it, their reaction was electrifying, and one that accorded him the extraordinary privilege of entering as deeply into their culture as any European or missionary had been allowed:

> Can it be true! We have given you something! All the priests, all the religious who have come to the Congo always wanted to be 'fathers' and 'mothers', they wanted to give, give, give, only give. We could do nothing but swallow. We could give them nothing, it was forbidden. They did not want to be our 'sons'. You, on the contrary, you have become our son. What a great happiness for us! Now, we want you too to give us something, something of yourself.[1]

It would seem that Tempels's admission to the innermost regions of the minds and souls of these Congolese and of their culture was significantly related to his greater readiness to receive from them than the majority of his colleagues. One is forcibly reminded here of Marcel Mauss's classical anthropological work, *The Gift*. Mauss demonstrated that the exchange of gifts is primarily an expressive set of acts involving the transmission not only of something material, but, more importantly, of something interpersonal and symbolic as well. However, gift-exchange, in any given culture, is not totally spontaneous. A triple set of norms provides its structure: the obligations to give, to receive, and to repay, conceptualized by Mauss as 'symmetrical and reciprocal'.[2] Thus, under defined social conditions, an individual or a group is expected to offer a gift to a designated other. In turn, the person (or persons) to whom a gift is offered is expected to accept it. He, thereby, incurs some obligation to balance the exchange by giving the donor something equivalent to what he has received. As Mauss put it, 'The gift not yet repaid debases the man who accepted it.'[3] By and large, Belgian colonial representatives made it quite clear to Congolese that they believed themselves to be bestowing a superior civilization upon them. Kindled by religious fervour, missionaries were even more convinced that they were the bearers of the greatest gift that mankind had ever known, Christ's message as incarnated in Christianity, and more specifically in the Catholic Church.

[1] Ibid., p. 7.
[2] M. Mauss, *The Gift*, trans. J. Cunnison (Glencoe, Ill.: Free Press, 1954), p. 11.
[3] Ibid., p. 63.

Generosity, charity in the original Christian sense of the term, and certainty regarding their own cultural and spiritual superiority, all combined, in the words of the Congolese, to make them 'give, give, give—only give'. The continual receiving from missionaries and other Belgians not only triggered a need in Congolese to reciprocate, it also subjected them to strong social and moral pressure to do so. For the Bantu, as with most primitive or advanced primitive cultures, the primary form of exchange is gift-exchange, rigorously structured and regulated by the norms of giving, receiving, and repaying. Tempels's conversations with Congolese suggested that because of these norms many had experienced considerable strain owing to the pervasive non-recognition by missionaries and other Europeans of anything in their culture or religion of like significance or worth that they could proffer in return. In any case, it appears that through a trial-and-error process Tempels arrived at the insight that enabled him to provide Congolese with this opportunity. In keeping with Mauss's schema, the fact that he acknowledged receiving something of great immaterial value from them made them eager to accept a comparable gift from him.

Something like the sentiment linked with this custom of gift-exchange led Alioune Diop (the renowned Senegalese philosopher and editor of *Présence africaine*)[1] to write in his foreword to the French edition of Tempels's *La Philosophie bantoue*:

> Here is a book essential to the Black, to his *prise de conscience*, to his thirst to situate himself in relation to Europe. It must also be the source-book of all those who are concerned with understanding the African and engaging in a living dialogue with him. For me, this little book is the most important of those that I have read about Africa . . . We thank the Reverend Father Tempels for having given us this book, testimony to us of the humility, the sensibility and the probity which must have characterized his relations with Blacks.[2]

[1] The journal *Présence africaine* was founded and edited by Diop after World War II and published in Paris. It remains a distinguished intellectual journal whose chief contributors are African and French novelists, poets, philosophers, economists, ethnographers, and linguists; among them Aimé Césaire, Leopold Sedar Senghor, David Diop, François Atangana, Jacques Rabemananjara. Until 1955 its Comité de Patronage was made up of such personages as Sartre, Gide, Camus, and Mounier. *Présence africaine* has been an important voice in the Pan-African and Négritude movements.

[2] R.P. Placide Tempels, *La Philosophie bantoue*, trans. A. Rubbens (Paris: Présence africaine, 1961, 2nd edn., pages not numbered). The passages from *La Philosophie bantoue* cited in this book are all quoted from this edition.

La Philosophie bantoue first appeared in 1945–6 as a series of articles in *Band*, a Flemish language journal published in Léopoldville.[1] The articles were translated by Antoine Rubbens, the Katanga lawyer who had closely shared Tempels's concern with adaptation, and published in book form in Élisabethville in 1946. Subsequently, *Présence africaine* in Paris obtained the right to reprint the book, using Rubbens's French translation. It was for the 1949 edition that Alioune Diop wrote his celebrated foreword.

In essence, *Bantu Philosophy* is the systematized expression of the insights at which Tempels arrived through his interchange with Congolese. The basic premiss on which the work rests is Tempels's contention that the Bantu, like all peoples, have 'a set of ideas, a logical system, a complete positive philosophy of the universe, of man and of the things that surround him, of existence, of life, of death and of the hereafter'.[2] The Bantu, Tempels claims, and 'more generally . . . all primitives', have as the 'foundation of their intellectual conceptions of the universe several basic principles, and even a philosophical system, [albeit] relatively simple and primitive, derived from a logically coherent ontology'.[3]

According to Tempels, in Bantu ontology, the fundamental notion of their conception of 'being is the concept of vital force (*force vitale*)'. He went so far as to say that 'all endeavours of the Bantu are oriented toward vital force'.[4] In contradistinction to Western Aristotelian philosophy which looks upon force as an attribute of being, Tempels asserted 'for the Bantu . . . force is the very essence of being . . . being *is* force'.[5] The Bantu conception of force, Tempels argued, embraced all forms of being: God, all human beings, the dead as well as the living, animals, plants, and minerals. All beings of the universe possess their own vital force, and each being has been endowed by God with a certain force that can increase the vital energy of the strongest being of creation, man, human person, or *Muntu*. The Bantu are preoccupied with those agents and events that can augment or diminish the vital energy so crucial to them.

---

[1] P. Tempels, 'Bantu-Filosofie', in *Band*, 1945, vol. 4, no. 2, pp. 60–73; no. 3, pp. 93–102; no. 7, pp. 267–74; no. 11, pp. 413–22; 1946, vol. 5, no. 1, pp. 19–28. The Flemish edition of Tempels's book was published in Belgium, with the help of Professor Dr. A. Burssens, an ethnologist of the University of Ghent, after the first French edition had appeared in the Congo. See, P. Placied Tempels, O.F.M., *Bantoe-Filosofie* (Antwerp: De Sikkel, 1946).

[2] Tempels, *La Philosophie bantoue*, p. 14.

[3] Ibid., p. 15. [4] Ibid., p. 33. [5] Ibid., p. 35.

'The supreme happiness . . . for the Bantu is to possess the greatest vital force; the worst adversity for him . . . is the diminution of this force.'[1] Thus, all negative experiences such as illness, suffering, injustice, failure, and even death itself are considered a reduction of vital force. These misfortunes are believed to be inflicted upon individuals and groups by an external agent endowed with superior force who weakens its victims. It is for this reason that one of the basic properties of all magic to which the Bantu turn is its capacity to increase resistance against these noxious events by reinforcing the individual's vital energy. The Bantu are also acutely aware of what they believe to be the interaction of all forces. They attach great importance to the influence of one person on another and on their ontological interdependence. In the Bantu way of thought,

man never appears as an isolated individual, as an independent substance. All men, all individuals make up a link in the chain of vital forces, a living link, active and passive, attached at the top to the chain of his ascendant lineage and supporting underneath him the lineage of his descent. One could say that among the Bantu, the individual is necessarily a clanic individual. This does not only refer to a juridical relation of dependence or to kinship relations, this must be understood as a real ontological interdependence.[2]

As the several editions of *Bantu Philosophy* indicate, Tempels's work made a great impact on many people, and its influence extended far beyond the Congo and Belgium. Not only was it recognized as important by French African intellectuals, it was read with interest and enthusiasm by anthropologists. Nevertheless, *Bantu Philosophy* also met with much criticism, some of it very bitter and hostile. To begin with, it was pointed out by some social scientists and missionaries that although Tempels advocated that the understanding of Bantu culture be based on 'a thorough knowledge of the language, an advanced ethnological study, a critical examination of the law' and the like, in fact he had based his whole work on the conversations he had held with Congolese in the capacity of a religious teacher expressing a willingness to learn from them. Furthermore, these critics questioned the legitimacy of identifying as Bantu the way of thought that he discerned in what his Congolese interlocutors told him. For the persons with whom he had entered into dialogue were exclusively members of the Luba tribe of North Katanga.

---

[1] Tempels, *La Philosophie bantoue*, p. 31.   [2] Ibid., pp. 73–4.

Tempels not only implied that he was writing about all Bantu peoples but that, in so doing, he was describing 'the soul' of *all* 'primitive peoples'. This allegation regarding the universal applicability of the Bantu philosophy to non-literate societies raised more doubts about the validity of Tempels's thesis.

Other critics questioned whether the characteristic way of thought, set of beliefs and values that he had 'discovered' among Congolese could properly be called the ontology or philosophy of the Bantu. One of the major criticisms of Tempels's work was that he artificially and speciously forced Bantu culture patterns into the logical-rational framework of the Thomistic and Scotistic philosophical systems that he had learnt in the seminary.[1]

Still more sophisticated critics expressed some uneasiness over the assertively intuitive way in which Tempels documented what he affirmed was the central idea in Bantu philosophy. Specifically, Tempels's omission of at least the TshiLuba term for 'vital force' disturbed them, to the point where they were sceptical as to whether this admittedly key concept was understood by Congolese in precisely the way that Tempels developed it.[2]

The most serious opposition to Tempels's book came from Monsignor Jean Félix de Hemptinne, the Catholic Bishop of Élisabethville. He made his objections known soon after the first French edition of the work was published in Élisabethville. His concern was undoubtedly heightened by the fact that *Bantu Philosophy* was likely to attract more attention and be more widely read in French than in the form in which it originally appeared.

Ironically, the first official reaction to *Bantu Philosophy* that Tempels received from senior official Church sources was favourable. The Apostolic Delegate (papal representative) to the Congo, Monsignor Dellepiane, wrote Tempels what has been described as a 'very

[1] The Thomistic and Scotistic traditions of philosophy and theology were at a low ebb in the 1920s when Tempels underwent his training. One cannot blame him for not having been familiar with a revigorated, dynamic, and existence-oriented Neo-Thomism of the 1950s, nor with Hegelian Idealism or Heidegger's Existentialism that did not influence Catholic thought until after World War II. Thus, the conceptual framework in which Tempels developed the antithesis between Western and Bantu philosophies rests on a static, rational, essence-oriented Thomism.

[2] In the Bantu language with which I am most familiar, KiKongo, no word or term exists that could be considered identical with Tempels's notion of vital force. The closest to it would be *ngolo*, which means strength, power, force. This word generally applies to physical or moral strength, but does not necessarily connote an immaterial life-force that constitutes the very essence of being.

sympathetic' letter. This was before de Hemptinne had made it known to Dellepiane that he vehemently disapproved of Tempels's writings. It will be remembered that one of the characteristics of de Hemptinne's general attitude toward Congolese and their culture was a conviction that could be summed up as follows: 'The Blacks had no writing, therefore they had no thought of civilization.' One of his highest goals was to contribute to the achievement of a Latin, Christian civilization in Africa. He believed adamantly that whatever was Congolese either had no bearing on what he defined as civilization or was incompatible with it, and thus, ideally, should be superseded by a combined missionary and colonial effort. It need hardly be said that Tempels's insistence on the distinctiveness of Bantu thought, its inner logic, cogency, and its relationship to a universal humanity was the very antithesis of de Hemptinne's position. Tempels's work outraged him for this reason alone. In addition, he considered Tempels an audacious upstart. For, from his lofty position as bishop, member of an illustrious French-speaking family in the Belgian nobility, and a Benedictine monk from the aristocratic abbey of Loppem-Saint André in Belgium, he did not consider it appropriate for a Franciscan friar of humble Flemish origins to be instructing ecclesiastical and colonial authorities on a so-called Bantu culture. As one of Tempels's Franciscan colleagues put it, Monsignor de Hemptinne's attitude was: 'We don't need that little Capuchin coming here to give us lessons.' As a consequence of the Bishop's intervention, one month after Dellepiane sent Tempels an appreciative letter about his book, he wrote a second one to him, altogether different in tone. This time, he asserted that, contrary to what Tempels had implied in *Bantu Philosophy*, it was important that the doctrine of the Church remain 'pure', and that it be not 'contaminated by African elements'. He also informed Tempels that he intended to have his publication examined in Rome. Dellepiane sent a copy of this letter to de Hemptinne.

De Hemptinne continued to wage a personal campaign against Tempels's book. Working behind the scenes in Rome, he tried to influence the Holy Office to suspend the book on the grounds that it was heretical. Although he did not succeed in this manœuvre, he was largely responsible for the fact that Tempels's return to the Congo at the end of his regular leave of absence from the mission in 1946 was postponed until 1949.

It is sociologically significant that a local bishop should have exercised such influence over the papal representative that he reversed his position regarding the orthodoxy and importance of Tempels's book, and paved the way for the bishop's impact on a central church agency in the Vatican. Part of the explanation lies in the impressive personality of de Hemptinne and the powerful effect that his blazing vision of himself as a 'Prince of the Church' had on others. However, as we shall see in Chapter VIII, this was not the last time that Tempels was destined to be disciplined through the mechanism of a religious superior stretching his prerogatives and personal influence so far as almost to override the position of Roman authorities. It would seem that this recurrent pattern is a potential force in the social control system of the Catholic Church as it applies to its ecclesiastical personnel (including religious Brothers and Sisters, as well as priests). We shall have further occasion to discuss this phenomenon.

Tempels's 1946 leave of absence in Belgium took on the aspect of a temporary exile. Actually, it was never described as such and was ambiguously imposed on him by his Franciscan superiors in Belgium, who for undisclosed reasons continually detained him from returning to the Congo mission. Despite the stress that Tempels experienced under these circumstances, he had the satisfaction of receiving public appreciation and support from a number of persons important to him. One of them was E. Possoz, who wrote a eulogistic article about Tempels's ideas. Later, looking back on the influence that his 'friend' Tempels had had on him, Possoz attributed his own research on 'universal primitive law' to the philosophical discussions he had with Tempels via correspondence in 1943–4 and to his subsequent reflections on *Bantu Philosophy* after it was published.[1] Possoz, in turn, introduced Abbé Joseph Cardijn, a close friend of his, to Tempels's writings. Cardijn made it informally known to Tempels through Possoz that he was very favourably impressed with his book. Cardijn, a diocesan priest of working-class Flemish origins, was already an international as well as a national figure in both labour and church milieux. He was founder and director of the Young Christian Workers movement. Like Tempels, Cardijn was a man of great personal and religious charisma. He attached great value to direct, human communication between priest and lay people about the everyday realities of their lives, in

---

[1] E. Possoz, 'Études Claniques', in *Revue juridique du Congo* (1964), 41ᵉ Année, no. spécial, pp. 215–33.

particular, their work. He also believed that this was not only an important realm for religious action, but, in contrast to many of his colleagues, that it was 'sacred' rather than 'profane'. Over the years, the two men developed a close friendship and later, as we shall see, during a much more critical period in Tempels's life, Cardijn, by then a cardinal, elected to defend Tempels at the highest level of church government in Rome. A glimpse of how many fundamental convictions Cardijn and Tempels shared is afforded us in the opening paragraphs of *Notre Rencontre*, a collection of essays, based on Tempels's religious teaching in the Jamaa, which he published in 1962.[1]

One day, Monsignor Cardijn set forth his views on the apostolate and the teaching of religion: 'Taken as a whole, the clergy has taken the wrong path. Priests are not guilty, but rather they are victims of their education. They emerge from the seminaries swollen with philosophy and theology, and climb into the pulpit where no matter what theological fact they take up, they develop it in two or three points. They talk well above the heads of the faithful, without having taken a close look at them. Instead of beginning from on high, one should begin from below, from the reality of living men. What do you do? Where do you work? Are you satisfied with your job? How much do you make? Are you married? Do you have children? And what do you think of life? What are your desires? etc. On all this, people have their opinion. It is their personal life. These thoughts and aspirations constitute their universe . . . and that's where God is. When one begins like this, one will find that, little by little, understanding and sympathy are born, and finally . . . love.'

Cardijn was one of three churchmen who encouraged Tempels to go on with the line of work he had begun, in the face of whatever criticism it might evoke. Pierre Charles, a Jesuit priest, was another. He was a professor of theology at the Jesuit house of studies in Louvain, an expert and innovator in missionary theory, whose highly expressive writings and speaking style had attracted a large following among the laity as well as the clergy. Because of Charles's standing, it was particularly important to Tempels—both personally and officially—that Charles presented a favourable analysis of *Bantu Philosophy* before the distinguished body of scholars in the Belgian Royal Colonial Institute, and that it was later diffused more widely in the form of an Institute publication.[2] The third famous churchman

---

[1] Tempels, *Notre Rencontre*, p. 9.

[2] R.P. Pierre Charles, 'Note relative à l'ouvrage du R.P. Tempels, intitulé "La Philosophie Bantoue" ', Institut Royal Colonial Belge, *Bulletin des Séances*, no. 2 (1946), 524–32.

who supported Tempels was Dom Celestin Lou, a Chinese Benedictine, member of the abbey of Loppem-Saint André, near Bruges.
Lou's entrance into the Benedictine Order had attracted much
attention, since in lay life he had been a distinguished diplomat and
scholar. The fact that he was author of a well-known comparative
work on Eastern and Western philosophy and religion[1] added significance and prestige to his advocacy of Tempels's thought.

But the most important event that occurred during Tempels's
prolonged stay in Belgium was more personal and mystical in nature.
It was a meeting that he later identified as the happening that ushered
in the third phase of his missionary life—the phase of 'encounter'.
One of his colleagues considered it 'the source of the Jamaa'.
According to Tempels, for many years he had hoped to experience
such a spiritual and human meeting. A few days before it happened,
a Hindu woman, with whom he was discussing religion, prophesied
that it would soon take place. The Indian woman made the prediction
in response to Tempels's despairing remarks about how incomprehensible, and even existentially absurd, he still found the search for
Nirvana, for absolute nothingness and total non-relatedness. She
enjoined him to continue his search and told him that before long
what he was looking for would be given to him. Several days later
Tempels met Sister X, the person he immediately felt to be 'the
other' with whom he was destined to have the critical encounter of
his life. Without any forewarning, Tempels had been sent briefly
to relieve the Franciscan chaplain of a hospital in a provincial city
in Limburg. Sister X was a patient in this hospital, and from the
moment they met it became a 'real encounter'. They told each other
many things about their personal lives. The Sister confided her
deepest religious beliefs and experiences to Tempels. She told him
that she viewed the Holy Trinity as the centre and source of her whole
life, and that she tried to actualize the triple love of God in all that
she did. She described a personal encounter she had had with
Christ, which to her had been a purification and had led her to
a deeper understanding of love. That encounter with Christ had
taken place in the spirit, yet had been very human and, in a sense,
corporeal.

[1] Dom Lou, *Souvenirs et Pensées* (Bruges: Desclée De Brouwer, 1945). Trans-
lated by Michael Derrick and published under the title, *Ways of Confucius and of
Christ* (London: Burns, Oates, 1948). For an interesting biographical note on
Jean Jacques Lou Tseng-Tsiang (1871–1949), see Édouard Neut, *Jean Jacques
Lou: Dom Lou* (Brussels: Éditions Synthèses, Supplément, nos. 192–3, 1962).

The religious meaning of Tempels's encounter with Sister X is movingly recounted in a personal document on the history of the Jamaa, probably written by Father Frans, the Franciscan priest most closely associated in the movement with Tempels. The vocabulary he uses to describe this meeting resembles Tempels's characteristic style, and suggests that it is a verbatim rendering of an interview with him. The encounter provided Tempels with:

a new vision on the whole of Christianity, a new discovery of Christ, or perhaps, a first discovery of Christianity, of God's good tidings to mankind. [Tempels] became conscious that man is created for the other, that man came only to self-realization, to really being man, in encounter with the other. Man, in order to be really man, has to change,[1] has to take the other into himself, has to give himself to the other. Only then does man become truly man. From then on, the whole creation, revelation, incarnation and redemption are seen [by Tempels] in the perspective of the encounter: the encounter of God with man, Christ with humanity (which is crystallized in Mary), encounter and rejection of it by the first man and the first woman. From now on, Christ's presence in the world can only be explained in the sense of an offer of encounter . . . Redemption [is] . . . a real encounter with Christ which, most of the time, or only, is realized with a person or a group of persons.

After a few days of hospital duties, Tempels returned to the local convent, where he started a voluminous correspondence with the Sister. His superior was struck by the frequency with which Tempels sent letters to the Sister and became suspicious about the nature of the correspondence. He exercised his prerogative of opening mail sent or received by members of his house. The letters were interpreted as personal expressions of mutual love, and the matter was referred to both Tempels's Provincial and the Sister's superior. The superiors reacted very strongly. Tempels was transferred to a convent near Antwerp and was forbidden to write to the Sister. She was put under pressure to register the kind of formal complaint against him at the diocesan chancery that normally would initiate juridical procedures against him in the Church. However, she refused to do this. And Tempels, in his own words, 'decided to remain faithful to his first human encounter that brought him light', his meeting with Sister X.

Tempels passed through a time of deep depression. Then, one night, he had an encounter with the Virgin Mary, comparable to

---

[1] In Dutch or Flemish, the verb *veranderen* (to change) has as its root the term *ander* (other, the other).

the one that Sister X had experienced with Christ. To Tempels, this was confirmation of the authenticity of his encounter with Sister X and of its deepest inner meaning. He confided the whole experience to Abbé Cardijn and Dom Lou. Both men were impressed with the spiritual significance of this meeting for Tempels and encouraged him to continue and develop his relationship with the Sister. They also suggested that he try to apply the insights that he had gained from this encounter and those on which *Bantu Philosophy* was based to the area of catechesis, and work out a Bantu catechism. This Tempels proceeded to do. By the time he left Belgium in 1949, he had written a small brochure entitled *Catéchèse bantoue*.[1]

In 1949 Tempels was finally granted permission to return to the Congo. The ecclesiastical sanctions that had been imposed on him in response to Rome's adverse reaction to *La Philosophie bantoue* and his Belgian superiors' punitive attitude toward his relationship with Sister X had taken an emotional toll on him. He arrived in the Congo in a dispirited frame of mind. He had hardly settled in Kabondo-Dianda as an assistant pastor when his mission superior received news from Belgium that the Congregation for the Propagation of the Faith at the Vatican had issued a formal interdiction forbidding Tempels to resume his missionary work in the Congo. The superior decided that it made no sense to ship Tempels back to Europe in response to this belated communication, but he did inform Tempels that such an order had been issued. Feeling himself to be a *persona non grata*, Tempels became more depressed. Though he conscientiously fulfilled his duties as assistant pastor, teaching catechism to schoolchildren and adults, he did so in a listless, routine way that dramatically contrasted with the creative and ebullient manner of his adaptation period of 1943–6. Nevertheless, the fact that he was once again in the Congo engaged in the activity of giving religious instruction to men, women, and children seems to have progressively revived and healed him. After a time, colleagues noted that he had begun to tape-record indigenous songs from various tribes of the area, and they interpreted this as the first real sign that he was emerging from his depression. In true Tempels fashion, what had begun as a casual, personal project gradually became a collection of no less than 2,000 songs that he later contributed to the National Radio Institute in Brussels.

[1] P. Tempels, *Catéchèse bantoue* (Bruges: Abbaye de St André, Les Questions missionaires, 2e série, fasc. 6, 1948).

Over the course of the next few years Tempels was rapidly moved from one short assignment to another. These included: Kajeje, a small mission centre 40 miles from Kabondo-Dianda (1952); Le Marinel, a labour camp for Congolese workers employed in the construction of a dam on the Lualaba river, 60 miles north of Kolwezi (March–May 1953); and Ruwe, a suburb of Kolwezi, where he worked from 1953 to 1956 in various capacities. At first, he was director of an experimental, inter-racial technical school in Ruwe, that was founded and organized by Union Minière. That project rapidly failed. Europeans and Congolese in Katanga were not ready to participate in such a racially integrated endeavour. Tempels was subsequently named head pastor of the Ruwe parish, where he was also appointed professor of religion at the teacher-training school. And it was at Ruwe that the Jamaa was born.

It was during this period in his missionary career that Tempels achieved what he considered to be a true encounter with Congolese. For him, it was the culmination of all that he had learned and experienced from the first two phases of his life as a missionary, and from his meeting at once synthesizing and transcendent, with Sister X. Now, in his dialogue with Congolese, he not only listened to their deepest thoughts and aspirations, and gave of himself to them in the same way, but he also discovered with them a 'common truth' and a 'common being':

Listen, if these are your aspirations, your thoughts, well then, I must tell you that, in spite of all the subtleties and all my formulas imported from Europe, I am beginning to discover the same things, the same aspirations, the same thoughts, the same desire for full, total, intense life; for fecundity, paternity; for union with others. Yes, it seems to me that I am discovering in myself the same sentiments that you have![1]

Once this 'discovery of our common truth' had taken place, Tempels felt that it was now possible to search together for a 'common solution to our common aspirations'. In his own words, 'I was supremely surprised to note that Christianity—the Christianity that I wished to teach—had just been born from this encounter.'[2] What Christianity meant to Tempels and his Congolese interlocutors in this encounter was first of all a personal meeting with Christ who (according to Tempels) said, 'I have come so that you may have life and have it abundantly . . . I am the life! Life for you is communion with

[1] *La Voix*, p. 7.   [2] Ibid.

Me, and I have come so that you may have it, abundant and total.'[1]
Through this meeting, they became one with Him, with God the
Father, and with each other. 'That is exactly what we were looking
for', these Congolese were convinced, Tempels wrote, 'what we are
trying to be: "one". We do not want to be like strangers among us,
and we do not want to be strangers to you; we want to know ourselves and to know one life [together].'[2] As Tempels and his earliest
followers recount it, this was the notion and experience of unity
out of which 'a movement that called itself the Jamaa' emerged.

[1] Ibid., p. 8.   [2] Ibid.

CHAPTER III

Social Organization and Development of the Jamaa

THE origins, spread, social organization, and ambience of the Jamaa cannot be fully understood without some knowledge of South Katanga. This province of the Congo is not just a specific geographical area and politico-administrative unit; it is a distinctive Congolese subculture.[1]

South Katanga is located on a plateau 4,000 foot high. Its climate is semi-tropical, alternating between a seven-month dry season (April–October) and a shorter rainy season. During the dry period there is an autumnal crispness in the air (the average temperature is 77 °F.), a cutting wind blows over the open plains, the sky is an electric blue, and the dazzlingly clear light gives everything a brilliant, etched look. This throws into bas-relief the essentially barren nature of the Katanga savannah. The climate is not favourable to agriculture; the soil is so poor that trees and crops do not thrive on it; only bushes, shrubs, and huge, fifteen-foot-high ant-hills decorate its bleak surface. All this is in sharp contrast to the numerous rivers, churning with rapids and waterfalls, that flow northward through the valleys of the area toward the great Lualaba-Congo river. One feels the vast untapped potential for hydroelectric power in these waterways.

The fecundity of Katanga lies below the surface. '[Even] at night [one sees] immense open pits, blazingly white under the floodlights, electric powered excavators, pursuing with an unbroken rhythm their ceaseless work, and long electric trains filled with ore, gliding silently . . .'[2]

[1] Two reliable works that throw light on Katanga are: Jules Gérard-Libois, *Katanga Secession*, trans. Rebecca Young (Madison, Wisconsin: The University of Wisconsin Press, 1966); and Crawford Young, *Politics in the Congo* (Princeton, N.J.: Princeton University Press, 1965).

[2] Union Minière du Haut-Katanga, *Union Minière du Haut-Katanga, 1906–1956* (Brussels: L. Cuypers, 1956), p. 209.

South Katanga is the great mining area of the Congo. Whereas, at the time of independence (1960), Katanga's agriculture represented only 10 per cent of the total agricultural output of the country, 75 per cent of the total mining production of the Congo originated in Katanga. The value of Katanga's mining output amounted to approximately 12 billion Belgian francs (U.S. $240 million). The bulk of the mining production consisted of copper (302,297 metric tons), zinc (162,540), manganese (206,932), cobalt (8,222), plus an assortment of rare metals, such as germanium, palladium, cadmium, tungsten, wolframite, colombo-tantalite, and uranium.[1] In order to appreciate the magnitude of these figures it should be pointed out that the Congo is the world's leading producer of cobalt (60 per cent) and ranks sixth among the world's copper-producing nations.[2]

Looming over this impressive mining activity was Union Minière du Haut-Katanga, a mammoth enterprise, which was a subsidiary of the leading Belgian holding company, Société Générale de Belgique.[3] Right from its inception in 1906, Union Minière was the chief employer in all Katanga. On 31 December 1960, for example, it had on its payroll 1,755 management personnel (of whom 86 were Africans) and 20,876 manual workers (all of whom were Africans).

In at least two major respects, the company was a nucleus of industrial and commercial development. By the end of 1954, it had been instrumental in launching no less than 2,600 firms in the area. Furthermore, its portfolio included participation in 17 Congolese, 10 Belgian, and 5 other foreign companies. The location of Élisabethville (Lubumbashi), Jadotville (Likasi), and Kolwezi, the three principal mining centres of Union Minière, in the heart of Central Africa necessitated the building and maintenance of a vast network

[1] Banque Nationale du Congo, *Rapport annuel 1967* (Kinshasa, 1968), p. 53. The principal producer, Union Minière du Haut-Katanga, was nationalized on 1 January 1967, and is now known as Gécamines (La Générale des Carrières et des Mines). According to the *Bulletin* of the Banque Nationale du Congo (VII, no. 4, 1968, p. 23), by 1968 the production figures were: 326,000 metric tons of copper, 150,675 tons of zinc, 187,180 tons of manganese, and 10,540 tons of cobalt. The proportion of mineral products in the Congo's export earnings climbed from 58 per cent in 1958 to 83 per cent in 1967. Copper, cobalt, and zinc account for approximately 80 per cent of the value of the mining production.

[2] Gécamines is the third-largest copper corporation in the world, after Kennecott and Anaconda.

[3] For more detailed economic, financial, and policy information on Société Générale and Union Minière, see: *Morphologie des groupes financiers*, 2nd edition (Brussels: Centre de Recherche et d'Information Socio-politiques, 1966), pp. 71–184.

of railways for the transportation of the ore and the metals. For example, Lubumbashi is 1,300 miles away from Lobito, the Angolan port on the Atlantic Ocean, 1,700 miles from Matadi, the Congo's main seaport, and 1,600 miles from Beira, the Indian Ocean port in Mozambique. The two main railway lines on which U.M. depended were the Belgian B.C.K. (Chemin de Fer du Bas-Congo au Katanga) and the Benguela Railway Company (Dilolo-Lobito). The principal shareholder in the Benguela Railway Co. is the Tanganyika Concessions Ltd. which until the nationalization of Union Minière held the largest single private block of shares in this company (14·47 per cent). The Union Minière complex also needed vast amounts of electric power, particularly for the electrolysis process in the refinement of the ore it mined, as well as for its transportation system.[1] Between 1930 and 1960, the Sogéfor (Société Générale des Forces Hydro-Électriques du Katanga), a subsidiary of U.M., built four power stations: Francqui (1930) and Bia (1950) on the Lufira river, Delcommune (1952) and Le Marinel (1956) on the Lualaba. Together, these stations provided South Katanga with 2·5 billion kWh of electric power.

South Katanga, then, is characterized by a high degree of industrialization, which surpasses that of other regions in the Congo and in Central Africa, and is second only to the Johannesburg area of the Republic of South Africa. Furthermore, as the vivid description of the Katangese mines cited above implies, the work at Union Minière is almost futuristic in the degree to which it is mechanized and computerized. The management takes special pride in the clockwork precision and exquisite control it has achieved through what it considers to be the ultimate in Taylorism.

It is not an exaggeration to say that virtually everything in South Katanga other than its mineral ore and its ant-hills was imported, planted, built, or manufactured by Union Minière. Even the African population is largely an immigrant labour force, brought from other Congolese districts or provinces to South Katanga. Before the arrival of Europeans in this part of the Congo, the area had the lowest population density in the Congo.[2] Two local tribes predominated,

---

[1] One ton of copper produced by this method requires 2,350 kWh, one ton of cobalt by the same method 6,000 kWh, and one ton of cobalt processed by the electric furnace uses up to 10,000 kWh.

[2] Even at the end of the 1940s, Katanga had a density of only 2·4 inhabitants per square km; the national average was 4·6. See Ministère des Colonies, *Plan décennal pour le développement économique et social du Congo Belge* (Brussels: Les

the ALunda and the BaYeke. The first wave of workers that Union Minière brought to South Katanga in the early 1900s came from Northern Rhodesia. During the 1920s and 1930s, workers were recruited in North Katanga, Lomami, and South Kasai. Up to the present time, Congolese from the Kasai constitute a majority of the labour force. Members of the Luba tribe are especially numerous and successful among them. Surveys made in Élisabethville in 1956, for example, show that 53 per cent of male workers in that city were 'Kasai' people, overwhelmingly Luba.[1] Since, as will be shown, many members of the Jamaa are of Luba origins, it is noteworthy that, according to another study,[2] the total number of BaLuba in Élisabethville in 1956 amounted to 44·9 per cent of the African population: 26·8 per cent were Luba from Kasai and 18·1 per cent were Luba-Shankadi from North Katanga. Even higher proportions obtain in the Kolwezi area. For example, in the two company towns, Musonoi and Metalkat, BaLuba from Kasai and from North Katanga represented 70 and 80 per cent respectively of the population in 1963.[3]

Beginning in 1927, Union Minière, like a number of other large industrial corporations in the Belgian Congo, adopted a policy of 'stabilizing' its African labour force. Among the measures it instituted at this time were a voluntary basis for the recruitment of workers, the offering of a three-year, renewable contract, and the provision of monetary and other help to young workers contemplating marriage. As a consequence, the proportion of married workers progressively increased and the rate of labour turnover decreased.[4]

Éditions De Visscher, 1949, tome 1), p. 9. According to Anatole Romaniuk, the figures for the period 1955–7 were 3·0 for Katanga and 5·5 for the whole country. Katanga still had the lowest density of the Congo's six provinces. Total population of the Congo in 1956 was estimated at 12,777,000. For the best demographic data on the Congo, see Anatole Romaniuk, 'The Demography of the Democratic Republic of the Congo', Chapter 6, pp. 241–341, in William Brass et al., The Demography of Tropical Africa (Princeton, N.J.: Princeton University Press, 1968).

[1] E. Toussaint, Congrès Scientifique d'Élisabethville, VI (Aug. 1950), p. 45.

[2] Jacques Denis, 'Élisabethville: matériaux pour une étude de la population africaine', in Bulletin trimestriel du Centre d'Étude des Problèmes Sociaux Indigènes (CEPSI), no. 34 (1956), 167.

[3] Personal fieldnotes, 4 Feb. 1964.

[4] Maurice Robert, Contribution à la géographie du Katanga (Brussels: Institut Royal Colonial Belge, Section des Sciences Naturelles et Médicales, tome XXIV, fasc. 3, 1954), pp. 11–12 and 61. By 1955, 90 per cent of the U.M. labour force

At Union Minière, as in other large companies, the late 1920s also marked the beginning of an all-embracing policy of industrial or corporate paternalism. Housing, family allowances, hospitals, schools, churches, *foyers sociaux*, and canteens were created by the company for the workers and their families. The camps and communities established were 'total institutions'[1] in several senses. Until the mid-1950s, residence in them was obligatory and the use of outside facilities was restricted. Camp authorities substituted for the normal civil administration and were supported by a Union Minière police force. Even the Catholic clergy who carried out religious, educational, and social functions were engaged and paid by the company. Union Minière's policy was to limit the missionary personnel it permitted to work within its confines largely to Belgian Catholic priests, Brothers, and Sisters.

One of the primary motives of this paternalism, beneficient though it was in many regards, was to 'keep a select labour force at work in [the] mines and . . . plants for as long as possible'.[2] Perhaps the most authoritative statement of Union Minière's social policy for its 'indigenous' employees was its memorandum issued in 1946 as a monograph. The introduction to this document sets forth its basic principles:

Each agent must effectively and sincerely collaborate in the pursuit of the Company's goal; he must take care not to jeopardize the reputation of being a good employer in the eyes of the Blacks that [the Company] has established and, each one in his sphere of action must be a moral as well as a technical educator for the Blacks whom the Company entrusts to him.

The colonizer must never lose sight of the fact that the Negroes have the souls of children, souls which mould themselves to the methods of the educator; they watch, listen, feel and imitate. Under all circumstances, the European must show himself to be a calm and balanced chief, good without weakness, benevolent without familiarity, active in method and,

was considered 'stable', 45 per cent of them being in the employment of the company for a period of ten years and more. See *Union Minière du Haut-Katanga: 1906–1956*, p. 254.

[1] See Erving Goffman, *Asylums: Essays on the Social Situation of Mental Patients and Other Inmates* (Garden City, N.Y.: Anchor Books, Doubleday, 1961), especially pp. 3–124, 'On the Characteristics of Total Institutions'.

[2] L. Mottoulle, *Politique sociale de l'Union Minière du Haut-Katanga pour sa main-d'œuvre indigène et ses résultats au cours de vingt années d'application* (Brussels: Institut Royal Colonial Belge, Section des Sciences Morales et Politiques, tome XIV, fasc. 3, 1946), p. 5.

above all, just in punishment of misbehaviour, as in the reward of good behaviour.

Every agent of the Company who does not thoroughly assimilate these principles or who acts counter to them risks impeding, and sometimes wiping out results that have been laboriously achieved, and, in the eyes of the Company, is an uninteresting, and even bad agent.

The Board of Directors of the Company states as a principle that anything that can harm the physical, moral or social well-being of the workers is contrary to the true interests of Union Minière.[1]

Union Minière aspired to and succeeded in dominating every aspect of the lives of their workers as completely as they did the South Katangese landscape. (In their more ironic moments, Congolese referred to this policy and its enactment as *mupolishi*, an allusion to the private police force of Union Minière.) The company created an artificial, manicured world of houses, graduated in size and quality according to the workers' status in the company's occupational hierarchy. It bounded them with asphalt avenues and highways, planted orderly rows of bougainvilleas and jacarandas around them, and flanked them with community buildings from which the social services were dispensed.

In many inward and outward ways, the Africans who lived in these company towns were transmuted by them as well as by the Taylorized universe in which they worked. Yet their kinship system, ethnic identity, religious and magical beliefs did not yield as easily to the impact of Union Minière as the Katangese terrain did to the company's gigantic shovels, scrapers, and bulldozers. As a consequence, life in these towns was a unique blend of traditional and modern, which one astute observer called 'rustic-industrial'.[2]

All this was physically as well as socially separated from the much less populated, but more luxurious world of the Europeans. These were largely Belgians, engineers, technicians, administrators, and executives of Union Minière and its subsidiaries.[3] The houses, hospitals, and churches of the European personnel were also built and provided by the company. A feature of their lives was the *Cercle*, a clubhouse, fitted out with tennis courts, swimming pool, playground, bar, and restaurant, where the white population congregated.

---

[1] Ibid., pp. 5–6.   [2] Personal communication, Father Frans, Aug. 1963.
[3] In the city of Élisabethville, there was also a sizeable number of independent settlers, primarily professionals and merchants.

The thoughts and conversations of these Belgian Katangese centred almost obsessively on their possessive love of what they considered their piece of Africa. Their living-rooms displayed a collection of choice Congolese *objets d'art*. In a master-to-servant manner, they were involved in the lives of their 'boys' (household employees) and their boys' kin. They constantly regaled each other with anecdotes about these servants and about those *évolués* on whom they proudly claimed to have had a 'civilizing' influence. Their cocktail and after-dinner conversations brimmed with anthropological exotica about Congolese tribes and traditional customs. And their facile observations on the basic personality of 'the Blacks' echoed the conclusions on this subject codified in the company's manual. Despite their preoccupation with things African, and their daily contact with Congolese in their industrial, educational, and social service functions, these Europeans were barricaded from the Black community by the caste system that they themselves created.

As suggested in our account of the stages of social and religious evolution through which Father Tempels passed, the Catholic missionary clergy in Katanga shared many of the attitudes towards Congolese that characterized the Belgian community.[1] The fact that the Catholic Church and its personnel were so closely entwined with the activities of Union Minière was an important regional manifestation of the more general colonial interconnection between the government, the Church, and big business described in Chapter II. In Katanga, industry was so dominant that it commanded some of the usual powers of the State. It also co-opted some of the influence of organized religion in such a way that it significantly blurred the demarcation in Katanga between the spheres of the sacred and the profane.

Three major groups of Catholic missionary priests had primary ecclesiastical responsibility in the dioceses of South Katanga: Franciscans, Benedictines, and Salesians. In 1963, they numbered

[1] I do not mean to imply by my concentration on the Catholic missionary clergy that I am indifferent to Protestant missionary activity in Katanga. My focus is dictated by the fact that the Jamaa was 'born' inside the Catholic Church in Katanga. The Protestant presence in this part of the Congo is significant, and antedates the arrival of the first Catholic missionaries. The first Protestant mission established in Katanga was set up by the British Garanganze Evangelical Mission in 1886. The most important Protestant mission in Katanga today is the Methodist Mission of South Congo, founded by American missionaries. See E. M. Braekman, *Histoire du protestantisme au Congo* (Brussels: Éditions de la Librairie des Éclaireurs Unionistes, 1961).

80, 66, and 57 priests respectively. We have already indicated that the priests closely associated with the Jamaa were primarily Franciscans and Benedictines, and that the strongest European subcultural influence upon the movement came from the Franciscans. In this connection, and with respect to the larger Katangese milieu in which the Jamaa fits, the social origins of these two groups of priests are significant. By and large, the Franciscans were recruited from Flemish Belgian families of working- and lower-middle-class status, residing in villages and small towns. In contrast, the Benedictines belonged to predominantly French-speaking Belgian families, professional and industrial, *haut bourgeois*, and noble. They were members of the same social strata that provided the Société Générale and Union Minière with their higher management echelons.

The chief groups of religious sisters in Katanga were the Benedictines, the Sisters of Charity (of Ghent), the Canonesses of the Roman Union, and the Sisters of Mary (of Pittem). The Benedictines and the Canonesses had social backgrounds similar to those of the Benedictine monks; the Sisters of Charity came mostly from Flemish middle–middle- and lower–middle-class origins; the Sisters of Mary were mainly daughters from Flemish peasant and working-class milieux. The relatively few nuns who became Jamaa were randomly distributed between the first three groups of sisters.

In so far as the impact of the Catholic Church on the African population is concerned, throughout South Katanga the Luba, from both Kasai and North Katanga, constituted the most dynamic segment of the Congolese laity. Parish activities and all kinds of Catholic religious movements depended heavily upon their participation and zeal.

No socio-historical survey of South Katanga would be complete without mention of a cardinal event that had a traumatic effect on Congolese and Belgians, clergy and laity. It also influenced the Jamaa's recruitment and diffusion, and played a critical role in shaping the Katete aspects of Jamaa doctrine and ritual. The Katanga Secession officially began on 11 July 1960 and ended on 14 January 1963. However, the impetus for the province's autonomy extended as far back in time as 1910, when the Minister of Colonies, Jules Renkin, suggested that Katanga should depend solely on Brussels, rather than on Boma, the Congo's capital at that time. Over the course of the next fifty years, Katanga's European society exerted continuous pressure on Belgian authorities to acknowledge

Katanga's unique economic importance in the Congo in the form of a privileged political autonomy from Boma and subsequently from Léopoldville, to which the seat of the colonial government was transferred in 1926. From the first, it would seem, these Belgians looked upon Katanga as a small independent country, a state within a state, which they themselves had discovered, developed, created in their own image: a land where they had staked out their lives and which they were ferociously determined to defend, even to the point of death.

In 1958, with the birth of the Conakat (Confédération des Associations Tribales du Katanga), a Congolese political party made up of so-called 'authentic Katangans' (Lunda, Luba-Shankadi, Yeke, Sanga, Tshokwe, Tabwa, Ndembu, Bemba, etc.), these leanings toward autonomy and federalism ceased to be a monopoly of European residents. One of the main features of the Conakat was its organized fears about the success attained by 'foreigners' from Kasai who had come to Katanga to work in its urban and mining centres. In particular, the founders of the Conakat were concerned about the Luba-Kasai, who now occupied the lion's share of whatever high-ranking positions were open to Congolese in civil administration, banking, trade, and industry. Partly as a reaction to this development, the Conakat allied itself with those Europeans who supported the notion of 'an autonomous and federated' Katanga, headed by 'authentic Katangans or men of good will who have given proof of their devotion to the cause of Katanga'. Originally, the Conakat also included the Association of the BaLuba, the Balubakat, founded in 1957. At that time, the Balubakat defined its twofold goal as the promotion of mutual aid among BaLuba and harmony with their Belgian 'civilizers'. However, the increasingly vehement anti-Kasai position of the Conakat, and its progressive identification with Belgian Katangese alienated the BaLuba from the Conakat. In November 1959, the Balubakat broke away, militantly rejecting their thesis of separatism and affirming support for 'unity for the Congo'. This bitter, ethnically complicated tug of war over the political future of Katanga took place on the troubled eve of Congo's independence. Katanga declared its secession from the Democratic Republic of the Congo only eleven days after the Congo had officially become a nation-state.

I will not go into further details of this historic episode and the subsequent administrative, political, and military intervention of the United Nations in the Congo. Life became dangerous for the BaLuba in South Katanga. By the end of 1961, approximately 100,000 men, women, and children (65 per cent of them Luba) had taken shelter in a refugee camp on the outskirts of Élisabethville and placed themselves under the protection of the United Nations armed forces.[1] Over a three-month period, May–July 1962, about 70,000 of these refugees were airlifted to Kasai and North Katanga by the U.N. authorities. Among the 'refugees' who spent time in what came to be known as the BaLuba Camp were perhaps 400–500 members of the Jamaa. There, along with the other inhabitants of the camp, they were exposed to many frightening and degrading experiences. Principal among these was the violence unleashed by the Jeunesses Balubakat, ferociously angry young Luba men committed to guerilla warfare against all whom they defined as their enemies. These included the non-Luba Katangese, African as well as European, and even the U.N. forces whom they regarded as allies of their persecutors. The wrath of these youths fed on itself in such a way that they established a reign of terror in the camp that affected Luba and non-Luba alike. They looted, pillaged, raped, committed sexual atrocities, and, in some instances, engaged in cannibalism. In the face of such brutality, one of the responses of the Jamaa people was to draw closer together and to offer each other support. They were also attracted to other inhabitants of the camp for whom religion was of central importance. For many of them, it was the first time that they had had any meaningful contact with Congolese who belonged to Protestant churches, or with members of indigenous religious movements, such as WaApostolo, Kitawala (an African version of Jehovah's Witnesses), etc. There is a consensus among members of the Catholic clergy with close connections to the Jamaa that, partly because the Jamists were ill-prepared for these encounters they appended to their own religious beliefs and practices fragments of these other religious systems that attracted them. The Jamaa observers contend that the 'deviations' of the Katete, for example, are syncretisms of this sort, especially influenced by the notions and practices of the Kitawala. However, on the basis of my knowledge of other Congolese religious movements,[2] I feel that this

[1] See Jules Gérard-Libois, *Katanga Secession*, pp. 264–5. For a more partisan, U.N. view, see *To Katanga and Back: A U.N. Case History* (New York: Grosset & Dunlap, 1962) written by Conor Cruise O'Brien, former United Nations Representative in Katanga.

[2] In addition to my personal, first-hand knowledge of several Congolese religious movements, with Professors Renée C. Fox and Jan Vansina, I have

influence has been exaggerated; for I am struck by the recurrence
of beliefs, symbols, rites, and behaviours similar to those of the
Katete in numerous of these movements. I am more inclined to
regard these phenomena as patterns that again and again emerge
when Bantu religion and Christianity meet, than to attribute them
so specifically to the impact that the adherents of particular religious
groups had upon Jamists.

When the United Nations flew the thousands of Luba back to
Kasai, many Jamists were among them. They disembarked at the
Mbuji-Mayi airport and made their way back to their villages of
origin. These *bena-avions* ('people of the airplanes'), as the local
people called them, began to teach the doctrine and the way of life
of the Jamaa. To some extent, they were invited to do so by Catholics in the region who had already heard of the existence of the
Jamaa in South Katanga. The local clergy was also receptive to the
teaching and the religious life style that the Jamists conveyed. And so
it was that the movement spread from South Katanga to South Kasai.

In 1963, the total Jamaa membership in the three urban centres
of South Katanga, namely Lubumbashi, Likasi, and Kolwezi, was
roughly estimated at 1,600 baba and mama. Since married couples
generally enter the movement together, this means that Jamists tend
to be equally divided between adult men and women. However, there
was a slightly larger group of women than men in the Jamaa, owing
to the fact that a small number of widows and women separated
from their husbands had been admitted to full membership. Jamists
constituted approximately 10 per cent of the Catholic married couples
in the area, out of a Catholic population that represented about
35 per cent of all inhabitants of these three urban agglomerations.

The tribal origins of Jamaa baba and mama were fairly representative of the Congolese population in South Katanga. Whereas
BaLuba constituted 60 per cent of the African inhabitants of the
region, they made up about 70 per cent of the Jamaa membership.
The latter proportion is consonant with the greater numerical
representation and participation of the Luba element in South
Katangese Catholicism than any other ethnic group.

analysed some 3,000 pages of documentary material on movements that occurred
in the Kasai region of the Congo, from the early 1900s until 1960. See Willy
De Craemer, Jan Vansina, and Renée C. Fox, 'Religious Movements in Central
Africa: A Theoretical Study', *Comparative Studies in Society and History*
18, no. 4 (Oct. 1976).

As far as occupation is concerned, a clear majority of the men in the movement, some 60 per cent, were skilled workers, most of whom were employed by Union Minière in positions such as miner, mechanic, fitter, electrician, welder, machinist, driver of heavy mine equipment (20-ton dump trucks, electrical shovels, cranes, scrapers, bulldozers, etc.). In general, these men belonged to the stable core of Union Minière's work force, having been steadily employed by the company for 15 to 20 years. Those workers who were not in the employment of Union Minière worked for B.C.K. and other large enterprises (Metalkat, Sogéchim, etc.) that are subsidiaries of U.M. or Société Générale. In a sense, Jamaa men formed an occupational élite in the Union Minière cosmos. They held the highest ranking blue-collar jobs open to Congolese. This category of position comprised no more than 10 per cent of the corporation's total African labour force. It is worth noting that these statistics on the number of Jamaa men who were skilled labourers contradict the ideological belief held by both clergy and laity, in and outside the movement, that the membership of the Jamaa has been drawn predominantly from the lowest occupational strata of Katangese.

The next largest number of Jamaa men, about 20 per cent, were engaged as unskilled workers and domestic employees, mainly in the service of Union Minière, its affiliated firms, and their European personnel.

In every parish where there was a Jamaa, some at least of the men associated with the movement held white-collar jobs in government or business organizations, while, on average, two or three others occupied teaching positions, as *moniteur* (primary school teacher), director of an elementary school, or instructor in a trade school. Taken together, these two groups, white-collar employees and teachers, accounted for 10 per cent of the baba in the Jamaa. The teachers played a crucial role in the Jamaa, since their training and experience qualified them for inclusion among the most important and effective instructors of the *mafundisho*. Both the white-collar workers and the teachers belonged to occupational categories that were among the most prestigious of those open to Congolese inhabitants of Katanga before 1960, when the Congo gained its independence. Furthermore, the majority of these men had received more than a primary school education, another uncommon phenomenon in pre-independence Katanga. Thus, as regards its social stratification, this male constituency of the Jamaa, even more than the skilled workers in the movement, belied the notion that its membership was recruited from the humblest echelons of local Katangese society.[1]

The mama of the Jamaa, like most Congolese women in Katanga, were wives and mothers, and had received a minimum of formal education. Very few of them were graduates of primary school, or were gainfully employed in any way other than petty roadside or market trade. These occupational and educational attributes were as much a reflection of the traditional status of women in Congolese society, as they were consequences of Belgian colonial policy.

The social structure and organization of the Jamaa cannot be fully appreciated without some mention of the various kinds of activities in which the movement involves members, and the extraordinary amount of time that the baba and mama devote to them. To begin with, there is a weekly schedule of *mafundisho* meetings. This includes one general meeting, open to the public, two meetings for Jamists in the early stages of initiation, and another one for advanced members of the third degree. In addition, Jamists participate in several forms of religious worship. Not only do they attend Mass every Sunday, but many go to Mass every morning during the week before beginning the day's work. In some parishes, each day during the months of May and October, members gather in the church for extensive devotions to the Virgin Mary. It is also common practice for many members to make a novena, i.e. a prayer meeting in the church during the first nine days of each month.

These formal, scheduled, relatively large-scale Jamaa functions do not exhaust the members' involvement in the movement's activities. Baba and mama hold private meetings in their homes several times a week. They make calls on Jamists and non-Jamists to exult or mourn with them at times of birth, illness, or death, and to offer them material assistance (help with household chores, food, money, etc.) when needed.

No Jamaa meeting or activity lasts for less than an hour, and most of them go on for two or three hours. Private meetings in Jamaa

[1] Mention should be made of one other very small occupational group in the Jamaa, particularly in connection with the idiosyncratic profile of one Jamaa in a Kolwezi parish. Here, most of the 100 male members of the movement were engaged in commerce, mainly as small, independent shopkeepers. The fact that the occupational structure of the community was autonomous from the Union Minière complex accounts for this pattern.

homes sometimes stretch throughout most of the night. No tallying of hours is needed to make clear how committed Jamists are to their movement and what demands this commitment makes on their time and energy.

As the foregoing implies, the fact that the Jamaa came to fruition in the land of Union Minière rather than in smaller, more rural and traditional, inland communities is of major sociological import. Although, as will be shown in Chapter VI, living and working in the urban centres and industrial camps of South Katanga did not necessarily dispel traditional Congolese attitudes, beliefs, and behaviours in the realms of kinship, religion, and magic, it did importantly modify the occupational experience and outlook of Jamists and non-Jamists alike in the South Katangese population. Furthermore, it might be said that one of the most far-reaching impacts that the economic characteristics of South Katanga had on the Jamaa was its very fluid pattern of horizontal labour mobility. For Union Minière continually moved its Congolese work force from one site to another according to its programme of extraction and production which, in turn, was contingent upon fluctuations in demand and supply of copper on the world market. The dissemination of the Jamaa was greatly facilitated by the policy of systematic displacement. Jamaa priests (Father Tempels included), as well as baba and mama, carried the message of the movement as they travelled from one community to another on the wave of this labour migration. In this way, and chiefly through personal contact, they 'engendered' new 'spiritual children' of the Jamaa.

The case history that follows epitomizes the process underlying the Jamaa's diffusion from its birthplace in Ruwe to a sequence of other communities throughout South Katanga. It also exemplifies many of the characteristics of the social background of Jamaa members that we have cited, as well as their high commitment to the movement. Finally, it throws light on charismatic aspects of the Jamaa that are primarily Congolese in origin; in this respect, it is especially relevant because its protagonist is a Congolese founder-leader of the movement.

Baba Gaston Mukendi is one of the Congolese leaders of the Jamaa. He and his wife do not belong to the small circle of seven married couples who were Tempels's first disciples and the founders of the movement. However, baba Gaston was one of the earliest persons who entered the Jamaa under the dual influence of Tempels, its prophet leader, and the seven couples. He became a Jamaa adherent in late 1954, the year of the movement's inception. To this day he is considered one of its most exemplary members and also one of the most active teachers and disseminators of its message.

Baba Gaston is now forty-nine years of age. He is a member of the Luba tribe of North Katanga. In his youth he received a primary school education. His wife, mama Marcelline, forty-three years old, is also Luba-Katanga and her formal schooling consisted of three years of primary education at a Catholic mission. The couple were already baptized Catholics at the time of their marriage in a local parish church. They have seven children.

In 1954, when they became members of the Jamaa, they were living at Dilala (2 km from Ruwe) in the workers' camp of Entrelco, the electric power company for which Gaston worked as an electrician and foreman. At that time, Entrelco was in charge of the electrification programme of the Katanga railway system. Through the informal network of his relations with other couples in the area, Gaston had occasion to meet and observe the Jamaa founders. He was deeply impressed with the quality of the relationship that existed between these husbands and wives, as well as between the couples and Father Tempels. 'I was astonished by the life of these couples . . . by their union . . . Ever since I was a small child, my ideal was understanding with others. I wanted to realize this ideal understanding with my wife . . .' He sought out Father Tempels, eager to learn from him how he could achieve this kind of oneness. However, he wryly admits that at this stage in his spiritual evolution, he still imagined that he would retain the traditional status and authority of a *bwana* (master) over his wife. Father Tempels agreed to teach him and his wife together. 'Bring your wife . . . You wish to find this unity . . . Your model will be the house of Nazareth.' At the end of one week of instruction, Tempels advised the couple to become a part of the Jamaa group. In this group, according to Gaston, 'We learned to know and to love each other.' In the course of 1955, the group attracted a number of other couples.

During the period 1956–9, Gaston and Marcelline were personally responsible for the spread of the Jamaa into several other communities in South Katanga. This was made possible by the fact that during these years Entrelco moved Gaston and his team from one community to another as the work on the railway progressed. In December 1956, Gaston was transferred to Tenke. Although he spent only nine months there, he succeeded in establishing a local Jamaa cell in the area. When his work obliged him to move once more, he delegated Bruno Ngoi to lead and develop the Jamaa that he had begun. Gaston contends that he did not really choose Ngoi. For this was a man who lived the precepts of the Jamaa in such an outstanding way that 'the group said "He must be the baba of us all, when you go."' In turn, Ngoi made contact with the Jamaa group in Kolwezi, thereby creating a direct link between the two Jamaas.

Gaston's next assignment was in Lubudi, where he took residence in May 1957. There, he launched another branch of the Jamaa. This time it had to be negotiated with the local missionary priest, who gave his consent on the condition that 'It will not be done in secret, but in broad daylight, so that I can keep an eye on you.' The reluctant attitude of the priest gradually changed, to the point where he turned over his own office to the Jamists and began to listen to the *mafundisho* that Gaston and Marcelline taught, along with the lay people who came to be instructed by them. In 1958 Gaston had to leave Lubudi for his new assignment in Mutshatsha. Once again, he chose a delegate, Paul Makanda, to take over responsibility for the local Jamaa.

The experience of Gaston and Marcelline in disseminating the Jamaa in Mutshatsha was more mixed than in the previous communities where they had lived and worked. They made home calls to many families with whom they talked of the Jamaa and prayed. As Gaston put it, the Jamaa 'took' with certain couples. As many as fifteen working-class families grouped themselves around baba Gaston and mama Marcelline. But other families proved more impervious. In retrospect, Gaston believes the critical factor that deterred these others from joining was that they did not have an opportunity to observe the special kind of union and understanding in which he and his wife were living. This hypothesis seems to be largely influenced by the experience that originally led him and his wife into the Jamaa.

Gaston spent the early part of 1959 in Kasaji where, under his influence, another Jamaa was started. When he moved on to Élisabethville in December 1959, he designated Marc Kabamba to succeed him as baba of the group. Kabamba, like Makanda, was recognized by the Jamists as a natural leader. He not only took charge of the Kasaji group, but was instrumental in beginning a Jamaa in Kisenge, the seat of the B.C.K.-Manganese mining centre.[1] Later, in 1961, the same man 'engendered' a Jamaa in Dilolo, an important railway town on the Angolan border.

Gaston's job finally brought him to the city of Élisabethville, where he, his wife, and his children reside to this day. In his customary way, he began to teach the Jamaa *mafundisho* to interested Congolese couples in various parishes of the city. A highly respected Benedictine missionary, Dom Thomas Nève, gave him a great deal of encouragement and support. The community in which Gaston worked most intensively was St Guillaume, a quasi-parish in the B.C.K. labour camp. However, Gaston and his family lived in another part of the city, Commune (borough) Albert. He attributes his initial failure in attracting people to the Jamaa to the fact that he preached in one place and resided in another: for, he explains, 'The people did not see me, my wife and me', by which he means that because the religious sense in which they are 'ONE' could not be observed, his message did not convert his listeners. For the same reason, he feels, he was equally unsuccessful in Katuba, another Élisabethville parish. It was not until he was joined by baba Daniel Kalala and his wife, mama Béatrice, that 'the Jamaa began to take'. This couple were the spiritual children of Gaston and Marcelline, who had initiated them into the Jamaa during their stay in Mutshatsha. The fact that Daniel not only taught the Jamaa way in the B.C.K. camp, but also worked and lived there, seems to have been the decisive element in the spread of the movement. At the same time Gaston made progress with the Jamaa in his own parish. He also rekindled the Jamaa activities of Victor Ngandu, a primary school teacher and one of the founding baba of the original Ruwe group, who had arrived in Élisabethville a few years earlier.

Gaston subsequently became an automobile mechanic, employed at the provincial government's garage. He was and still is noted for his skill and conscientiousness at work, and the overtime he puts in, even when he is not compensated for it. The religious faith of Gaston and Marcelline is almost legendary. A story frequently told by other Jamaa members to illustrate the quality of this couple's Christian commitment turns on their response in the face of a major adversity. In the early 1960s they were robbed of all their clothing

[1] B.C.K. is the Lower-Congo to Katanga railway company (see above, p. 40).

and their life savings of 20,000 Congolese francs ($400). Instead of displaying grief or vindictiveness, they publicly prayed that God would fill their hearts with 'kindness and forgiveness, not with revenge', and that the thief would not suffer too greatly for his deed. They are also considered remarkable for the magic-free way in which they meet difficult life challenges. For example, their eldest child, a nineteen-year-old boy, is afflicted with sickle-cell anaemia, and will probably not live long. So far as is known by other Jamists, Gaston and Marcelline have never consulted a witch-doctor or used traditional *dawa* (magical charms) to deal with this problem. Instead, they have placed the matter in God's hands, and within the framework of this religious acquiescence, have done everything possible to give their son a meaningful, if abbreviated life. Although his health does not permit him either to attend school or to work, his parents have arranged with a priest that he be involved in a modified way in boy-scout activities. This has become his all-consuming interest.

Baba Gaston and mama Marcelline are renowned also for their boundless hospitality. Innumerable Jamaa meetings are held in their modest house, and a constant flow of Jamaa delegations from distant communities (some coming from as far as 600 miles away) stay with them for extended periods of time. The problem of lodging and feeding the visitors assumed such proportions that the local parish priest took the initiative of obtaining supplementary housing and a small subsidy from the bishop to help them meet these demands.

Like many Jamaa couples, Gaston and Marcelline are so deeply engaged in Jamaa activities that the amount of time and energy they can devote to their children is restricted. However, in contrast to other Jamists, they make a conscientious effort to take their children on family outings and, above all, to encourage their education and schoolwork. With the exception of their eldest child, all their sons and daughters are attending good schools and earning high grades. Gaston and Marcelline do not know enough French to help their children with their homework and Gaston admits that occasionally, when he does try to assist them, he is likely to lose his patience and temper. Nevertheless, the parents have set aside a room in their small, crowded house for the six children to do their homework together, sitting around a common table, often until quite late at night. The children say their prayers and sing some religious songs before retiring.

Their modest formal education notwithstanding, Gaston and Marcelline's religious understanding and status are so advanced that they have personally taught the Jamaa *mafundisho* to two Catholic bishops (one Belgian and one Congolese), as well as to half a dozen priests, black and white, and several members of lay religious institutes. In addition, mama Marcelline has a reputation for being a powerfully outspoken person on religious and moral issues, no more timorous when speaking to high-ranking church officials on such matters than she is with ordinary lay people.

Gaston and Marcelline are pivotal members of a jamaa within the Jamaa. They are the spiritual progenitors of five members of an important Jamaa subculture, clustered in Lubumbashi: baba Daniel and mama Béatrice, Miss Renée Van Houten, an organizer of and adviser to the Katanga branch of the J.O.C.F. (Jeunesse Ouvrière Chrétienne Féminine, the female branch of the Young Christian Workers' movement), Benoit Leclerc, a Benedictine Father, and the archbishop of Élisabethville, also a Benedictine missionary priest. In addition, Xavier De Winter, a Belgian Jesuit, also belongs to this genealogical in-group by virtue of his having been taught and initiated into the Jamaa by baba Daniel and mama Béatrice.

We now turn to the beliefs and rites that profoundly affected the lives of baba Gaston, mama Marcelline, and their fellow Jamaa members. These cultural dimensions of the movement constitute the core of its social and religious meaning.

CHAPTER IV

Jamaa Beliefs and Rites

FOR a number of reasons, the belief system of the Jamaa is not easy to define. In the first place, various of the movement's leaders hold the typical charismatic view that the essence of the Jamaa cannot be expressed in an impersonal, intellectualized, codified way. They maintain that it must be felt-understood: discovered, lived, and shared in and through the spiritualized intimacies of intense, personal relations. 'Before anything else, all religious teaching is a personal encounter.'[1] These are experiences, they contend, that can neither be grasped nor communicated purely through words. At the same time, the Jamaa attaches a special kind of importance to keywords, compressing into them a complex of ideas, beliefs, and associations that are never made explicit. In this regard words constitute a symbolic code that transcends the verbal and that are difficult for anyone not initiated into the Jamaa to decipher, no matter how close to the movement and identified with it he may be. This form of nominalism is primarily Congolese and is yet another of the Jamaa's characteristics that makes a coherent statement of its doctrine problematic. In keeping with a more general tendency of Congolese culture, the movement accords a higher value to symbols and rites and their enactment than to systematic doctrine.

Partly as a consequence of these attributes of the Jamaa, the limited educational background of the greater part of its membership, and also of some of the characteristics of its founder, Tempels, very few formal writings about the movement, by leaders or adherents, have been produced. Strictly speaking, the only extant writings that fall into this category are four works by Tempels himself: *La Philosophie bantoue*, published (in 1949) ten years before the inception of the Jamaa; the pamphlet *Catéchèse bantoue* (1948); *Notre Rencontre* (1962), a collection of basic religious lessons taught by Tempels in the Jamaa that he was persuaded by his priests-lieutenants to make available to a larger public; and a second

[1] Tempels, *Notre Rencontre*, p. 84.

volume of these lessons, *Notre Rencontre II*, that was not cleared for publication by authorities of the Catholic Church.

The numerous other kinds of writings on the Jamaa do not provide easy clarification of Jamaa doctrine. For the most part, they fall into three categories: personal documents written by Catholic clergy, affectively involved with the Jamaa, in which they express their changing understanding of the movement and their positive and negative feelings about it; testimonies by baba and mama as to how the Jamaa transformed their lives as well as a dozen *mafundisho* taught by them, recorded by persons other than Tempels; several theological and social scientific evaluations of the Jamaa, informally commissioned by church authorities, concerned with the question of 'how Catholic' the movement is, and what kinds of action, if any, the official Church should take regarding it.

Two other factors complicate the identification of the Jamaa's belief system. First, as its members pass from one stage of initiation and conversion to another, there is a tendency for them to feel that their comprehension of what the Jamaa is about changes, deepens, and becomes more authentic. Second, as we have seen, almost from the movement's inception, there was a group of Congolese members, later to crystallize as the Katete, whose conceptions of Jamaa doctrine and rites significantly differed from what Tempels and his first disciples believed they were transmitting.

In sum, the difficulties of codifying and analysing Jamaa beliefs are not purely methodological in nature. Rather, they are significant indicators of the fact that the Jamaa is at once a Congolese and a Catholic movement, charismatic, highly dynamic, relatively non-routinized, led and catalysed by mystically oriented men and women who emphasize religious experience, and around which there has been much controversy over its relationship to the institutionalized Church. These attributes must be taken into account in any attempt, sociological or otherwise, to describe and interpret the Jamaa's belief system.

The core concept and central religious experiences of the Jamaa turn on 'encounter' (*rencontre*), 'vital union' (*union vitale*), and the state of being ONE (*UN*, or in Swahili, *umoja*). Its essence lies in the emotional and spiritual unity that progressively comes to pass when, in marriage, a man and a woman open their thoughts and feelings to each other in a mutual search for a deep understanding of Christian love, and for the ability individually and collectively to actualize it in all aspects of their lives. In Jamaa terms, such a relationship is 'fecund'. From it new spiritual children are engendered. These children are not the biological offspring of the couple, but adult persons who, through intensive spiritual contact with a Jamaa baba and mama, are 'born' into the vital state of Christianity that the movement represents. Conversion to the Jamaa and initiation into it are effected by a chain of encounters and births of this kind. Each couple constitutes a fertile micro-jamaa, contributing to the development of an ever-growing, larger spiritual family. Jamists regard the Catholic Church as the superordinate Jamaa which, ideally, ought to be an ecclesia of 'living stones', animated and integrated by the kind of spiritual kinship between its members that characterized primitive Christianity.

Jamaa adherents believe that the first and most ideal Jamaa, the one from which all others developed and to which all ultimately refer, is the 'union of love', the encounter between Christ and the Virgin Mary. They are assumed to have given themselves to each other in such a perfect and total spiritual way that they became transcendently ONE. 'Christ did not wish to belong to God the Father all alone, in the isolation of His soul without allowing anyone to be in communion with Him . . . He wished to give Himself to God, together with Myriam.'[1] Christ is the 'new Adam', Mary the 'new Eve', free from the original sin of the first couple: isolation from God was a consequence of their failure to attain the union with each other in love that God expected and commanded of them.[2] Through their union, Christ and Mary repaired this original sin.

The Virgin is variously referred to by her Hebraic name, Myriam, her Christian name, Mary, her Bantu name, mama Maria; she is also called 'the new Eve'.[3] In this symbolic way her name spans the Old and New Testaments, Jewish, Christian, Catholic, and Bantu traditions.

Christ and Mary are viewed as bound to one another in a triple, mutual love that exemplifies the interpersonal relations between the Father, Son, and Holy Spirit in the Trinity. According to Jamaa belief, they were 'more than' mother and son; in a mystical sense, they were also linked as father and daughter, and husband and wife. From their love-filled 'plenitude' the first two Jamaa child-disciples

[1] Tempels, 'Le Renouveau communautaire', unpublished essay, 1967, p. 2.
[2] Tempels, *Notre Rencontre*, pp. 64–5.   [3] Ibid., pp. 131, 171–2.

were born: Mary Magdalen and John. In turn, out of the encounter
with each other, Mary Magdalen (sensual-corporeal love purified)
and John (spiritual celibate love) became mama and baba of other
children.

As the foregoing implies, the Jamaa attaches particular importance
to the humanity (*bumuntu*) of Christ, and to that of the Virgin Mary
and the most intimate associates of Christ and Mary. The fact that
'for thirty years in the house in Nazareth, Christ lived the life of a
layman . . . the life of an ordinary man' is emphasized.[1] He is depicted
as 'a magnificent, majestic man, in the full force of young adulthood'.[2]
And it is explicitly stated that it was only in the last three years
of his life, on the eve of his death, that he assumed an explicitly
priestly role.[3]

Jamaa members are interested in the homely, human details of
the life that Mary, Christ, and his disciples led: how their house
was furnished, what they ate, what they looked like, how they
dressed, how they spoke, what they said to each other, and so on.
This commonplace and terrestrial conception of Christ's presence
among men conveys another basic belief of the Jamaa: a special
relationship between the first and second commandments.

In Jamaa doctrine, the love of one's fellow men and an encounter-
in-love with particular baba and mama among them comprise a
precondition for an encounter with Christ and Mary, through which
love of God is experienced and attained. Thus, the Jamaa not only
preaches the symbiotic relationship between the first and second
commandments, but it also implies that the second is a prerequisite
for the first.

The Jamaa regards conjugal love between a man and a woman as
the prototype of love of one's fellow man. In this regard, and
through the significance that the movement accords the relationship
between Christ and Mary, the Jamaa underscores the unique and
indispensable spiritual role that the woman plays. It is emphasized
that God 'wished to be born, to be born into human nature, born
of a woman, of this Woman . . .', and that she was not created
'merely as a *means* for Him to be born as a human being . . . [Rather],
He wanted and conceived her for Herself . . .'[4] According to Jamaa
belief, Mary is at one and the same time the medium of union with
Christ, the source through which love, unity, and humanity are

---

[1] Tempels, *Notre Rencontre*, vol. II, pp. 70–1.   [2] Ibid., p. 34.
[3] Ibid., p. 71.   [4] Tempels, *Notre Rencontre*, pp. 106–7.

given and received; 'the other' (*l'autre*) through which the divine is
approached and one's vocation realized; 'the fertile one' (*la féconde*)
who gives birth to children, spiritually as well as physically. She
personifies and symbolizes the fact that without the presence of the
woman man is alone, incomplete, sterile, loveless, and likely to
engage in egoistical, dangerous, and destructive forms of behaviour
that, in effect, serve Satan:

> In all these examples of encounter between men, we note the presence
> of things, landholdings, possessions, blood bonds, racial bonds, ideologies,
> ideals or common slogans, and at the same time we notice the absence of
> ... the woman. All these man-to-man encounters are not bad ... but in all
> these encounters, however beautiful they may be, an element of depth,
> an element of fullness are missing . . . the presence of Eve. All these
> male encounters, the good ones, must exist, but they cannot replace
> Adam and Eve's encounter . . . They often prove to be incomplete, more
> or less sterile, or even dangerous because of . . . the absence of the
> woman . . .[1]

Christ and Mary, John and Mary Magdalen are virtually the only
persons in the New Testament on whom the Jamaa focuses. Joseph,
Mary's husband, is only occasionally mentioned in Jamaa writings,
but in the oral teaching of some communities he is presented as the
patron of the movement.

Considerable importance is attached to Satan, who is viewed as the
antithesis of the holy union of the Trinity and of the triple relationship between Christ and Mary. In Jamaa doctrine Satan is the most
magnificent, powerful, and intelligent of the angels created by God.
He has become a vehicle of hate and destruction because, in his
pride and self-adulation, he refuses to become one in love with the
other angels. As a consequence, he lives in a state of terrible isolation
(*upeke*), an eternal hell in which he is isolated from God and all
those who are capable of loving. For Jamists this isolation is a form
of death.

In keeping with the significance that the Jamaa assigns to union-
in-love, it places special emphasis on two sacraments, marriage and
communion. Baptism is only mentioned in passing and infrequent
reference is made to the sacrament of penance. In fact, the Jamaa

[1] Tempels, *Notre Rencontre*, vol. II, pp. 66–7. The dots in the text that precede
phrases like 'the woman', 'the presence of Eve', 'the absence of the woman' are
Tempels's own. They denote pauses for suspense and emphasis, and probably
resemble the manner of Tempels's oral delivery of his *mafundisho* to the people.

primarily concerns itself with one form of sin: the negation of love
and thereby of God, through failure to meet the other in the deepest
human and spiritual sense. The meaning and impact of the sacraments are considered to depend on more than their inherent spiritual
power. Jamaa members subscribe to the orthodox Catholic belief
that sacraments performed by a priest are non-contingently effective.
But they feel that the effect of the sacrament is enhanced by the
quality of interaction between priest and faithful, and by his human,
as well as spiritual, oneness with them. 'How can we be united with
what takes place on the altar, if we cannot be ONE with you, who
are on the altar,'[1] exclaimed a group of Jamaa members, when a
priest advised them to try to participate more actively in the events of
the Mass. The priestly counterpart to this sentiment is expressed in
the statement by Tempels:

> As a priest, I must offer on the altar the body and the blood of Christ,
> his human being, given in love. On the other hand, the baba and mama
> ask me to offer their encounter on the altar, their gift of mutual love.
> I would be a strange kind of priest, if I were to find myself between this
> double offering of the love of Christ and of the baba and mama, all the
> time remaining an isolated being, without encounter. As an isolated being
> I would hardly feel present in the offerings that I have between my hands.[2]

As the foregoing implies, the role of the priest is defined by the
Jamaa in its own way. In certain respects, it is based on an orthodox
Catholic conception of the priesthood. The priest is consecrated as
'the other Christ'. He is 'the sacred man who can bless, anoint,
purify, sanctify, illumine, vivify, who can grant divine pardon and
give communion with God, with the personal and living Christ,
body and blood'.[3] However, the Jamaa places almost as much
emphasis on the human qualities and life experiences of the priest as
on his sacerdotal status. As already indicated, the Jamaa underscores the fact that it was not until Christ had lived thirty years of an
ordinary, non-priestly, 'human and religious' life, that he began to
preach the message he had come to bring. 'The human Christ had
to have a plenitude of human life, and then a plenitude of religious
life to make his priestly plenitude possible . . .'[4] In the Jamaa view,
ideally, the priesthood should be a 'crowning' and a 'fulfilment'
based on a human existence that has been rich enough to allow for

---

[1] Tempels, *Notre Rencontre*, vol. II, p. 74.   [2] Ibid., p. 74.
[3] Tempels, *Notre Rencontre*, p. 44.
[4] Tempels, *Notre Rencontre*, vol. II, p. 71.

self-knowledge, personal growth, and the kind of encounter with
one's 'neighbour' that is a precondition for one's humanity.
Tempels goes so far as to state that it is only after this phase of a man's
development is well launched that he finally comes 'to feel the
necessity of the absolute expressing itself ritually, the necessity of a
consecration, the necessity of the priesthood'.[1] For the priesthood
to precede these humanizing experiences is not only regarded as
a personal and religious deformation, but also as a condition that
impoverishes all aspects of a priest's activities, his sacramental functions included. Tempels illustrates this conviction from his own
history as a priest, confessing that 'one made ritual gestures, celebrated the sacrifice of love and of the gift of oneself, without being
oneself love in human and religious plenitude, without belonging
totally to . . . another, to my neighbour'.[2] The priest's oneness with the
lay person takes on added significance in the Jamaa because there
is a real sense in which each facilitates and augments the union of
the other with Christ. Priest and faithful, then, are mutually dependent. The priest needs the baba and the mama to grow in priest-
liness, just as the baba and the mama need the priest to offer on the
altar their gift of love. 'The baba and the mama become a reason
for his priesthood. And the mass becomes their communal mass.'[3]
They are also spiritually equal, in the sense that the priest does not
possess a truth that is different from or superior to that of the laity.
An implicit parallel is drawn between the fact that Christ's great
religious insights were not based on specialized priestly training and
the fact that simple baba and mama may possess spiritual understanding that equals and, in some cases, even surpasses that of the
priest. 'He [Christ] did not have a teacher, nor a specialized education,
and nevertheless he spoke like a doctor. Without being a priest
according to the law, without being a doctor recognized by Israel,
he spoke like a doctor, he spoke like a prophet, he spoke like a
religious innovator.'[4] In fact, as this quotation suggests, Jamaa doctrine tends to be charismatically romantic about how much closer to
God the 'natural' man or woman is likely to be than those who are
more educated and routinized in formal church structures. The baba
and mama of the Jamaa are considered to be all the richer because
they are not only 'basic' people, 'divested of any sort of uniform,

[1] Ibid., p. 72.   [2] Ibid., p. 73.
[3] Letter from Tempels to a Congolese priest, 21 Mar. 1963.
[4] Tempels, *Notre Rencontre*, vol. II, p. 70.

veil or ornament', but also because they are members of the Bantu culture. Their heritage is seen as analogous to the Jewish origins of Christ and Myriam. In these respects, the Jamaa borders on reversing the usual hierarchical conception of the relationship between priest and lay person, implying that by natural and cultural endowment, baba and mama are often spiritually superordinate to the priest. This is epitomized in the child-like status that the priest assumes when he is being instructed in the Jamaa way by a baba and mama, who initiate him progressively into the movement.[1] In a letter to a colleague, a priest-member of the Jamaa describes this relationship, with its accompanying spiritual costs and even greater spiritual gains:

I wrote you earlier that I was going to a baba and a mama to be instructed. Little by little, that has given me deeper insight. The main thing is not to let oneself be instructed, but to have a baba and a mama whose child one really becomes: people who are going to influence one's whole life and with whom one becomes one. The first experience I gained was this: people are extremely delicate and discreet. On my own I reached the point where I felt that to be 'mwana' is impossible unless there is total openness vis-à-vis the people. It cost me quite a lot, and I have not yet completely achieved it: but, many things that earlier in my life I did not feel were wrong or things that I neglected have become clear to me thanks to them. Secondly, it [the whole experience] brings about a great simplification. All those years in the Congo, even through the worst ones, I have tried to remain faithful to the required morning meditation, and . . . I have not failed that often. But since I go to these people, this is no longer a painful and often boring search. It becomes a prayer, and a clearer insight in what is lacking in my life. Thirdly, through these people a contact with the whole 'life' of the parish is growing slowly. When I go to sleep, I am really with the people, I think consciously of those many households with whom I am in contact, with whom I live and sympathize, first and above all, of this baba and this mama. In the morning, my very first thoughts are for them. There is nothing forced in it: quietly and very spontaneously I feel one with them, with their prayer, with their life, with their sorrow and joy. That experience, without any doubt, has touched something very deep in me.[2]

This account of a particular missionary's dynamic encounter with his baba and mama highlights several other aspects of the priest's relations with other people, which are advocated by Jamaa doctrine.

---

[1] The *mafundisho* and the initiation rites into the Jamaa will be discussed more fully later in the chapter.
[2] Letter from Father Frans to Father Jerome, 23 Nov. 1961.

In Tempels's words, those who are 'given to God' as priests need
not and should not become 'cold, closed and unreachable'[1] persons.
If they wish to be absolutely faithful to Christ, they should not be
living more individually, but rather more communally in contact
with others, most especially with lay people. Tempels makes explicit
a general belief in the Jamaa that by and large, partly because of
their vows of celibacy, priests have lived out their religious vocation
'in the solitude and isolation of their inner beings . . . separated
from the world and from their neighbour.' This has been as im-
poverishing to them spiritually and emotionally, as it has been
perplexing and unfulfilling to the faithful they are supposed to
know, love, and serve. Ideally, the Jamaa priest is one who, sociologically speaking, has realized the functional equivalent of Christ's
oneness with Mary and of a husband's unity with his wife in marriage.
If it is spiritually fecund, his union with a particular baba and mama
will progressively widen and deepen his relationship with all the
baba and mama of his parish. As the excerpt from a Jamaa priest's
letter indicates, the kind of oneness that a priest ought to experience
with his people should take the form of a deeply felt identification
with the everyday, commonplace details of their lives, as well as with
their more exceptional moments of great joy and sorrow.

Here, as in other facets of Jamaa doctrine, particular emphasis is
placed upon the valuable contribution that the 'religious thought of
the woman' can make to the development of the priest. Christ's
relationship to Mary is invoked in this regard, and in one passage,
Tempels goes so far as to say that:

He wished to belong to God, together with Myriam, He wished to
belong to us, together with her, whom He took as a collaborator, as a
co-redemptress . . . Christ was indeed the first priest-religious and She
was indeed the model of all women, of all religious sisters. They are the
most perfectly given and consecrated to God. They were and are so, 'together'. To wish to do better than they easily leads to an erroneous
perspective, to a super-perfection in which one ends up feeling the uneasiness of failing to achieve a perfect solution.[2]

The primary rites of the Jamaa are the stages of initiation, called
'ways' (*njia* in Swahili) or 'degrees' or 'thoughts', through which
lay persons and clergy progressively enter the movement. As we
shall see, there are minor but none the less significant differences
in the initiation of baba and mama, on the one hand, and religious

[1] Tempels, 'Le Renouveau communautaire', p. 2.   [2] Ibid., p. 2.

personnel on the other. Furthermore, although the essential meaning of each of the 'ways' is relatively constant from one initiate to the
other, there is some variation in the ceremonies carried out at each
stage. One of the sources of this variation lies in patterned differences
between the manner in which Tempels conducted the 'ways' and
their subsequent enactment by the several priests, baba and mama
whom he delegated as his charismatic representatives. Finally, there
is incontrovertible evidence both in Tempels's correspondence with
Jamaa priests and in the letters that one of the two priests, who could
be considered his successor, wrote to a close colleague that, at least
until the year 1963, the legitimate initiation process consisted of
four ways. After that, for reasons that we will specify, the fourth
way was officially dropped and initiation became a three-phase
sequence. Numerous Jamaa members, however, claim either that the
fourth way never existed in the first place, or that it is only practised
by an aberrant group of 'deviationists' in the Jamaa.[1] The reasons
why the fourth way is controversial will become apparent once it has
been described and analysed.

Jamaa members prefer not to disclose to outsiders the full details
of the content and experiences associated with each of the 'ways'.[2]
This attitude and policy have several sources. First, there is a
traditional Bantu tendency on the part of its African members to
feel that the more a thing is kept secret, the more it is valued. Second,
secrecy is the hallmark of the traditional Bantu associations that
have initiation rites. It enhances the meaning and importance of
the initiation's constituent elements, the words and acts. Third,
those who have passed through the stages testify that it is an 'extraordinary experience' which cannot easily be described, and which
perhaps will be drained or deformed by attempts to do so. This sentiment, for example, was expressed by a Jamaa priest who had just
been initiated into the first way and wrote about it to his closest
friend:

I am not going to write you that much about it [the initiation]: only
this, that, if one can do it without any ulterior motive, without the desire to
know, but purely and simply to become one with the people, it is an extraordinary experience. I do not like to write about it. Besides, it would not
work. And I would not want to mislead you. But I am endlessly happy

[1] The nature of doctrinal and ritual 'deviations' in the Jamaa will be discussed
in the next section of this chapter.
[2] This obviously constituted some methodological difficulty in getting the
data.

that for months I have tried to really become child of [those] people, and that I have done this in all integrity and honesty.[1]

Fourth, there are those who contend that Tempels, its founder and leader, institutionalized in the Jamaa a certain need for and enjoyment of secrecy that are a part of his basic personality structure. The lay people who join the Jamaa are already baptized Catholics before they are introduced into the movement. By and large, they enter the Jamaa two by two, as married couples. In some cases, a woman may wish to become jamaa, while her husband is either indifferent or resistant to joining. She may pass through the first way alone, but cannot progress to the other degrees of initiation until her husband agrees to accompany her on this spiritual journey. The essential vectors that carry initiates from one phase of their induction to another are the so-called *mafundisho* (lessons), and certain prescribed encounters, dreams, and visions. The *mafundisho* constitute the process of non-didactic instruction through which the spirit, as well as the message of the Jamaa, are transmitted. *Mafundisho* are given in Swahili, and are of two types. In their most formal expression they consist of weekly presentations of key aspects of Jamaa doctrine given to large gatherings of persons who either belong to the movement or are interested in it. The teacher usually is a Jamaa baba or priest. The kind of audience participation invited by the teacher consists of encouraging those listening to him to echo back vital words or phrases, or collectively to respond in the expected fashion to a rhetorically phrased question. The second type of *mafundisho* takes place in a more informal and intimate context, chiefly between the couple who are being inducted into the movement and the Jamaa baba, mama, or priest who is instructing them. These are the *mafundisho* directly conducive to the encounters, dreams, and visions that must be experienced. They take the form of a continuing stream of highly interactive dialogue and discussion between the baba, mama, and the priest when he is present. These interchanges centre on the Jamaa doctrine presented earlier in this chapter. They are rich in African images, expressions, and proverbs; they often go on for hours without interruption; and though they are typically characterized by the almost musical repetitiveness of language, at their very best, they are spontaneous, original, and even creative.

[1] Letter from Father Frans to Father Jerome, 17 Dec. 1961.

The goal of the first way (*njia ya kwanza*) is to achieve personal knowledge of Christ and the Virgin Mary, and to experience a living encounter with them. According to Jamaa doctrine, baba and mama who have 'received the visit' of Christ and Mary ought not to keep this grace for themselves alone. They should share this union and the consequent spiritual richness of their inner life with other persons. The baba should seek out a man, the mama a woman, who will become, in effect, their 'spiritual children'. Once this contact has been made and mutually assented to, 'parents' and 'children' will then meet regularly in their homes. In these meetings *mafundisho* are taught to the initiates by the baba and mama; both couples recount extensive personal histories; painful and joyous intimacies are shared; and religious experiences are reported and analysed. In some cases, these meetings take place several times a week, in others, as often as everyday; each may last anywhere from one to three hours.

Eventually, the baba and mama who are inducting the new 'children' into the movement decide that they have received enough instruction and made sufficient spiritual progress to be, what Tempels calls, 'introduced into the first way'. In effect, this means that the initiates have successfully passed one phase of the first degree and are deemed ready to be launched on a second, more advanced and mystical, phase of this way. The preparation for this transition typically takes from one to two years. There are more 'drop-outs' in this stage of initiation than at any other subsequent point, mainly because many candidates fail to meet their baba and mama's criteria of childlike simplicity, increasing candour and openness, and consistency between professed beliefs and insights, on the one hand, and personal conduct, on the other.

The second part of the first way begins with the baba and mama confiding in the initiates exactly how they have come to know Christ and Mary: how they have met them, seen them and spoken to them, and how, ever since these encounters, Christ and Mary are real persons in their lives, loving presences in all they do. The baba and mama then proceed to tell their children how they also can meet and come to know Christ and Mary. Throughout this period when the initiates are trying to make their first living contact with Christ and the Virgin, they are encouraged frequently to recite the following prayer: 'Lord Jesus, give me the Virgin Mary; Mary, give me Jesus.' Through this repeated prayer and all that has preceded it in the first way, the male initiate eventually meets the Virgin, in dream or vision, and She, in turn, introduces him to Christ. The female initiate encounters Christ in the same manner, and He helps her to meet the Virgin. These double encounters may occur more than once for the entering couple. They are described by those who have experienced them as 'total' meetings that take place both in spirit and in a 'very human, corporeal way'. The initiates testify that from these encounters they gain a deeper understanding of love and a sense of purification from sin.

After these meetings the initiates are considered ready to undergo the rite that signifies their full passage through the first way. Ideally, if there is a Jamaa priest available, he conducts this rite along with the baba and mama; if not, the baba and mama perform the ceremony themselves. As already stated, there is considerable variation in the content of this ceremony. In general, it consists of: prayers, asking God to bless the candidates with the grace and the force to live up to their new life; an exhortation to them to offer regularly certain prayers, such as the Hail Mary, the act of contrition, etc.; and an enjoinder to keep the initiation secret. At the end of the ceremony the initiates kneel to receive a final blessing in the form of the imposition of hands on their heads. The initiates then offer a reciprocal blessing to their baba and mama. When the ceremony is ended, it is not uncommon for some kind of communal meal to be served.

The goal of the second way (*njia ya pili*) is the total union, affective and spiritual, between the husband and wife being initiated into the Jamaa. As Tempels put it, it is the time for the two of them to 'encounter and marry each other more profoundly, husband and wife, in their house . . . [the time] when, together, they receive Christ and the Blessed Virgin in their house, in their marriage, in their encounter.'[1] This state of 'being ONE' comes to pass through the couple's mutual encounter with Christ and Mary.

When a baba and mama have 'known' Christ and Mary for a certain time and each has experienced in his own way meetings with them, their spiritual parents bring them before a Jamaa priest for their initiation into the second way. The primary criterion of their readiness is that the presence of Christ and Mary has become so intimate that it transforms and animates their daily lives. Whereas, often the husband and wife are introduced to the first way at different times, it is essential that they enter the second way together,

[1] Letter from Tempels to a Congolese priest, 21 Mar. 1963.

for, as already indicated, the central meaning of this degree is based on this togetherness. The priest summarizes for the couple the *mafundisho* they have received since the first initiation, and reviews their efforts to put these instructions into practice. He then exhorts them to become one in the manner required by the second way. The following is a verbatim account of what Tempels said to couples on this occasion. Although other Jamaa priests might address the initiates somewhat differently, the content of the message they deliver at this turning-point in the second way is much the same.[1]

Baba and mama, until today you have been two persons who live together, but who were not completely one. You know one another, but you do not know each other to the very depths of your hearts. Baba, did you know how your mama is in her heart when she prays, when she is united with God, when she talks with Christ and the Blessed Virgin? Surely, you would like to know how she is in her heart, and you would like to know each other perfectly. From now on, baba, you are going to give your whole heart to your mama, and you are going to tell her everything: you will tell her how you pray and how you know the Virgin. You will give her everything.

Mama, if your baba gives you his whole heart, do you think that he will deny the Blessed Virgin? No! Rather, he will consider you, you and the Blessed Virgin, as the same person. The love, the respect that he has for the Blessed Virgin, he will transfer them upon you. And you should know that from this day on you take the place of the Blessed Virgin for him, that you give him the Blessed Virgin. At the same time that you give yourself to your baba in all your life and in your love, give him also the Blessed Virgin. When you give yourself to him, in all your love, give him at the same time the Blessed Virgin. And pray for him, say to the Blessed Virgin: 'Holy Mary, receive my husband totally in your love.'

Mama, do you wish to know your husband totally, and also to know how in his heart he is with God, with the Blessed Virgin and with Christ? From this day on, give your whole heart to your husband, without ever giving it to anyone else, and tell him everything.

Baba, will your mama in acting this way deny Christ? No! From today on, you should fully realize that you take the place of Christ for her. Carry Christ in you and understand that, united with Christ, you take His place beside her. The respect, the love that Christ had for Mary, you must also carry in you. In the love which unites you with her, you will pray, saying: 'Lord Jesus, receive my mama in all your love!'

And to live this, henceforth each evening you will say your prayer together. You will prepare yourselves so that the love of Jesus and Mary will live in you both; in order that you will be able to see them together,

---

[1] Letter from Father Frans to Father Erik, 5 Sept. 1963.

and that you will have the same dreams together; in order that Christ and Mary be together in your love. From now on, you must change your prayer, you must no longer pray with two hearts, but your prayer will be a single and same prayer from the two of you together. Husband, carry your wife in your heart when you pray. And you, wife, carry your husband in your heart when you say your prayers. And even when you are not together, when your husband has gone to work, watch over him through your prayer, stay close to him in your heart. Husband, wherever you go to do your work, carry your wife with you in your heart and in your prayer. Thus, your marriage will be a holy marriage, that can never be shattered.

In the early stages of the Jamaa's development, Tempels himself was the spiritual gatekeeper who personally initiated candidates into all the ways, and determined when and if they were ready for each passage. However, as the Jamaa grew in numbers, and became more geographically dispersed, it was more difficult for Tempels to be solely responsible for the initiation process. His role was further complicated by his definitive departure from the Congo in 1962, although he maintained a voluminous correspondence with Jamaa members and clergy. On the eve of his return to Belgium, he designated certain baba and mama whom he judged to have sufficiently assimilated the Jamaa spirit to admit new members to the first and second ways. He also conferred these same powers of initiation on two priests who had themselves become full members of the movement. In addition, they were given the sole right and responsibility to induct persons into the third way. 'Before Placied left, he told the people: I am going, but [Father] Frans is staying with you. From now on, you yourselves may do the initiating for the first and second ways. But the third way unifies the priest with you, and for that you have to go to him.'[1] These two Fathers maintained close contact with Tempels through letters and periodic visits to him in Europe, and they consulted him on every ambiguous, complex, or troublesome issue that arose in the Jamaa. As mentioned earlier, these two men can properly be considered not only Tempels's closest priestly disciples, but also the two major candidates for succession to the charismatic leadership of the movement.[2]

After a baba and mama have made individual contact with Christ

[1] Ibid.
[2] This will be more fully analysed in Chapter VII on the subculture of Catholic priests in the Jamaa.

and Mary, and have met each other in depth, they are ready to offer these two sorts of encounter to God. This offering, mediated by a Jamaa priest who knows them intimately, constitutes the third way (*njia ya tatu*). The principal goal of this way is the union of baba and mama, as individuals, with the priest. When this happens, in the words of Tempels, together they become 'perfectly jamaa . . . church in plenitude'.

In the period when Tempels was the priest who conducted this phase of initiation, the third degree was carried out in a way that was infused with his person and details of what he considered to be the most important encounter of his own life: the encounter with the religious sister that was the seminal experience out of which the Jamaa grew. In the context of the third way, Tempels called this sister 'Mama X'. He required the mama to receive him in her thoughts; in turn, the baba was to receive 'Mama X'. In the same manner, and through her unity with Tempels, she would link the baba with him. According to Tempels, through these encounters, baba, mama, and the priest would become unified with each other and with Christ and Mary in the following way:

> In the end the priest will understand that he must commune with Christ in his love for this baba and mama. He will realize together with his baba and mama that as Christ gave His Blessed Mother . . . to the priest and to this baba, so the baba, in order to commune more intimately with his priest, wishes to give him by the force of the spirit his mama, in order that he and the priest be ONE, in love for the Virgin and in love for *their* mama. The mama will wish to be able to commune with the Blessed Virgin in her love for Christ, through her love for her baba, and equally, through her love for the priest who receives her. By the grace of God, priest and baba and mama will become ONE. And that is the third way, the third degree, or the third thought . . .[1]

Initiation into this third way was modified by the priest chosen by Tempels to replace him in this function. The story of Mama X is no longer recounted. The union of baba and mama with the priest, though deeply personal, is less autobiographically oriented. It is now more directly linked to the initiates' oneness with the priest not only as the official representative of the Catholic Church, but also as someone directly commanded by Christ to be one with the baba and mama, as He was one with Mary and mankind.

[1] Letter from Tempels to a Congolese priest, 21 Mar. 1963.

Here is how one Jamaa priest talks to a Jamaa couple when they come to him for the third initiation:[1]

Together we have sought love. We have achieved union with Christ and our Blessed Lady. We have received Christ and Mary. Later we introduced Christ and our Blessed Lady into our home, and we became conscious of the fact that in our home we take the place of Christ and our Blessed Lady. But we still have something more to accomplish. When Christ left His apostles, He said to them: Go and do what I have done. As I was ONE with all of you, with Mary, with the people, so you must go and be ONE with them. Be ONE with the baba and the mama whom I entrust to you. In the same manner Christ wishes that from now on I myself as a priest be ONE with you.

But in order for us to become ONE we must know each other. First I will make myself known to you.

At this point in the exhortation the priest recounts his life history. These are the personal details that one Jamaa priest shares with the initiates:

I tell them at this point that ever since I was a child I had a vocation to the priesthood, and how I knew for certain that I would become a priest. When I had been ordained a priest I lived from the thought of working for Christ. I tried this, but there were many things that went wrong. Pride, ill will towards the people, harshness, and other wrong things. I further tell them the story of how I arrived in N., and how, little by little, I started searching for union, and how this further developed.

Once this confession has taken place, the priest addresses the baba and mama in the following manner:

Now you know me. Now that we know each other in this way, I ask you to accept me as Christ accepted Mary: to accept me, to love me, as your child whom you must care for, help and protect. Accept me also as a father, who in his mass, prayer and teaching wants to give you the life; accept me in your love. That I too may be in your love. I also accept you as my children, as my father and mother, and I accept you as participant in your mutual love, I give you all that I received from Christ. My priesthood included, and the task that Christ entrusted to me: to spread love among men. You also, go now and carry the love in your home to people who do not know love. This fecundity is a fecundity of all of us together. The children that you engender are also mine, and mine are also yours. Now let us bless each other and think of each other that we may consciously live that union and that Christ may show it to us in thoughts.

[1] Letter from Father Frans to Father Erik, 5 Sept. 1963.

The purpose of the fourth way was for baba and mama together, as a unified couple, to experience a living encounter with Christ, Mary and the priest. Tempels explained that 'as the second way is two people together becoming one with Christ, so the fourth way is two people together becoming one with the priest'. Because of its ephemeral, secret, and controversial nature, we know less of the details of this way than of those that preceded it. It would seem that some of the most important *mafundisho* associated with this way focused on the relationships between Christ, Mary, John, and Mary Magdalen, as explained in our earlier discussion of Jamaa doctrine. There is also direct testimonial evidence given by Jamaa priests and couples that initiation into this degree entailed some amount of mutual bodily exposure. The meaning of this part of the ritual was for baba, mama, and priest to come to know each other corporeally, as well as spiritually, and to bless each other's body, and become physically one. When this happened it was said that the priest had been 'born in the house': consummated as a spiritual child of the baba and mama. There were some members of the movement who expected the priest who had passed through the fourth way to share and transmit the 'light' and 'Holy Spirit' he had received through this stage of the initiation by subsequently 'being born in other peoples' houses'.

For a priest entering the Jamaa, certain of the initiation rites and their symbolic significance are different from those for a lay initiate.[1] The priest enters the first way very much as a baba and mama do. In Tempels's words, 'This priest enters the house of a baba and his mama and becomes the child of both of them when they succeed in also introducing him into the first way, namely to know Christ and the Virgin as they know them.'[2]

Strictly speaking, the second way (in which the baba and mama together experience an encounter with Christ and Mary) is designed for a married couple, rather than for a priest. However, Tempels felt that there was spiritual value both for the couple and for the priest if the latter could vicariously, but directly, have 'respectful knowledge' of the encounter between a baba and mama 'in the Jamaa spirit'. This is the essence of the second way for the priest. Its

---

[1] Other variations exist for Sisters and lay people having taken religious vows, mainly due to the fact that they are celibate, rather than to their sacramental status and power.

[2] Letter from Tempels to a Congolese priest, 21 Mar. 1963.

spiritual benefits ideally are threefold. Sharing their mutual encounter with the priest deepens the union of the baba and mama. It also enables the priest to understand better how the baba and mama are living. And, by virtue of his communion with his 'spiritual parents' and his knowledge of the second degree through which they have passed, the priest becomes more truly and fully their 'child' (*mwana*). In principle, as Tempels conceived the initiation sequence, the Jamaa priest should have passed through the third and fourth ways in a manner complementary to that of lay members. So far as we know, only one priest, Father Frans, began this part of the initiation under the aegis of his baba and mama, which was guided through correspondence from Belgium by Tempels. This still experimental phase was aborted when the priest was confronted with the fact that being 'born into the house' of his baba and mama entailed a mutual bodily blessing and bodily union with the couple through the mama. Somewhat later, he learned that, once this was completed, he would also be expected to be born into the houses of numerous other Jamaa couples, thereby 'transmitting and distributing the Light, the Holy Spirit'. A flurry of letters was exchanged between Tempels, Father Frans, and his baba and mama, in which both the indications and counterindications for these rites were discussed. Although Father Frans seems to have gone through the first part of this process, apparently, the conclusion that he, Tempels, and his Jamaa parents reached is that it would not be advisable for priests to do so in the future. Father Frans was never born in the houses of other baba and mama. Before this could happen, in response to an agonized letter sent by Father Frans, Tempels wrote that he had 'erred' in having devised the rite. As he put it, the priest 'could not be distributed further, so long as [he] did not have somebody who totally belonged to [him]'.[1] As we understand it, this was Tempels's metaphorical way of acknowledging that celibacy imposed certain limits on the extent to which the priest could be expected to achieve union with the people, and on the manner in which he could express his oneness with them.

It now appears, in retrospect, that from the very inception of the Jamaa certain of Tempels's teachings were understood by some of his Congolese followers in a way other than that he himself intended. These 'misunderstandings' were not random. For the most part, they concerned interpretations of various episodes in the Old and New

---

[1] Letter from Father Frans to Father Erik, 5 Sept. 1963.

Testaments. They were similarly expressed in rites as well as beliefs by Jamaa baba and mama in communities in Katanga and Kasai. They surfaced at about the same time in these different localities, in the second half of 1963. They were sufficiently recurrent and identifiable to be collectively labelled 'the deviations' by Catholic clergy, both Jamaa and non-Jamaa, who became increasingly concerned about their heterodoxy. And gradually, belief in these interpretations became organized by particular baba in a way that constituted the basis for the Katete movement that we have described in the preceding chapter. Between 1963 to the present time, these beliefs and rites have become more pervasive and paramount in the Jamaa.

Although all Jamaa members do not subscribe to or participate in these so-called deviations, they are believed to be legitimate patterns by a substantial number of Jamaa members who adhere to them. These patterns appear to constitute an institutionalized variant of the movement's doctrine and ritual.

This orientation in the Jamaa seems primarily to derive from the way that Congolese members interpreted the implications of Tempels's emphasis on life, fecundity, love, union, and the trinary relationship, parent–spouse–child. As we have seen, Tempels developed these ideas chiefly around the persons of Christ and Mary and their relationship to one another. In his *mafundisho*, Tempels tried to make it clear that Christ and Mary's love, unity, and fecundity, though very human, were totally spiritual. Nevertheless, he seems to have evoked a more corporeal notion of their relationship than he either intended or recognized. The reasons for this will be elaborated more fully later in this chapter. In brief, their origins were: Tempels's choice of language and its connotations; the ambience his words, gestures, and person created; some of the latent feelings he inadvertently communicated to his audience; and, not the least, some of the ways in which Bantu culture shaped the reactions of the people to his teachings. Here, for example, is one of the ways he presented the idea that 'God the Father, the Son and the Holy Spirit . . . thought of the Virgin . . . before all eternity, saying: "I want to communicate to you all my love of paternity, of filiality and of union with you" ':

It happened that God sent the Virgin Mary an angel who informed her how God had thought of her since all eternity. And God Himself gave the light to Mama Maria so that she might know that God wished to be with her as Father, as Child and as 'one same thing' (*kitu kimoja*), and to be united with her in these three thoughts [ideas] of love. Doubt seized Mary; how can God who is without body be love with her, in what way; on the one hand, [there is] God who is without body, who is pure Spirit, and on the other hand, she, the Virgin with her humanity. Nevertheless, she believes in God, and so it is, that she crushed the head of Satan. Then, it came to pass that God who is pure Spirit (having not yet entered into the womb of the Virgin Mary) and the Virgin Mary, who is only a human being, unite in complete love. Then, it happens that God consents to become child of the Virgin Mary, child of her thoughts and of her spirit, and even of the fecundity of her body, of her womb.

Tempels's disclaimers notwithstanding, through expositions like this, numerous Jamists received the message that fundamental 'unity', 'being-one-thing' (*kitu kimoja*) achieved its full realization only when baba and mama became one through sexual intercourse, as they were convinced Christ and Mary had done. Uniting through physical relations made 'totally pure by the Love of God' is viewed by such Jamaa members as a sign of the highest, most spiritual form of love. Furthermore, they have taken this belief and applied it to figures and events in the Old and New Testaments of special importance in Jamaa teaching. Thus, running parallel to the orthodox understanding of these key biblical episodes are the following 'Katete' ways of interpreting them:

—Adam and Eve: There are at least three Katete versions of the story of Adam and Eve's original sin. The first one goes like this. God did not allow Adam to have conjugal relations with his wife, Eve. Thus, Adam suffered loss of semen. Satan succeeded in catching that semen and escaped with it into the depths of hell. Immediately after His death, Christ descended into hell, where He retrieved Adam's semen from Satan's power.

—The second version has it that God imposed a prohibition on Adam and Eve: 'Do not look at your own genitals or those of your neighbour.' But the snake in the tree told Eve: 'Take a good look at those parts of your body, and you shall know everything.' From then on Adam and Eve lived together, before God had given them permission to do so.

—The third interpretation of the Garden of Eden story is as follows: God had given Adam and Eve permission to live as man and wife. The snake taught Eve how to get full sexual satisfaction without Adam as a partner. Eve then taught this to Adam.

— Cain and Abel: Adam and Eve watched their two sons grow up and become adults. They noticed that they were losing their semen. In order to prevent that, Adam asked Eve to have sexual relations with their sons.

Eve gave herself to them both, but favoured Abel. And this explains the jealousy of Cain.

—Angels have wives. Lucifer refused to give his wife to certain angels. Thus, he was ejected from the company of the good angels.

—Joseph and Mary had a normal, ordinary married life. They had sexual relations like all husbands and wives. They had other children in addition to Jesus. But it was Jesus who taught his parents 'true' love.

—As a young man, Christ showed no interest in girls. That caused Joseph and Mary great concern, so much so that they called a family council together to discuss the problem.

—At the wedding of Canaan, Jesus transformed water into wine. His purpose in doing so was to make everyone drunk. He then gave a public demonstration of exchange of wives, beginning with his own mother. Jesus gave his love to the bride, Mary gave her love to the groom, and this exchange enhanced their union.

—At the inception of Jesus's public life, He asked His mother to 'become mother of his children'. Mary was stunned, but Jesus told her that from that moment on He stood in another relationship to her. They became one flesh.

—The temptation with which Christ was faced in the desert during his forty days of fasting had to do with women. Satan wanted to offer him a woman so that Christ could not give himself to his mother. Jesus refused. It was not until after the fast in the desert that He was able to offer himself to his mother.

—Mary Magdalen was Christ's mistress. They were 'united corporeally'.

—Mary Magdalen and John were physically united with each other, and with Christ and Mary.

—Jesus washed the feet of the apostles. Some maintain that it was not their feet He washed, but rather their private parts. Christ, then, gave his love to the apostles. He did this by having sexual relations with their wives.

—Nicodemus: In order to be born a second time, Nicodemus had to take another wife, and she had to sleep with his first wife.

—At the Last Supper, John was reclining on the breast of Jesus. This conversation took place between them:

John: 'Jesus, pardon me, when I saw You with Our Lady, I always thought that You took her as your wife.'

Jesus: 'Wait . . . tomorrow you'll understand.'

—On the Cross, Christ entrusted his mother to John, saying: 'Behold thy mother!' And from that hour, John lived with Mary.

—In the Eucharist, the bread and the wine are no longer bread and wine, but something else . . .

—At Pentecost, after receiving the Holy Spirit, the apostles united corporeally with the women of the congregation.[1]

Several themes that occur in these reinterpreted Bible stories should be mentioned here. To begin with, the extent to which they focus on sexual relations, genitalia, and bodily secretions associated with sex and procreation, particularly semen, is extraordinary to a non-Bantu observer. Even the most basic and sacred symbols of Christianity, the bread and wine of the Eucharist, are equated with this 'something else'. Not only are such holy figures as Mary and John, who in Catholic tradition are believed to be virginal and celibate, depicted as persons who have had extensive sexual experience, but also Christ Himself. It is equally important to note, however, that their sexual activity is viewed as having occurred within a restricted circle of persons, who constitute something equivalent to an extended, clanic family. Christ, Mary, Joseph, Mary Magdalen, John, and the other apostles make up this biological-and-spiritual Jamaa, linked to and descended from Adam and Eve, and their sons Cain and Abel, who are regarded as primary ancestors. The criss-crossing web of sexual relations that unite them are seen as more than physical. They express, consummate, intensify, and widen a collective familial love that is considered more spiritual, creative, and perfect than 'ordinary' love. All this is consonant in significant ways with the Bantu emphasis on myths of origin, kinship, clanic solidarity, and fecundity. The vision of a transcendental love present in the stories appears to be more explicitly Christian. These tales also recurrently express strong taboo-like disapproval of masturbation and the spilling of semen, and great anxiety about them. Here, Bantu beliefs converge with those of the Old Testament, so that these acts are construed as dangerous and undesirable because they entail ritual impurity and loss of vitality, and jeopardize fertility.

There are at least three aspects of these stories that cannot be accounted for either in Bantu or Judaeo-Christian traditions. It is more than implied that an incestuous relationship existed between

[1] These Katete renditions of biblical stories have been abstracted from a letter written in August 1963 by Tempels and Father Benoit to Jamaa baba and mama of Katanga, and from a memorandum reporting on the Katete development in Kasai, written by a missionary priest in that region, associated with the Jamaa.

Christ and Mary, His mother. Something closely resembling homo-
sexual love is described as uniting Christ, John, and all the apostles.
Finally, numerous exchanges of sexual partners between Christ,
the two Marys, and the apostles are reported to have occurred. The
incest taboo prohibiting sexual relations between parents and
children is one of the strongest taboos among the tribes from
which Jamaa members have been recruited. Homosexuality is both
rare and strongly disapproved of. The exchange of sexual partners
is synonymous with adultery, which is condemned. The only traditional patterns that have any possible relationship to the kinds of
sexual exchanges that are depicted in these modified Bible accounts
are, on the one hand, the Luba-Katanga custom of offering one's
wife to a visiting brother as part of the hospitality extended to him,
and, on the other, highly ritualized sexual relations with a designated
woman other than one's spouse as an integral element of initiation
into certain secret religious or professional associations among the
Luba. Some of the factors that may have contributed to those Katete
interpretations which are deviant for Bantu peoples, as well as
for Western European Christians, will be examined in a subsequent section of this chapter. Here, we will only state that many of
the Jamaa members who subscribe to the Katete interpretation do not
regard the relations between the New Testament personages that
they depict in their stories as problematic. For they feel that holy
individuals who incarnate 'divine love', most especially Christ and
Mary, are lifted above and exempted from the prohibitions and
taboos that apply to ordinary human beings.

Predictably, these Katete variants of Jamaa beliefs have their
counterparts in the Jamaa ritual system. They promote the interpretation and enactment of union in each of the 'ways' as both
physical and spiritual. In some instances, the baba and mama being
initiated into the Jamaa pass through the rites in a state of nudity.
Husbands and wives have been known to pray together on their
knees, without any clothes on, in front of a burning candle and
a statue of the Virgin Mary. It has been reported that sometimes
entrance into the second and third degrees of the Jamaa has not only
entailed sexual relations between the married couple being initiated,
but also between them and their initiators. When this has occurred, it
has taken the form of an intimate public ceremony, and has been understood as a sign of perfect love and union. Finally, these Katete conceptions have encouraged Jamists to think of the priest as a 'giver

of life'. Some members have sought magico-religious life from him in the form of physical contact and even sexual union.

Partly because of the charismatic nature of Tempels's personality and the movement he created, very few members of the Jamaa recognize the extent to which it has been shaped by Franciscan and Flemish as well as by Christian, Catholic, and Bantu cultural traits. Even the most learned Jamaa priests are not fully aware of the way that these elements have been creatively synthesized in the movement; for they are at least as preoccupied with the special qualities of Tempels as are Congolese adherents, if not more so. Most Jamists regard the movement as a divinely inspired outgrowth of the unique, compelling, and endlessly fascinating characteristics of Tempels. This tendency has been reinforced by Tempels's own insistence on the antithesis between the kind of existential search and discovery represented by the Jamaa, and what he has disdainfully referred to as a search and apprenticeship through books. Through this invidious comparison, he has implied that he is not indebted to his formal training or earlier socialization for the insights on which the Jamaa is based. Quite the contrary, as we have already shown, Tempels felt that it was not until he laid down the manuals that epitomized the form of Belgianness and institutionalized Catholicism in which he had been schooled that he became sufficiently Christian, priestly, and Bantu to create and enter into a jamaa. His Congolese followers attribute Tempels's gift of grace to both Catholic and Bantu priestly powers. The Belgian Fathers and Sisters in the movement also consider him to be a highly endowed priest. In addition, they display a Continental European tendency to explain Tempels's life history, attitudes, beliefs, values, and behaviour as unique products of a unique personality, almost to the exclusion of historical, social, and cultural influences. All these elements converge to perpetuate what might be called a charismatic myth about the sources of Jamaa beliefs and rites.

In significant ways, the Jamaa is consonant with the Franciscan tradition out of which Tempels comes. Franciscan theology[1] is christocentric. It not only accords a greater primacy to Christ than other schools of Christian theology, but it also emphasizes his human nature and humanity. Closely associated with this insistence on the personhood of Christ is the equally characteristic Franciscan veneration

---

[1] St. Bonaventure (1221–74) and Duns Scotus (1265–1308) are the principal architects of the Franciscan school of theology.

of his Mother, Mary. As a contemporary expert on Franciscanism has pointed out, 'It is not by chance that Scotus, one of the
two greatest Franciscan theologians, bears the title *Doctor Marianus*
for his services in explaining the doctrine of the Immaculate Conception.'[1] The Franciscan conception of God is one of pure, generous, transcendent love. God is viewed as virtually synonymous with
love. St. Bonaventure has presented the mystery of the Trinity as
an outpouring of God's love. And in Franciscan thought, God is
depicted as wanting man to be 'his partner in love'.[2] In a sense, there
is no distinctive system of Franciscan theology. Rather, it is formu-
lated in what modern philosophy would call existential and personal
terms. It also focuses in a special way on the Scripture. St. Francis
himself asked no more than that men should follow the gospel and
do what it asks. Finally, the renowned Franciscan love of nature is
a specific expression of a more general characteristic of Franciscanism: its positive outlook on things of this world, because God
is considered to be present in them. It is stressed that in all creation
man can see and meet God. The 'exemplarism' of Franciscan theology propounds that what God had created was prefigured in his
'mind', and thus existed in thought before it appeared in concrete form.

It can be seen, then, that in critical respects the centrality of
Christ and Mary for the Jamaa is in keeping with the Franciscan
spirit. In the Jamaa, too, as in Franciscanism, great importance is
attached to the fact that Christ and His Mother lived a terrestrial,
human existence. The very essence of the Jamaa lies in the search
to meet God, Christ, and Mary in love, and to be rendered more
loving thereby. For Jamists, as for Franciscans, the Bible and
various of its personages have what might almost be termed a folk
religion importance. Certain parts of the Old Testament and all
of the New Testament are especially valued not only because they
are believed to embody the most sacred of religious teachings and
messages, but also because they are thought to contain some of the
most compelling insights into the humanity of Christ, Mary, Mary
Magdalen, the apostles, and their biblical progenitors. Certainly,
the Jamaa also represents a highly personal, deeply existential, but

---

[1] Friedrich Wetter, 'Franciscan Theology', in Karl Rahner, *et al.*, eds., *Sacramentum Mundi: An Encyclopedia of Theology*, vol. II (New York: Herder and
Herder, 1968), p. 349. This succinct essay (pp. 346–9) is a remarkably lucid
analysis of the distinctive attributes of Franciscanism.

[2] Ibid., p. 348.

none the less communal sort of religious orientation in which men and women are inspired to seek a face-to-face and unifying encounter with God in love.

Some of these attributes also characterize the Flemish cultura tradition out of which Tempels comes. The Virgin Mary holds a special and cherished place in Flanders. She is affectionately referred to as *Onze Lieve Vrouw*, 'Our Beloved Lady'. Her presence is visible in niches built into the brick walls of old Flemish houses[1] and in roadside shrines. Countless churches and parishes bear her name. She is a favoured subject of Flemish painters and poets, who generally depict her romantically as a beautiful, young, fine-boned woman with shiny, flaxen hair, richly garbed in a crimson cape draped gracefully over an azure-blue dress, bordered in precious jewels. Although she is often portrayed with the Infant Jesus in her arms or at her breast, in contrast to the Italian Madonna, one is less inclined to think of her as a maternal figure than as a nubile Flemish maiden.[2] In some of the most famous paintings of the Flemish Primitives, she is shown with a red apple, voluptuously reminiscent of the Garden of Eden and/or with a red rose, as evocative of the medieval tradition of courtly love as of spiritual perfection.

The style in which Tempels recounted Bible stories to the members of the Jamaa with vivid, homely, verbatim, and, in numerous ways, fictitious detail also has its precedent in Flemish painting and literature. The artistic tradition to which it seems to have a significant relationship has often been referred to as one of 'sensual mysticism'. An almost perfect parallel to Tempels's fashion of narrating critical episodes in the life of Jesus, for example, can be found in the folk story, *The Christ Child in Flanders*, by the Flemish novelist, Felix Timmermans. 'With some poetic licence and much pleasure in embellishment I have portrayed the divine adventures of the Child Jesus, of his sweet mother and excellent foster-father against the background of our own good and beautiful Flanders',

[1] In the city of Bruges in medieval times, one of the requirements for being admitted to a guild as a Master craftsman was the making of a statue of the Virgin Mary with the primary materials of one's craft (wood, metal, lace, etc.). This statue was then placed in a niche over the Master's front door, as a sign of his calling and status. It was supposed to confer blessings on the man and his family.

[2] For a sensitive and masterful analysis of the symbolism and psychological significance of the Madonna in Southern Italian culture, see Anne Parsons, *Belief, Magic, and Anomie* (New York: The Free Press, 1969), especially pp. 16–24, 45–7, 95–6, and 274–5.

he wrote in the preface to his tale.[1] What Timmermans did with his pen, transposing the gospel to the earth of Flanders, Flemish painters did with their brushes. Here, for example, is a scene in the home of Joseph, Mary, and the Child Jesus, as presented in the lyrical and mysterious, earthly and luxuriant prose of Timmermans:

It was in September, and the smell of fruit was everywhere. Along the edge of the fields the scarlet potatoweed fires wove drowsy skanes of smoke through the trees. A solitary bat fluttered blackly away.

In the white cottage where Joseph and Mary and the child lived together in deepest peace, the windows were open. There was as yet no light inside, but the honeyed fragrance of dark roses swung deep into the twilight of the rooms and hovered over the supper table on which lay the folded hands of a man and a woman. And while the man's voice, rumbling like a great bumblebee, droned heaven's blessing over the food, a pudgy child's fist banged lustily with the wooden spoon upon the table.[2]

This kind of naïve delight in the descriptive details of every-day life and appreciation of the art of the raconteur is part of the Bantu oral tradition as well. Thus, Tempels's way of recounting Bible tales had resonance for Congolese, and in some respects was familiar to them. They, in turn, elaborated these stories. What Tempels has called the 'triple aspirations' of Bantu peoples— fecundity, union, and vital force —became central themes in their interpretations of Old and New Testament episodes, and, beyond that, in Jamaa beliefs and rites more generally. Tempels has recounted the process of dialogue and encounter with Congolese men and women through which he came to understand their primary values and yearnings. We have no reason to doubt the historical validity of his account, and on this basis we can say that the Jamaa's preoccupation with fecundity, union, and vital force is predominantly Bantu, albeit catalysed by Tempels.

Various other attributes of Jamaa beliefs and rites seem to be primarily Bantu. These include the initiation process and the secrecy surrounding the exact nature of the various 'ways'. Tempels recognized that such rituals and mystery were germane to traditional

---

[1] Felix Timmermans, *The Christ Child in Flanders* (Chicago: Henry Regnery, 1961), no page number. (The original Flemish publication appeared in 1917.) In connection with our attempt to link certain Franciscan and Flemish culture traits with attributes of the Jamaa, it is interesting to note that one of the most renowned novels of Timmermans is a semi-fictitious account of the life of St. Francis, entitled *De Harp van Sint Franciskus*.

[2] Felix Timmermans, *The Christ Child in Flanders*, p. 197.

religious associations, and he semi-consciously designed these aspects of the Jamaa to be compatible with the culture.

It will be remembered that prescribed dreams are a crucial part of these initiation rites. Experiencing certain kinds of dreams and sharing them with one's spouse, with other baba and mama, and with Jamaa priests are also important modes of interaction and communication in other Jamaa contexts. The role of the dream in the Jamaa appears to be largely Bantu. Dreams are 'vehicles of symbolic messages' for Congolese, and in present-day as well as in traditional society they play a key role in individual and group life. For Congolese, dreams are 'real', not 'imagined'. 'Just as there is a continuum between body and soul, life and death, Congolese believe, so there is an unbroken thread between sleeping and waking experiences. Through dreams and in them, the individual makes contact with the shades of the ancestors and with the spirits.'[1] The African-inspired preoccupation with dreams in the Jamaa seems to have triggered deeply buried cultural associations with the dream in the Belgian priests who belong to the movement. They have become newly aware of the fact that God often communicated with man through the dream, as recorded in the pages of the Bible, and from time to time they raise pensive questions about why God no longer talks to them this way. They have also been re-sensitized to the dream-like, imagistic quality of the literary and, especially, the artistic Flemish tradition out of which nearly all of them come. As a consequence, both manifestly and latently they have re-inforced the tendency of Congolese Jamists to attach special significance to dreams.

Closely related to the Bantu belief in dreams is the characteristic attitude of the Bantu towards the spoken and written word. This has been described as a form of nominalism.[2] In effect, messages expressed in various forms (the dream and *mawazo*, or thoughts, included) are reified. They are believed to have an essence of their own and to be infused with supernatural power to exert a beneficent or noxious influence on events and persons. This orientation to 'words' is associated with a culturally determined sensitivity to the deeper sentiments and motives of persons who are delivering 'messages'. This is perhaps one of the paramount sources of some of the so-called deviations in the Jamaa.

[1] Renée C. Fox, 'The Intelligence behind the Mask', unpublished paper, 1968, p. 39.   [2] Ibid., p. 38.

On the one hand, despite Tempels's extraordinary grasp of Bantu Luba culture in some respects, he apparently used certain words and concepts without being fully aware of the way they would be understood and acted upon by his Congolese interlocutors. Notably, for example, the symbols water, blood, house, and gift of life as used by Tempels were interpreted by numerous Jamaa members in what Europeans would consider highly erotic ways. The meaning that Jamists have attached to these symbols does not seem to be arbitrary, or necessarily deviant, irreligious, or perverse. One could cite numerous religious movements other than the Jamaa that have occurred in Congolese history in which the coming together of Bantu, Christian, and Western influences have produced phenomena similar to the katete expressions.

Finally, some of the Katete beliefs and rites seem to have originated in Congolese members' perception of certain confusions and ambiguities contained in Tempels's teachings, and in their subsequent cultural elaborations upon these. Above all, Tempels's presentation of a husband–wife as well as a reciprocal parent–child relationship between Christ and Mary does suggest incest, although he intended it to signify the triple love of the Trinity. Secondly, as we have indicated, Tempels talked a great deal to Jamaa members about his encounter with Sister X. While he was in the Congo, the third way in the initiation sequence consisted of the baba receiving Mama X in thoughts, and the mama, Tempels. Congolese seem to have understood from these experiences that Tempels and Christ and Mama X and Mary were to be equated in certain ways, and that what was being expressed through these rites was partly the husband-and-wife-like love that this priest and sister bore for each other.

In what sense, if any, this may have been true is hard to document. To what extent Tempels was aware of the fact that some of the Katete beliefs and practices grew in part out of this presumed insight, and to what degree he himself participated in them is unclear.

CHAPTER V

Jamaa Symbolism

IN the *mafundisho*, dreams, and life histories narrated by baba and mama of the Jamaa, certain themes, images, and symbols occur frequently. As might be expected, one source of these common patterns is the system of beliefs and rites on which the movement is founded. Thus, in the dreams and stories that Jamists recount as well as in the lessons they teach, Christ and Mary, man and woman, encounter, union, and fecundity are central themes.

However, a closer examination of these expressive materials not only provides confirmation that the primary Jamaa beliefs and rites we have identified are deeply internalized by the members of the movement; it also reveals the forms in which traditional and Bantu conceptions are interwoven with modern and Christian themes in the psyches of the African men and women of the Jamaa. When compared with most other religious movements in the Congo during this century,[1] the Jamaa is notable for the predominance and profundity of its Christian orientation.[2] Nevertheless, in its conscious and unconscious expressive symbolism, imagery associated with core elements of Bantu culture—especially its underlying cosmic view—recurs.

At the heart of this cosmic outlook lies what we term the 'fortune–misfortune constellation'.[3] Bantu Africans are continuously pre-

[1] For my knowledge of the major religious movements in the Congo from 1900 to 1970, I am especially indebted to the collection of primary materials on 'secret sects' in the archives of the Kasai province in colonial Congo, to which I made a footnote reference in Chapter III. My first-hand sociological research in association with the Centre de Recherches Sociologiques from 1962 to 1967 gave me access to another whole body of primary data on Congolese religious movements, both contemporaneous and historical. In addition, my earlier work at Kisantu, Lower Congo (1952–4), brought me into direct contact with several religious movements in that region. The most significant of these was Kimbanguism, which is probably the Congolese religious movement that is most widely known in Africa and abroad. It is the only indigenous movement that is officially recognized as one of Zaïre's national churches.

[2] There are only two other Congolese religious movements that we would classify as comparably Christian in orientation: Kimbanguism and the Apostolo movement.

[3] This concept is drawn from Willy De Craemer et al., 'Religious Movements in Central Africa'.

occupied with the problem of explaining why and how felicitous and adverse happenings befall human beings. Health, longevity, wealth, fecundity, status, power, and psychic peace are primary among the experiences constituting good fortune. Illness, death, poverty, sterility, degradation, and dissension epitomize misfortune. Both good and bad fortune are believed to be predominantly metaphysical in origin, caused by the workings of ancestors and spirits. These spirits, in turn, are triggered into action by the conscious and unconsious thoughts and feelings of significant persons in one's social entourage. Africans are particularly concerned about the harm that can be done to them by means of witchcraft or sorcery, that is, through the evil sentiments of others or through their deliberate use of ritualistic means to inflict damage. Both witchcraft and sorcery are conceived to emanate from pride, envy, malice, hostility, and the like. The shared conviction that other persons are the vehicles of misfortune creates a social as well as psychic atmosphere of generalized distrust and vigilance. A concomitant of this cosmic outlook and of the existential anxiety inherent in it is the proliferation of purification rites, taboos, and charms in the traditional religious system. These are designed to avert or cause misfortune, or to maximize good fortune. They are also related to the Bantu African concern about acquiring and maintaining as much life force as possible in order to deal with and succeed in the face of omnipresent danger.

As we have seen in the previous chapter, the Jamaa view differs strikingly in a number of significant ways. It associates the ultimate and proximate significance of life and death with Christ and the Virgin Mary, and, to a lesser extent, with God the Father. In contradistinction to Bantu cosmology, it does not attribute the good and bad happenings of everyday life to their intervening in human affairs the way spirits do. Rather, the Jamaa emphasizes that the quality of one's own and of each couple's encounter with these supernatural figures has a diffuse effect on the ambience in which one's life as a whole evolves. Furthermore, in the Jamaa the institutionalized apprehensiveness of Bantu culture is dispelled by the movement's stress on working towards and praying for open and trusting human relationships. These aspects of the Jamaa, in turn, seem to infuse members with sufficient psychological and spiritual confidence to dispense with the use of charms or other traditional ritual objects.

Despite the fundamental differences between Jamaa and Bantu

religious perspectives, there are a number of significant parallels. To begin with, the positive goals to which the Jamaa aspires are compatible with the values that are defined as good fortune in the traditional culture. In fact, the Jamaa attaches special importance to some of these, notably to fecundity and inner and outer harmony. (However, in the Jamaa context the notion of fecundity has been extended to include spiritual as well as biological procreation.) Although Jamists no longer use charms, there are times when their attitudes toward Catholic religious objects, such as the chalice, the communion wafer, religious statues, medals, and the rosary, are similar to those held towards Bantu religious objects. Finally, 'the three ways' of the Jamaa are explicitly influenced by the fact that initiation rites frame the most important events in the individual and communal life cycles of Bantu society.

This intricate blend of elements in the Jamaa can best be seen and understood through a close consideration of some of the expressive materials to which we have referred. Out of our collection of some forty dreams, *mafundisho*, and life histories, some have been chosen for analysis here. They have been selected because they highlight the primary images, metaphors, symbols, feelings, and themes that appear repeatedly in all Jamaa data of this sort. The dreams, *mafundisho*, and life histories presented in this chapter were gathered through my personal contact with some two hundred baba and mama. In addition, four Jamaa priest-leaders gave me access to the primary materials that they had collected from a sum total of approximately three hundred African Jamists in their local parishes.[1]

The following life history was related by Martin Kazadi, a Luba man in his mid-thirties, married and the father of four children, who worked as a mechanic for Union Minière. His account is also a testimony, because its primary intent was to demonstrate how membership in the Jamaa, through the spiritual understanding it provided and the psychic support it offered, had transformed his own life, and the lives of his wife and children as well.

My father was a man who made *manga* [medicines, magical charms]. He had all sorts of secret powers at his disposal. When he was locked up

[1] I gratefully acknowledge the help I received from the Revd. Bertien Peeraer, O.F.M., in assembling some of this documentation. He gave me access to his own rich collection of Jamaa dreams, *mafundisho*, and life histories. I would also like to thank Professor Theo Theuws, O.F.M. for sharing relevant personal letters with me.

in a hut, with guards posted all around, one suddenly saw him walking down the path. He could change into the form of a leopard or a lion, and he had medicines against all illnesses and against all misfortune. When I had grown up, my father wanted to transfer his powers to me. But, in the meantime, the Whites had arrived to our region. There were Whites who beat us and who extorted money. Other Whites came and gave us injections. There was also a white man who did not ask for anything, and who was friendly with the children.

We wanted to know what he was 'teaching' and at night we gathered around the fire with him. We wanted to know his village, and together with other adults, we undertook the trip, three, four days of marching in order to find out where he was living and what he was doing. He had talked about God, and so, I told my father, 'I don't want your things. I want the things of God.' My older brothers got angry with me because I had not accepted the things my father had offered me. In the meantime, I was baptized. My brothers started making [black magic] charms. They wanted to kill me. It was then that I began to feel fear.

In those days, I often went to the train to sell things. Senegalese often passed by. I asked fellow villagers to show me somebody who would sell me a charm which would protect me against my brothers' charms. I had put aside some savings, a thousand francs, in order to marry a woman, and to buy some goats. I used all my money to pay for the horns [receptacles for magical powder] and the preventive medicines of foreigners [Senegalese? Whites?], and I hid everything in a trunk in my house.

One day the Father, a priest, came to our village. So my brothers decided, 'We are going to tell the priest that he has charms, because now ours are powerless. The priest will take away his charms, and then we will be able to kill him.' That day, in the evening, the priest called me and he asked me if I had charms. I confessed immediately. The priest called in the Catechist, who started scolding me. The priest said, 'Don't scold him; he has confessed immediately.' That night the priest came to my house. He had a prayerbook with him and a flashlight. I showed him the charms. He asked me how I had got them. He said, 'Wait, I'll give you a piece of paper for the White man of the State [Government], so that he can arrest those men and force them to repay you the money.' But I replied, 'In buying those charms, I have sinned. Let the money be lost, then, as penance for my sin.' The priest insisted, but I did not give in.

Later, I took my wife into my house, and we had a child. We were both Christian. My brothers became jealous again, and they started to make charms again to bewitch me and my family. I broke my leg, and I had to crawl over the ground to go to the bush. My wife fell ill. My child, and the others too, became sick. We all became very afraid. We went to the diviner, to the charm-makers, and we became so poor that we did not even have clothes anymore. We had to walk around in the village, naked. But the illness did not disappear. It stayed around our house.

My eldest brother wanted my death and the death of my children. But a younger brother who was boarding there was favourably disposed towards me. He was going on a long journey. Before leaving, he was going to write down in a book where the charms were hidden. I was to go to my eldest brother and read in the book and find there where the charms were. But my eldest brother did not let me enter his house. I sent others to look in the book, but there was nothing written [there]. That night I saw my brother in a dream, the younger one who had gone on a journey. He said, 'Get up tomorrow morning at five; go on the road to the place of the dead [cemetery] and stand on the spot where the wind comes from all sides. That will be the place where the charms are hidden.' I went, but terror seized my body. And then, I felt myself being driven to the place and there I knew where I had to dig. I started digging and found a whole basket full of charms. Again, I went to the sorcerer. He made me new charms; he pushed a piece of a needle into my forehead and two other pieces into my upper arm. He made me plenty of charms so that I would no longer feel any blows and would be invulnerable, and no evil powers would be able to touch my house. Then we became the poorest people in the village.

Once again, the priest came [to the village]. I was ill. The priest said, 'I am going with Louise [the narrator's wife] to the mission.' My wife was pounding cassava. She came to tell me. I was ill. The priest came to me and said 'I am going with Louise. You stay here, but tomorrow you get up, take your stick and drag yourself to the mission.' My wife went with him. She carried the sick children. The next day I got up. I dragged myself to the mission. There, once again, the priest took all my charms away from me, and he blessed me so that the needles in my forehead and my arm would no longer influence my thoughts.

And so, later on we came to Katanga. What made our faith so weak was terror of the dead. We had them in our sleep; they asked sacrifices from us; they gave us orders. And we didn't know in what state the dead were. And the priest didn't know either. But now that we know that the dead are living, and that they are our friends, and that we can help them, our fear has disappeared. And we are one with each other: the two of us and our children, and our *bankambo* [dead ancestors]. We help them with our prayers; we are with them in the Mass; and there, we also are one with the priest. We are no longer alone . . .

The foregoing narrative is a classic expression of some of the major elements in the Bantu magico-religious system, and of the existential terror that its beliefs, practices, and world-view can evoke. Underlying the story is the conviction that the good and the evil events occurring in the lives of individuals and groups are primarily attributable to the thoughts and feelings of others. The significant others who have the greatest capacity both to safeguard one against misfortune and to cause one harm are one's closest kin. Thus, the anger and jealousy of Martin's oldest brothers not only filled him with fear, but also 'bewitched' him so that he, his wife, and children were afflicted with illness, accidents, and poverty. On the other hand, the fact that Martin's younger brother was 'favourably disposed' towards him, protected him against the full impact of his older brothers' wrath and envy. Through his appearance in Martin's dreams, as well as the aid he offered in a waking state, this younger brother led Martin to the 'whole basket full of charms' that were working an adverse alchemy over his existence.

The sources of the older brothers' vindictiveness are complex. It seems to spring from the fact that their father chose Martin, rather than one of them, as the son to whom he wished to transfer his mystical powers; from their resentment that Martin had rejected traditional African ways by not accepting 'the things' his father offered; and from the fact that, in their view, Martin had identified with the ways that Whites exploited and abused Africans, as well as with their medical and other beneficent activities by converting to Christianity.

Implicit in the brothers' rancour, too, was their apprehensive belief that Catholicism and its priests provide its adherents with supernatural force greater than that of the most powerful African charms. Through their actions the brothers implied that the harmonious, fecund marriage and the prosperity that Martin enjoyed before his troubles began resulted from the efficaciousness of Christian *manga* and the forces they harness. In this latter regard, to this day, Martin's attitudes toward the powers of Catholicism and its clergy are not completely at variance with those of his brothers. Throughout his narrative he clearly expresses the conviction that the counsel and assistance of the priest and the sacraments he administers are the only forces strong enough to overcome the malignant impact of black magical charms.

It is significant that in his account of a visit from the priest who helped him, Martin emphasizes his arrival by night and refers to his prayerbook and flashlight. This image brings to mind several associations. It is compatible with the central elements in a type of religious movement that recurs in the Congo, known as *Mitumbula*. This movement tends to occur at times of intense collective anxiety. It is accompanied by an epidemic-like spread of the belief that harmful spirits, teleguided by the white man, are appearing at night in various guises. One of the earmarks of the presence of these spirits is that they come bearing a blinding light (a flaming torch, a flashlight, headlights of a car, etc.). Their intent is to 'capture' the body and soul of the Africans whom they accost and abduct.[1] The fact that Martin also remembers the priest's prayerbook suggests that his feelings about it are similar to those manifested in the Congo Rebellion of 1964–5 both by rebel soldiers and by villagers throughout the country. The rebels often took or stole priests' missals, breviaries, and other prayerbooks. Though many villagers were moved to return the books to priests when they found them, they commonly demonstrated apprehension about touching the 'holy books'. Like Congolese caught up in the *Mitumbula* phenomenon, the rebels, and villagers, Martin shows his bivalent beliefs toward the priest's powers. On the basis of the foregoing, it seems probable that the priest's night visitation, his flashlight, and prayerbook signified to Martin that he was both the conveyor and dispeller of evil spirits.

One aspect of the Catholic clergy's metaphysical influence about which Martin feels no ambivalence is the priest's ability to deal with the dead. Before his conversion to Christianity and his entrance into the Jamaa, Martin was literally terrified of the *Bankambo*, spirits of dead ancestors. This, too, is traditional. Departed spirits, including those of ancestors, are believed to intervene in the minor as well as major affairs of the living. If placated, these spirits can be helpful to the living; but if they are disturbed or alienated by the attitudes or actions of living persons, the spirits will cause them great harm and, in extreme cases, kill them.

Involvement in the Jamaa seems to have altered Martin's fear of the dead. With the help of periodic reassurances from a priest, he now views the dead primarily as 'friends', with whom he, his wife, and children, the priest, and even Christ, are 'one'. In another text I have examined, Martin confides a relevant dream he experienced to a Jamaa priest. Here Martin found himself in a house 'as big as a hall', filled with men and women who were 'lying everywhere.' Gradually he recognized them. They were spirits of the dead from the village in which he was born and raised. As he and the Jamaa priest

[1] A recurrent theme in *Mitumbula* movements is the frightened belief that white men are sending out black agents to abduct Africans, in order to kill them, and can and purvey their flesh as corned beef. The veiled allusions to cannibalism and to the slave trade are intriguing aspects of this collective belief.

agreed, if he had had such a dream in his pre-Jamaa days, Martin would have sought the protective help of a powerful sorcerer. But now he feels sufficiently confident of his mutual-aid relationship with the spirits that he does not need to do so. Nevertheless, it is notable that the spirits of the dead still figure importantly in Martin's dream life, and that he is inclined to share dreams about the dead with a priest when they occur.

Several other beliefs and practices to which Martin refers in his narrative are integral to the Bantu magico-religious system. They include the belief that metaphysically endowed persons can change their form and that certain rites, charms, and actions, such as the insertion of needles in the forehead and arms, can confer invulnerability on a person. From his account, it appears that Martin is still convinced that such powers exist, though in his present state of psychic and spiritual security he is no longer as awed or threatened by them as he once was.

Finally, the last sentence in Martin's story ('We are no longer alone . . .') is a condensed statement of an orientation fundamental to Bantu social structure, culture, and personality. Solidarity with kin, with all non-relatives with whom one has significant social relations, with the ancestors and other spirits of the dead is indispensable to one's identity, integrity, and equilibrium. Without this solidarity a Congolese person is not only susceptible to all kinds of affliction, but he virtually ceases to exist psychically, spiritually, and socially. Thus, to be alone, as Martin implies, is the worst, most life-threatening fate that a Congolese man or woman can experience. At the end of his story, when Martin laconically affirms that he, his wife, and children are no longer alone, he is saying that they have been restored to humanity and to life through their reintegration with themselves, significant others, and the spirits.

The following two dreams come from Suzanne Kalala, a Lulua woman, married to an industrial worker employed by one of Union Minière's subsidiary plants, and the mother of four children. At the time that she communicated these and other dreams, Suzanne was a mama of the Jamaa's 'third way', and a prominent member of her local parish. In these dreams, as in Martin Kazadi's life history, Bantu, Catholic, and explicitly Jamist elements are intermixed. As indicated in Chapter IV, the sleeping and dreaming life of Congolese is as real to them as their waking life. Dreams are actual events in which the dreamer participates. Although not all dreams are considered to have a deeper meaning, the greater part of them are believed to contain a supernatural message that it is important to decipher. Thus, in her descriptions of her dreams, Suzanne speaks alternately of the fact that she is 'in *mawazo*' or that she 'receives *mawazo*'. Here she has applied an at once traditional and Jamist concept to the communications that she receives through her dreams. The fact that Suzanne was willing to tell others about these particular dreams suggests that she interpreted them as the type of dreams that has significance for a group, rather than as the type that conveys a private message.

Another day, I begin to sleep. I receive *mawazo*. I see light coming out of the headboard of our bed, which goes like this. [She makes a gesture extending her arm forward.] Then, there in this light I see a man who follows that light. This man says to me, 'Pray the prayer of contrition in exactly this way'. I pray the prayer of contrition. 'Pray the prayer of profession of faith in God.' I pray this prayer of faith in God. Then he says, 'Say the names of the saints Peter and Paul.' I pronounce their names. He says, 'Say the name of Saint Noah.' I say the name of this saint. After having prayed this prayer, they come and show me, saying, 'Receive this statue in your *mawazo*. Receive this statue. Open your hands.' I place my hands so. 'Say, I will receive this statue. This statue will begin to protect you even against all the evils which enter your house. This statue will begin to protect even your entire house and the children whom you engender in your body. This statue, at the interior of this statue there are stars, there is the moon, there is the glory of the name of the Father. This statue, receive it. You will put it in the middle of your own bed, baba and mama.' I put my hands like this . . . I see my hands, they go 'weee'. [She shows how she put her hands on the bed . . .] I put them so. My hands on the bed. Then, I remove them like this. They say, 'Receive the light of the purity of your soul.' I put my hands like this, 'weee'. I am like this. I put them down between us, like this, three times. Then, they say to me, 'This statue, it will close your mouth in front of the baba and mama, in front of all the brothers in the whole world. Through [the power of] this statue you will bear children for God. And you, you will succeed in being saved now, as the Lord Jesus has achieved redemption. He worked for God saving the world.' . . . They showed us this statue, and in it, these stars and this moon. 'It will begin to illumine you, and you will begin to illumine all your brothers who are lost, who remain in the traps of the devil. You will begin to save them.' This simply ends like this.

I was sleeping. I see, someone shows me, 'You, mama, you see now, you are about to receive the three *mawazo* of God the Father. Keep them in your [own] *mawazo*. What you are going to receive is the salvation of the whole world.' Then someone shows me a candle. I take that candle in my hand. There was another man there, with a newborn infant. Then I light the candle. I take it and put it in the infant's hand. Then I bless this child, saying, 'Satan, leave this child. Dirty Satan, leave it. You, child, receive the light in your soul.' This is the way I spoke. Then I had a thing in my hand. It looks like a glove. This thing is so, like a piece of hairy cowhide, as long as this [from hand to elbow]. Then I take this thing, I plunge it in water. Someone says, 'Do you see this child?' I say, 'This thing here, if a man is possessed by sorcery, or if he is [dangerous] in another way, you take this thing, you dip it in water and you sprinkle this man with it, saying, 'Vomit all these things that are in your soul. If it is sorcery or if it is something else, where you went to receive this *buloji* sorcery, I wasn't there." ' You will do thus upon this child or upon an adult man, and where he vomits his *buloji* things, you will not know it, no. Then you sprinkle him with water. And so it was, I was dressed in white clothes like the priest . . . I am completely dressed in this manner. Then someone shows me, someone says, 'It is truly the priesthood that you wish to obtain, redemption to save the world.' I return, I awake, I am in *mawazo*.

At the centre of Suzanne's first dream is the statue that she receives from the unidentified man with whom she converses. Ostensibly, it is a statue of the Virgin Mary, as suggested by its association with the stars, the moon, and the 'glory of the name of the Father'. However, the instructions that Suzanne is given about the statue and some of the properties ascribed to it are not those usually attributed to a Catholic statue of this sort. She is told to put it in the middle of her bed between herself and her husband three times before letting it rest there. She is assured that the statue will illumine and save her, the Jamaa baba and mama, and all mankind, that it will protect her and her family against evil, and that it will 'close [her] mouth in front of' those with whom she has contact. The attribution of this last power to the statue implies that it has the mystical capacity to keep Suzanne from uttering the kind of negative thoughts or feelings that in the Bantu way cause harm. What Suzanne's dream has in common with Martin's story is the belief that Catholic religious objects, like the statue of the Virgin, are potent antidotes to 'all the evils that [can] enter your house' through the workings of witchcraft.

Statues appear in the dreams of numerous Jamaa members. In some of these dreams, as in Suzanne's, the statues represent the presence of the Virgin Mary or Christ; in others they are less explicitly identifiable. But in all cases, certain details link the statues with traditional personages. In Suzanne's dream, for example, the statue of the Virgin can be equated with the statues of female ancestors, venerated in Luba and Lulua culture. This parallel is suggested by the prescribed ritualistic way in which Suzanne manipulates the statue and by the anti-witchcraft powers with which the statue is endowed.

The light that suffuses Suzanne's dream, radiating from the headboard of her bed and from the statue is influenced more by Christian than by Bantu conceptions. In myths, legends, and sculpture that are purely Bantu African this kind of celestial light is not found.

In Suzanne's second dream, Bantu, Christian, and Jamaa elements are mixed in a free-associational way. In the first phase, Suzanne is involved with God's three *mawazo*, a votive candle, a small child who could be the Infant Jesus, and with exorcizing Satan from the child. Without any apparent transition, she then finds herself in the next part of her dream, holding in her hand an African magico-religious object traditionally used in purification rites. She is told that in order for it effectively to counteract sorcery that affects either this child or any adult, the possessed person must be sprinkled with lustral water and 'vomit' all evil thoughts and feelings, while certain formulae are pronounced over him. Suddenly, in the last part of her dream, it is Suzanne herself who is performing these rites. But now she is dressed in the 'white clothes' of a Catholic missionary priest. She has become 'one' with the priest in the 'third way' sense of the Jamaa. The voice that tells Suzanne it is truly the priesthood and salvation of the world that she wants alludes to another meaning in her identification with the priest. Once again, a belief that Suzanne and Martin share with most Congolese is symbolically expressed here. It is the belief that the rites, the religious objects, even the garments associated with Catholicism, and especially the powers of the priest, have greater metaphysical force than any African charm, ceremony, or magico-religious practitioner.

Finally, we consider a *mafundisho* taught by Joseph Kabeya. He is a Luba man, who has special importance in the Jamaa, because he is one of its founding baba. Joseph is still a leader in the movement and one of its most influential teachers of Jamaa doctrine. The following *mafundisho*, addressed to an assembly of baba and mama in Musonoi, is concerned with the *bumuntu*. The word *muntu* means man in the generic sense of human being. *Bumuntu* is the term for the essential nature of a human being, the essence of his/her humanity, including its origin and destination. The distinctive logic of this *mafundisho*, its musical repetitiveness and its local imagery are characteristic of Jamaa materials and of Bantu oral tradition in general.

We were like lost men. We were lost because we no longer know our *bumuntu*. We do not know it any longer. We have forgotten it. We have completely forgotten our *bumuntu*. We look and we say, 'That one there is passing by.' We say, 'That man is passing; that man is passing.' We say, 'That man passes.' A man passes. We say, 'I don't know him.' That's the way it is, isn't it, baba and mama? We are in search of our *bumuntu*, isn't it so, baba and mama? Now, baba and mama, you must make a real effort to know our *bumuntu*. Only when we know our *bumuntu* will we have the true way. And perhaps there we will come to know ourselves well, and perhaps there we will become true men, or men of God [Christians].

We have seen an example in our own village, down there. A man was dying. Whether he was someone passing on the road or however it was, he was dying there on the road. Now, many people pass by him. They say, 'Eeeh, that man, someone go tell the men of God. Where are they?' That one there [dying] is also a man. Instead of burying him, they begin to question each other, 'Eeeh, go and tell the man who directs the prayers, go tell the man who teaches [the catechist], go and tell the men of God to come and bury this man.' Somebody passes by, and he speaks this way. Another passes by, and he speaks this way. Still another passes by and he speaks this way, too.

The ones who pass, are they not men, and the ones they call to bury him, are they not men, too? They all are men. Why did those baba pass without burying that man? Because knowledge of their *bumuntu* was lacking. They failed to know their human-being.

And now another example. We have also seen another example of the same sort. A stranger arrives. He turns around and around in a large village. He looks for a place to sleep. He doesn't find one. He is told, 'Go there, to the Christians, there near the church. Go there and look for a place to sleep.' Now, baba and mama, in the village where he passes, aren't they men? They are men. They are very, very much men. Look, they refuse him. Where they send him, what do these pagans think? They say, 'Those people there are the ones who know the men of God; they know their neighbour; they know the passers-by; they know the strangers.'

And so, baba and mama, when it comes to the matter of our *bumuntu*, this is a very big thing for us to try to know. People ask us, baba and mama, 'How many men pass on the road?' One says there are many people; another says there are two. Who are the two? A man and a woman, those are the ones who pass by from morning till evening. And we, too, we do not succeed in knowing them, that man and that woman. We do not succeed in knowing our *bumuntu*. Even when we are together and search together, we don't reach it. Thus, baba and mama, like those who pass on the road, they pass alongside of the man who is dead. They call on us, men of God, saying, 'Let them come and bury him.' Or, in the case of the man to whom they refuse a place to sleep, they look for us, saying, 'Go to the men of God; they are the ones who can offer you a place to sleep.' So, they address themselves to us in this matter. It is necessary, it is absolutely necessary for us to know our *bumuntu*, because there is a place from which that man comes. When they fail to help their neighbour, a man like themselves, they fail to know their *bumuntu*. They fail to know a very big thing: they don't know where man comes from.

So, if we don't have these ideas, that knowledge, do we know then where man comes from? No. Some people think this way: man is on earth; man comes from his father and his mother, those who begot him. This is how some people think. And if we think likewise, we forget Him who created us, and we forget where we come from. Sometimes, if we too forget about our *bumuntu*, we will not find the way to where we are going. . . .

Man is what kind of thing? What is man? Sometimes we answer, 'Man is thoughts, man is thoughts.' Then they question us, 'How can man be thoughts? We know that man is a body.' We say, 'Man is thoughts, but this man, where was he? This man-thoughts, where was he? One could say, for a long time, this man was close to God; for a long time, he was in God's thoughts. . . . At the moment that He thought man, He said, "I will make man." It was at that moment that man was close to God in His thoughts. God greatly rejoiced saying, "You, my man, I and my man, we will be one thing. I and my man, we will be in agreement; We will love each other; We will be united; We will be one thing." '

And we too, baba and mama, like them, we sometimes say that man is a body. But, what is a body? It is a tribe, this body is a tribe. This body makes many errors. It has many words. Sometimes, when we follow the body, we will forget each other. You will pass by a man like yourself. We will say about him, 'Aaah' [with disesteem]. Another will say, 'I am KaTshiokwe. This European has white limbs. That one is a MuKete, and that one a MuLuba. That one is not from our region.' So, this body of ours differs from the man who was in God's thought, because this man who was in the thought of God had no tribe. He had no tribe of his own. Where he was in God's thought, did he belong to a tribe? No, he was not of a tribe. To what tribe did he belong when he was with God? He did not belong to a tribe, because he was thought. He was thought, he was in accord with God. God loves His man in His thoughts. [Joseph Kabeya next develops the Jamaa theme that man has been granted the privilege of sharing the three great *mawazo* or thoughts of God: Life, Fecundity, and Love. He defines 'Christian-being' as living one's life according to these *mawazo*. He ends the whole *mafundisho* with the following summary and exhortation.]

These are our thoughts, baba and mama. We wanted to rethink them together today. If we want to remain distant from one another, what will our *bumuntu* become? In that case, our *bumuntu* will have no road. We will return to where we were long ago. You look at me and you say [with contempt], 'Aaah'. I see you and I say, 'Aaah, I do not know him.' And so, we will not be on the road of our Christian-being. These, baba and mama, are the ideas about our *bumuntu* of which we wanted to remind you, the way to seek to know our *bumuntu* that has been lost. We have lost our *bumuntu*, baba and mama, we have lost it, and we are lost. Who among you with beards and white hair still knows and says, 'I nursed at my mother's breasts. I was in my mother's womb. I acted this way and that way?' No one. We puff ourselves up. Sometimes we lack respect for this mother. Likewise we look at God this way, without knowing where we come from. Let us search, baba and mama, for our human-being. Here on earth, this is a very big thing.

This *mafundisho* intricately fuses Bantu and Christian ideas. The concept of *bumuntu* to which it is addressed is compatible with Bantu African beliefs about the nature of man and of man's life. Though the details of these beliefs may vary from one ethnic tradition to another, it is commonly held that man is composed of several parts. His physical or bodily being constitutes man's outer form and appearance. However visible and material it may be, it is not as real and vital as man's immaterial being. What is variously referred to as his shadow, his breath, or his soul is regarded as the essence of man, his ego, his real life, and the part of him that continues even after death. When Joseph Kabeya insists that man is not simply or principally a body, he is invoking this Bantu view of man. At the same time, his affirmation that man is essentially spiritual in nature is the expression of a Christian principle, that he, the baba, and mama have learned through Catholic and Jamaa teachings. Here, the two religious systems, Bantu and Christian, coincide and merge.

In the Bantu religious system, the search to fathom the nature of man is indissolubly linked with another metaphysical preoccupation: the question of man's origin or, as Joseph phrases it in his *mafundisho*, 'Man is thought, but this man, where was he?' The answer that Joseph provides is a traditional one. Man was created by God who 'thought' him into being. Here, the generalized Bantu belief that thoughts and feelings have the power to determine events and direct persons is invoked to explain the mystical relationship between what was in God's mind, the beginnings of man, and man's *bumuntu*. Joseph's lesson mingles this African religious view of the Creation and the origin of human life with the Judaeo-Christian version of it presented in the Book of Genesis. The two traditions are close enough in this regard, so that they can be blended without distortion, as Joseph has done.

The central concern of the *mafundisho* is with the alienation of man from his *bumuntu*, its causes, manifestations, and consequences. Joseph portrays this 'lost' state through anecdotes, which he vividly and repetitively recounts with dialogue and gestures, in the style of Bantu oral tradition. Those who are separated from their *bumuntu* are likened to villagers who pass a dying man on the road and refuse to help or bury him, or who do not offer a stranger a place to sleep for the night. They believe that they were created by their parents. They consider man to be essentially corporeal. And they extend their definition of man as a body to make invidious distinctions between different kinds of physical men, on the basis of tribe and race.

Joseph's story about the dying man and the villagers is reminiscent of the parable of the Good Samaritan in the New Testament. Given the awe with which Africans view the dead and their terror of displeasing the spirits of the dead, refusal to bury a man is one of the most dangerously irreverent acts that Joseph could have cited. His tale about the stranger who is denied shelter in the large village is a commentary on a flagrant deviation from the norms of African hospitality. And in his remarks on tribalism, he deals with a phenomenon deeply rooted in Bantu tradition that he considers antipathetic to both the African concept of *bumuntu* and the Christian concept of soul.

Joseph depicts all of humanity as men and women alternately dwelling in a village and travelling a road. In contrast to those who are one with their *bumuntu*, he implies, those who are estranged from it do not know where they live, where they come from, or where they are going. (The latter is an allusion to life after death.) The highest state of 'knowing' one's *bumuntu* is considered by Joseph to be synonymous with having a 'Christian-being'. He distinguishes this from simply being a Christian, as well as from being a 'pagan'. The person who has sought and found his Christian-being is an integrated and 'true man'. This is because he has received and 'kept' God's three great thoughts (Life, Fecundity, and Love), and he has actualized them in his existence 'here on earth'.

As the foregoing indicates, Joseph's *mafundisho* is as Bantu African as it is Christian. It identifies and develops much common ground between the two religious systems, and in a number of respects it unifies them. However, there are at least two major areas in which the Bantu African and the Christian ways are not easily reconciled by Joseph and the baba and mama to whom he preaches.

The first of these is the conflict between the universalism of the Christian vision and the particularism of the Bantu vision. In the Christian view, as Joseph phrases it, all men are 'very, very much men', they are men like ourselves, they are 'one thing'. This does not mean that persons who are baptized Christians will necessarily live up to the ideal. Joseph recognizes the potentiality for aberration even in the very pious baba and mama of the Jamaa, and in himself. ('We have lost our *bumuntu*, baba and mama, we have lost it, and we are lost.') But in the part of the *mafundisho* where he talks of God's three thoughts, Joseph does affirm that Christians have a particular obligation to be 'one'. '. . . And so it is, baba and mama, that we must seek to be 'one' on earth. Let us be 'one' man, we Christians, we men of Christ. . . . Let us be 'one' because of our Christianity. Let our Christian-being not be separated. . . .' In the Bantu view, great metaphysical, as well as political, importance is attached to the bonds of kinship, clan, tribe, and ethnicity. Solidarity is primarily built along these particularistic lines. As Joseph sees it, the fact that in this tradition men define themselves as KaTshiokwe or MuLuba, kin or stranger, can lead them to be 'distant from one another' and to regard each other with distrust, disrespect, and contemptuous pride.

The second major area in his *mafundisho* where Bantu and Christian orientations diverge concerns the assumptions in African culture about the effects of thoughts and feelings on events. Once again, in this *mafundisho* as in the life history and the dreams we have analysed, the conviction is expressed that negative words, sentiments, and thoughts can cause ill to the person towards whom they are directed, and also towards the person from whom they emanate. This appears in the *mafundisho* at several points. When Joseph says, 'This body makes many errors. It has many words', he means that the gossip and slander in which the non-spiritual part of man engages brings about adverse events. At a later point in the lesson he inveighs against the tendency both to 'puff ourselves up' with arrogance and to 'lack respect' even for one's closest of kin and one's elders. In the way that Joseph phrases this there is the implication that such arrogance and disrespect are among the attitudes that can harm. Finally, Joseph makes an explicit connection between evil thoughts and evil events in the section of his lesson on God's three thoughts:

. . . If you hate a man close to you because of his fecundity or anything else, because of his spiritual or bodily fecundity, when you seek to harm the children of God, those whom God has engendered, you seek to show them bad things or make them lose the way, you yourself lose your fecundity, because it is God who gave you fecundity.

The examination of these Jamaa materials had three aims. The first was to provide aesthetic and affective understanding of primary Jamaa symbols and themes, and of their expressive connotations. The second was to document and elaborate some of the Jamaa beliefs and rites presented in Chapter IV. The third was to show the intricate mixture of Bantu African and Christian elements that these beliefs and rites contain. We now proceed to another level of analysis, a consideration of the ways in which Jamaa doctrine, ritual, and symbolism affect the behaviour of its baba and mama in their relationship to one another and in that part of their lives that is not directly concerned with their religion.

CHAPTER VI

Impact of the Jamaa on its
Lay Members

THE impact of the Jamaa on its Congolese members is multi-faceted, stretching into every sector of their social life. Their attitudes and behaviour in their familial, economic, political, and educational roles, as well as their religious roles, are significantly influenced by the values, beliefs, rites, social structure, and organization of the movement. By and large, the effects of the Jamaa upon the baba and mama are profound. They are experienced as 'conversion'; they endure, and they seem to constitute an authentic desocialization-resocialization process.

The Jamaa attaches supreme religious importance to the family. This view is compatible both with Christian doctrine and with the central place accorded to kinship in Bantu culture and society. However, in a number of significant ways, Jamaa and Bantu conceptions of the family differ. The Jamaa regards the family as a human replica of the Trinity. It is especially preoccupied with the 'Family of Nazareth'. In these two respects, it is explicitly Christian. The Jamaa also focuses with special intensity on the husband–wife relationship; for, as shown in Chapter IV, it considers the married couple to be a miniature Jamaa. In its view, the Church and the larger society are super-Jamaas, of which married couples are the basic units and building blocks. In its emphasis on the monogamous conjugal family, and particularly spouses, the movement departs from the priority assigned to the extended family in traditional African kinship systems, and from their customary polygamous forms of marriage. Here, the Jamaa has been shaped by modern Western Christian ideas about the family and the ordering of relations within it. However, the Jamaa notion of the married couple as a living atom in a macro-Jamaa fits the Bantu definition of the nuclear family's relationship to the clan system. Nevertheless, the Jamaa has modified the Bantu way of looking at the extended kinship structure, so that membership in it is determined less on biological and particularistic grounds and more on the basis of a shared spiritual view and way of life.

Finally, the movement grants special status and attributes distinctive importance to the mama of the family. In Jamaa doctrine, she is seen as the incarnation and extension of the Virgin Mary and her love. In no sense is the Jamaa mama believed to be inferior to the baba, and it might even be said that in her symbolic role as spiritual generatrix she is elevated above him. But, in other respects, largely as a consequence of the Jamaa's insistence on encounter and union between husband and wife, distinctions between sex roles are blurred, and the usual degree of inequality between them is reduced. Ostensibly, this conception of the woman runs counter to the traditionally sharp division of labour that exists between the African man and woman, husband and wife, as well as to the woman's traditional subordination to the man. Such status and ranking of male over female is particularly prominent in patrilineal kinship systems, like that of the Luba, the ethnic group to which the majority of the Jamists belong. Nevertheless, as the honorific term 'mama' implies, even within the traditional framework the fecund woman was granted respect and privileged status. This is based on the entwined kinship-and-religion-associated conviction that 'the mission' of spouses is 'to engender children in order to survive and to respond to the desire of the dead ancestors to always have representatives on earth, and to have as many children as possible in order to enlarge the familial group'.[1]

There is one other major area in which the Luba woman traditionally occupied a position that vied with those reserved for men. Sorcery is a highly developed part of the Luba magico-religious system, and women have been the chief practitioners of this activity. (In the case of the Luba, the powers of the sorcerer or sorceress are considered non-hereditary, and are exercised and transmitted in a planned, deliberate way.)[2] From one point of view the spiritual predominance of women in the Jamaa is a continuation of their magico-religious power base in traditional society. At the same time, in that conversion to the Jamaa and initiation into it entail a rejection of sorcery, witchcraft, and the charms associated

[1] Léonard Mukenge, 'Croyances religieuses et structures socio-familiales en société luba: "Buena Muntu", "Bakishi", "Milambu" ', *Cahiers économiques et sociaux*, V, no. 1 (Mar. 1967), 83.
[2] Jan Vansina, *Introduction à l'ethnographie du Congo* (Brussels: Éditions Universitaires du Congo, 1965), p. 170.

with them, by becoming members of the movement women give up what is perhaps their most potent source of authority, prestige, and protection.

Jamaa couples universally attest to the transformation that their 'encounter' and 'union' have effected in their marriage. Being Jamaa, they affirm, has increased the mutual respect, concern, exchange, support, and love that exist between husband and wife. Couples say that they experience more serenity and fulfilment when they are together. They testify that deep inner motivation to be totally one with one another and faithful to each other 'grows like a blossoming tree'. Here, for example, is the way one mama describes the profound emotional and spiritual changes in her marriage:

> For a long time, my husband and I have been Christians. But when we were together, we did not get along. We did not know each other. No! . . . Sometimes I would want to explain something to him. He would refuse to sit down, even for a moment, to listen to me. He would reproach me. I would flee from him altogether. Then we began to have a better understanding, my husband and I. But I had a bad spirit within myself at home, without explaining it to my husband. Thus, it was on this matter that we looked for a path saying, 'This thing which separates us, where does it come from?' That is the way we are now, we understand each other. I tell him all the things that happen to me, all that is in me. It is like Adam and Eve who sinned before God. Then Adam began to tell all his faults to each child, to each baba and to each mama. It is thus that the tree flourishes because of its leaves, and the leaves grow well because of the tree.

The daily behaviour of spouses in their relationship to one another is significantly modified. Out of his new-found conviction that he is *mwana* (child) and *baba* (father) of his wife, rather than her *bwana* (master), the Jamaa husband shares activities and responsibilities, as well as thoughts and feelings, with his spouse. The couple make many family decisions together. Some husbands help their wives with the housework. Nor is it uncommon for a Jamaa man to plan the family budget with his wife, and even give over his entire monthly salary to her to administer. This new relationship tends to liberate the Jamaa woman in such a way that she behaves less deferentially and timidly than her traditional counterpart, speaks up more often and eloquently. She frequently makes public statements at Jamaa meetings, a form of behaviour that tribal custom would not have allowed.

Despite the apparently spectacular changes in their married lives, there is evidence that the Jamaa women continue to feel some apprehension about the depth and permanence of their husbands' conversion. For example, in one important Jamaa parish, this anxiety has been ritualized in the form of the 'one o'clock prayer'. Every afternoon at one p.m., the Jamaa women convene for an hour in the church, in order to pray together that the new ways in which their husbands now treat them will continue in the future. Invocations and testimonies are also part of this prayer meeting: 'Mama, do you want to return to the old times when your husband gave you 500 francs for flour, and when that was finished, he would give you no more, and accuse you of having spent it all for your own family?...' It is significant that there is no known group of Jamaa men who come together to pray about their wives in this way. In the Congo, as in all societies, women have a greater emotional vested interest in their marriage than men, not only because they are economically dependent on their husbands, but also because their socio-psychological definition as adults is determined to a greater extent by their marital status. The anxiety of the Jamaa women flows from this fact, and also from the high incidence of infidelity among husbands in the past. (In the latter respect, before they joined the movement, men who became Jamaa did not behave very differently from their peers in Congolese urban centres.)

The average Jamaa couple were somewhere between 30 and 45 years of age when they joined the movement, had already been married for many years, and had a typical Congolese *grande famille* of from six to ten children. Characteristically, husband and wife had lived out many turbulent times in their relationship to one another. Their entrance into the movement thus occurred in a mature period of their lives. Partly as a consequence of this, and partly because a fecund marriage is the mystical centre of the Jamaa, members tend to consider themselves superior to young, unmarried adults and to married couples who have not borne children. These attitudes also have roots in traditional Bantu culture. One of their consequences for the movement is that unmarried lay people are rarely admitted to the Jamaa.[1] In addition, teen-age boys and girls who are children

---

[1] One notable exception to this general pattern is a small quasi-religious community within the Jamaa located in Lubumbashi, and known as Emmaus House. Its members are elderly women, who are collectively referred to as 'widows'. In fact, many of these women have lost their husbands through death, but others are women whose husbands have deserted them. The Emmaus group

of the baba and mama, as well as those who are not related to them, report with some chagrin that Jamaa members regard them as 'incomplete, half-persons'. Again, this Jamaa view is wholly consistent with Bantu tradition.

Compared to Jamaa doctrine regarding relations between spouses, the movement's ideas about parent–child relations are much less developed. To give birth to children, and to become mama and baba in a spiritual and psychological, as well as biological, sense is one of the ultimate values and goals of the Jamaa. However, Jamaa beliefs encourage members not to attach more significance to children born of their flesh than to their 'spiritual children', who are the 'fruit' of a religious encounter between two persons. In Jamaa thought, all the baba and mama of the movement are also children of one another; and each member considers his (her) own spouse as the most important child.

One of the consequences of the priority assigned to the husband–wife relationship, together with this special definition of 'child', is that it contributes to the attitude of indifference and the negligence that numerous baba and mama seem to manifest towards their biological offspring. These tendencies are augmented by the amount of time and energy that a committed Jamaa couple ordinarily invest in the religious ceremonies, meetings, private and group teaching sessions, social service, and hospitable functions of the movement. They are also reinforced by the religious fatalism with which many Jamaa parents regard their children. One mama, for example, expresses this outlook: '. . . You were in the womb of your mother. Your mother was saying, "When this child leaves my womb, whether it will be a boy-child or whether it will be a girl-child is up to God. I put it [the child] in His hands. What He will do with this child, only He knows" . . .' This trusting attitude with respect to God's intentions for the child, along with the other factors mentioned, may lead a couple so totally to consecrate themselves to their Jamaa activities that to a considerable extent they disregard the psychological, intellectual, and even religious formation of their own children. This pattern is not characteristic of all Jamaa couples, as the case of baba Gaston, mama Marcelline, and their children cited in Chapter III illustrates. It is also true that the unusual understanding and harmony that Jamaa couples attain

tries to live up to the vow of poverty of religious sisterhood and its commitment to work among the most destitute and suffering people.

in their relationship have positive socio-psychological consequences for the security and identity of their children that partly offset those that ensue from their parents' preoccupation with each other and the Jamaa.

In the realm of economic and occupational activities, Jamaa men have established a reputation for steady, productive, high-quality work and for the moral commitment that underlies it. This is so strong a characteristic of the baba that even the directors of Union Minière were 'converted' to the idea that the movement was a salutary rather than a subversive development. At the outset, the management was apprehensive about the movement that had attracted a significant number of their best African workers. They thought of it as a mysterious, potentially rebellious sect, made up of 'cells' of members, who could easily infiltrate the Congolese ranks of the company. They asked for and obtained a confidential report on the nature of the movement from a Franciscan priest closely affiliated with it. Subsequently, after company officials had observed the Jamaa at first hand and, above all, noted the exemplary behaviour of their Jamaa employees, they became enthusiastic about the movement. Several directors went so far as to testify that, 'Thanks to the Jamaa, in our city [Kolwezi] we have never had any serious disturbances, disorders or conflicts.' From the point of view of Union Minière, which judges its workers according to the production standards and profit margins of a super-technological, capitalistic corporation, Jamaa men are model workers: efficient, obedient, respectful, loyal, and grateful to their employer, the Company.

Although this is not a distorted description, there is evidence to indicate that quite a few baba are more ambivalent toward Union Minière than their employers have perceived. The following incident, for instance, is revealing in this regard. In a certain parish of the Kolwezi area, a Catholic priest asked members of the local Jamaa whether they would help him distribute invitation cards from door to door. He saw this as a way of soliciting greater adult attendance at Mass and communion the first Sunday of every month. The Jamists refused to co-operate with this plan. 'Why are you using cards?' they exclaimed. 'That's what Union Minière does! Cards!' Jamaa employees do not express such sentiments, either by word or by deed, in the context of their work. But here, in a peripheral setting, they gave voice to unmistakably hostile sentiments about the degree of rationalization, bureaucratization, and control to which the Company subjected them.

As a result of the positive attitude and behaviour that Jamists exhibit on the job, their Company dossiers are excellent, their employment security high, and their chance of promotion better than that of most categories of workers. This means that the material well-being of their families is ensured. At the same time, the tendency of baba perfectly to conform to what is expected of them at work means that they are less disposed to negotiate or fight for improvements in working conditions, increases in salaries, and the like, than are some of their fellow workers.

Another aspect of Jamaa that affects baba at work is the importance that they attach to dreams and other supernatural communications. The most dramatic instance of this sort that I know is baba André's dream and its ramifications. Baba André, a member of the Jamaa, drove a 20-ton dump truck for Union Minière. His wife began to have worrying premonitory fears about his safety at work, which she shared with him in the Jamaa fashion. One night, baba André dreamt that he was inside his truck, which had become a gigantic horrible monster. The truck-monster had swallowed him up, and he no longer had any control over it. Both baba André and his wife were frightened by this dream, which he recounted to her. Subsequently, he fell ill and stayed away from work for the next few weeks. Finally, the day came when he returned to the mines and his truck. On his very first day back at work, he had an accident in his truck and was killed.

We will not attempt to make a religious interpretation of this dream and its sequels. However, the following would seem a reasonable psycho-cultural analysis. Baba André's wife intuitively sensed the increasing anxiety that her husband was experiencing behind the wheel of his truck. The beliefs and rites of the Jamaa to which they belonged reinforced their cultural predisposition to believe in the 'reality' of baba André's dream about his truck-monster; for, in the Bantu African culture, most dreams are communications carrying messages that are supposed to be deciphered and acted upon. The fact that this baba and mama were deeply identified with one another, as is common among Jamaa couples, quickened their mutual anxiety. Baba André's apprehension was not only augmented by his dream, but also by his wife's response to his account of it. Both husband and wife interpreted the dream as a bad sign. As the fatal accident that occurred dramatically indicates, this dream was a self-fulfilling prophecy, with the quality of a voodoo death. Without totally demystifying this event, it could be said that the psychological and existential disquietude to which baba André was subject played a causal role in his accidental death.

Thus far, in our discussion of the Jamaa's impact on the economic attitudes and behaviour of Jamists, we have dealt exclusively with those baba who are skilled or unskilled industrial workers. Some analogous observations on Jamaa men who are primary school teachers are in order. As indicated, such men constitute an important occupational minority in the movement, where one of their primary functions is teaching the *mafundisho*. There is thus a fit between their occupational and their religious roles. Yet, at the same time, the Jamaa makes such extraordinary demands on them that, in some cases, it saps their energy for teaching at school. For example, several *moniteurs* have been known to fall asleep at their desks, because they were exhausted from teaching *mafundisho* every evening for hours on end, and from the extensive travelling back and forth that this entailed. Another *moniteur*, who originally taught the seventh grade, at his own request was granted permission to teach the fourth grade instead. He wished to be more free to devote himself to Jamaa instruction. A certain amount of other-worldly motivation entered into his decision, both in his disengagement from getting on in his professional world, and in his imperviousness to traditional sensitivity about rank and the humiliation of demotion.

More generally, Jamaa attitudes toward material possessions and rewards are complex. Jamaa families are notable for the care with which they furnish and maintain their homes, however modest their habitations may be. With the exception of a small number of zealously fatalistic and ascetic Jamists, they respond with approval when their children do well at school, foreseeing the wider opportunities that 'the diploma' will bring. Yet, the encounter and union that the movement effects and the qualitative changes that they bring to pass in their social and spiritual lives are supremely important to the baba and mama. And they do not expect, or necessarily desire, that the religious progress they have made will result in material progress for themselves and their families. In a society in which gift-exchange still figures prominently, the most fervent members of the movement are conspicuous for the large sums of money they freely, but unflamboyantly, spend on various Jamaa activities, especially travel, hospitality, and contributions to *rites de passage* for such events as births, marriages, and deaths. Jamaa attitudes towards the polity range from indifference to hostility. In part this is a consequence of the strong emphasis that the movement places on universalism and egalitarianism. One mama eloquently expressed how these aspects of the Jamaa 'have changed our life':

Whether it is a Lunda, a Kasai, a Tshokwe who falls ill, we go to him to help him. In the past, each one lived for himself, kept to himself. Now, there are no longer *kabila* [tribes] in the Jamaa; there are no longer Whites and Blacks. We are all one, since God is our Father.

For many Jamists, politics are the antithesis of this outlook. As they see it, politics are invidious and divisive, and they destroy. There is a streak of other-worldliness in this attitude that antedates the events connected with the Congo's Independence and the Katanga secession. However, the turmoil, violence, and loss of life that accompanied these political happenings reinforced the conviction of many Jamaa members that politics are 'the devil's work'. In all these respects, Jamaa attitudes and behaviour concerning the polity contrast sharply with those of non-Jamaa Congolese citizens. Tribal and ethnic identifications still predominate in the Congo, and, especially among men residing in towns and cities, political careers are coveted because of the power, prestige, and wealth that accompany them.

Incidents in local parish life are sometimes indicative of the Jamists' anti-political sentiments. For example, in the summer of 1969, one of the bishops of South Katanga directed his parishes to establish local councils composed of lay men and women, representative of the various groups within the Catholic community. This was inspired by the recommendations of Vatican Council II that encouraged greater participation of the laity in decision-making processes of the Church. To his surprise, when Father Damien, a parish priest, asked members of his congregation to draw up a slate of candidates for election to the local council, he met with resistance from Jamists. 'Elections!' they exclaimed. 'That is politics! That comes from the devil!' Father Damien persisted and suggested that after a particular Sunday Mass each person write on a sheet of paper the names of five men and five women who he thought were 'good Christians', with 'mature judgement', and 'the interest of the parish at heart'. These nominations were supposed to be deposited anonymously in a bag, set aside for that purpose. Once again, the Jamists refused. Their influence in the parish was so great that the only 'democratic' way the pastor could think of for setting up the council was to invite six Congolese religious Sisters in the parish to select the ten members required. Although he explicitly instructed the Sisters to be non-partisan in their choice, the outcome of their selection was that the whole council was composed of Jamaa baba and mama. When Father Damien protested, the sisters replied, 'Yes, we know. But there are no other good Christians in the parish!' Thus, paradoxically, the conspicuous Christian zeal and commitment of these Jamists was responsible for the fact that they were elected to the very political religious offices to which they objected, by a process that was designed to simulate the one they had blocked.

On the whole, in the broader political arena, Jamists do not take an actively obstructionistic stand. Instead, they perform their civic duties of voting in city, provincial, and national elections in a passively acquiescent way. They do not get passionately involved in the ebb and flow of party politics, and they are not interested in running for any office.

One of the distinctive characteristics of the present-day Congolese population is the fervour of its belief in the importance and value of education. This conviction is so strong that families are willing to make heavy sacrifices in order to provide schooling for their children. And the young people themselves travel further and further away from the village in search of ways to advance their education from primary to secondary to university levels.

The attitude of the Jamaa as a whole towards the meaning and worth of education sharply contrasts with this development. To begin with, in his teachings Tempels minimized and even disparaged the significance of schooling and intellectualization for the attainment of the spiritual goals of the Jamaa. He often asserted that an 'apprenticeship through books' or 'searching in books' constituted a 'barrier' to the kind of deep religious understanding and life that the movement represented. In part his point of view arose from his personal and Franciscan tendency to assign a higher value to the non-rational and mystic than to 'cognitive rationality',[1] and to regard these orientations as antipathetic. In this respect, he is both anti-intellectual and fundamentalistic. Tempels's outlook was also related to his at once realistic and romantic appreciation of Bantu oral tradition and what he considered to be its inherent wisdom, humanity, and religiosity. In addition, Tempels was reacting against what he thought were the detrimental effects of the Mission-dominated educational system that the Belgian colonial regime imposed on young Congolese. As he saw it, teaching Congolese 'to read and write, to count and to add and subtract', to speak and to read what he disdainfully called 'ki-français', 'uprooted them from their ancestral tradition', 'ulcerated [their] basic vital wisdom', and turned many of them into an 'imitation-White'.[2] Finally, Tempels's depreciation of formal schooling and book-derived learning was associated with his notion, itself derived from Primitive Christianity, that the highest form of spirituality consisted of being so free from all worldly trappings that, in effect, one was a newborn child. Tempels inclined to the belief that uncontaminated Bantu culture brought one closer to this religious state than the form of modern Western civilization imposed on the Congo.

As already indicated, many of the Jamaa baba and mama are middle-aged couples who have had a minimum of formal education. Partly for this reason they have responded favourably to Tempels's repudiation of schools and books, but other less obvious factors have also contributed to this reaction. The baba and mama have experienced an enhancement of their sense of self-worth, thanks to the high value attached by Tempels and the movement to the oral tradition of Bantu culture and to spirituality that is dissociated from academic learning. Thus, in a society that is granting higher status and better occupational opportunities to persons with an advanced education, Jamaa couples have found what amounts to a socio-psychological island where they are eligible to be esteemed on the basis of other than school-produced qualities.

This is not to say that Jamists are so other-worldly or indignant as to reject totally the values of education. Their attitudes towards

[1] To my knowledge, the two first publications in which Talcott Parsons conceptualized this value-orientation are: T. Parsons, 'On the Concept of Value-commitments', *Sociological Inquiry*, 38, no. 2 (Spring 1968), 135–60; T. Parsons and Gerald M. Platt, 'Some Considerations on the American Academic Profession', *Minerva*, VI, no. 4 (Summer 1968), 497–523.
[2] Tempels, *La Philosophie bantoue*, pp. 19–21.

education are more complex. For example, as we have seen, *moniteurs* (primary school teachers) are important in the movement because they have special training for the *mafundisho*. In addition, couples like baba Gaston and mama Marcelline support and encourage their children in their schooling and homework. It is interesting that, in the case of this couple, their attitude toward the education of their children is largely the result of the influence of two Belgian Jamaa members: a Benedictine priest, who comes from an academic professional family background, and a young lay woman, eager to complete her own college education, who is a leader in a Catholic social action movement. Both the priest and the young woman were initiated into the Jamaa by baba Gaston and mama Marcelline and thus are their spiritual children.

Such couples as this one notwithstanding, it seems fair to say that the majority of Jamaa members are relatively unconcerned about their own education and that of their children.

Finally, we turn to the religious impact of the Jamaa on the personality and cosmic view of its members. The movement enhances the affectivity and expressiveness of its members in various significant ways. Baba and mama discover new dimensions of communication and communion in their marriage, and also new sources of satisfaction. Jamaa women emerge from the traditionally retiring, silent, and submissive role played by African women, especially in public contexts. They participate in the lessons, discussions, and other activities of the movement in a dynamic and creative way. Both the baba and the mama have brought new religious forms into being. Along with the Jamaa priests, they have invented a special vocabulary, and they have composed prayers, religious songs, and *mafundisho*. All members of the Jamaa, Congolese and European, lay and religious, report that the emotional and spiritual quality of their prayer life and meditation has been profoundly enriched and illumined by the Jamaa.[1] As an example, we may quote a baba's description of these qualitative changes in his relationship to God that the Jamaa has produced. In his experience the movement changed the face of God for him from White to Black, and turned Him from an object of a rote lesson to a live presence.

[1] See for example the letter from Father Frans to Father Jerome (23 Nov. 1961) quoted above, p. 64.

In the past, they taught us religion the same way that we learned French or algebra. But now, in the Jamaa God has become alive . . . God is no longer a God of foreigners, of Whites. The baba and mama feel themselves to be 'of God', on an equal basis with the foreigners, the Whites.[1]

In certain regards, the Jamaa seems to have a psycho-therapeutic effect on its members. The intimate and spontaneous discussions in which they are continually involved are cathartic. These group sessions provide them with a legitimate and non-threatening opportunity to express a wide range of deep feelings: anxiety, uncertainty, guilt, as well as love, gratification, happiness, and serenity. This aspect of Jamaa interaction does not consist of a simple discharge of strong feeling. Nor is it an agitated or frenzied experience. What is involved is a mutually trusting and peaceful exchange in the inner recesses of a spiritual family of even the most disturbing sentiments. Baba, mama, and priests respond enthusiastically and offer their moral support to those who need it, so that various difficulties and problems are resolved through a group process. In structure, content, and spirit, these facets of relations between Jamaa members are an extension of the relations that exist between Jamaa spouses.

One of the most eloquent testimonies to the liberating and supportive effect that the movement has on its members is to be found in the statements that Jamaa priests make about the changes it has wrought in them. They affirm that the movement has helped them to achieve more fully the ideal relationship which they feel that as missionaries they ought to have with the people whom they came to serve. Through the Jamaa, they declare, most of the misunderstanding, tension, alienation, and frustration that they formerly experienced in their encounters with Congolese has been dispelled. In short, their involvement in the movement seems to have provided them with a means of resolving one of the primary sources of strain to which they are subject in their role as missionary priests.

What is perhaps most impressive is the degree to which the Jamaa appears to have transformed the world-view of its Congolese members. The traditional Congolese thought and belief system is a deterministic one. Most of the events that befall man are considered to be either felicitous or adverse. Most experiences are regarded as either positive or negative. The concept of chance and the aleatory happening does not exist in this cognitive system. The principal causes of untoward occurrences are believed to be evil

[1] Personal interview with baba Daniel, 23 Feb. 1961.

thoughts, feelings, and motives of significant other persons. These have the capacity to harm, because they can mobilize the power of the spirits which exist in the spheres of the universe that lie between the Supreme Being, the ancestors, and Man. Thus, through the media of witchcraft, i.e. unconsciously motivated psychic acts, and sorcery, consciously motivated ones, harm and misfortune are always a threatening potentiality. Partly as a consequence of this set of conceptions and beliefs, the traditional Congolese world-view is 'pervasively apprehensive, anxious, suspicious, distrustful and vigilant. Brooding anger, envy and jealousy of the heart [that are believed to] harm and destroy . . . are [felt to be] incipient everywhere and in everyone: in the stranger, in one's self, and most especially in those with whom one has the closest relationship. And so one must constantly be on guard.'[1] John V. Taylor has called this Bantu 'vision' a 'primal world-view', poetically expressing it in the following way:

This is the ultimate horror and darkness of the primal world-view, that beneath the smiling face may lurk the hating heart. The traditional African community, for all its solidarity and the truth of its vision of Man, is corrupted by a twofold mistrust—mistrust of the stranger because he is outside the kinship bond and mistrust of the unknown witch because he is outside humanity.[2]

To a remarkable extent, the Jamaa has succeeded in dislodging this basic fear-ridden attitude from the minds and psyches of its members, replacing it with a sense of trust, protection, forgiveness, and love. In my informed opinion, in this respect the Jamaa has surpassed most (Protestant as well as Catholic) Church efforts to 'convert' Congolese to Christianity and specifically to its message of Love.

The belief in and use of magic by Congolese are integrally related to their traditional view. In the Jamaa, as indicated earlier, all forms of magic and fetishism are officially proscribed. All observers agree that Jamists resort to magic less often than most Congolese of similar background. At the same time, it is true that this dimension of Bantu culture is so tenacious that it has by no means been eradicated from the attitudes and behaviour patterns of Jamaa members. In Chapter IV, we have analysed some Katete beliefs and practices,

[1] Renée C. Fox, 'The Intelligence behind the Mask', unpublished paper, 1968, p. 66.
[2] John V. Taylor, *The Primal Vision* (London: S.C.M. Press, 1965), p. 192.

and saw to what extent they originate in the traditional magico-religious system. What is even more generalized in the Jamaa is the persistence of a belief in the danger of the life-force being diminished and in the cult of the dead, and a cleaving to the ritualistic practices that petition and appease the shades of the ancestors. In a moment of sharp insight into these aspects of the baba and mama's 'mentality', one Jamaa priest had this to say:

I have arrived at the conviction that it is impossible to talk witchcraft out of the heads of our people, not even the people of the Jamaa. What can be done, however, is to give them an idea about death of which Christ says, 'I will come as a thief in the night', an idea about the care God has for us, 'All the hairs of your head are counted'. But saying that there is no *buloji* [witchcraft], there one ruptures contact with the people. What you can explain is that the real *muloji* is the one who breaks up the unity between the people, who extinguishes love, who can kill both the body and the soul.[1]

The sense of relative liberation and security that the Jamaa confers on its members, who also feel themselves to have attained a profound understanding of encounter, union, and love produces yet another set of religious attitudes among the baba and mama. These have been referred to as 'Super-Jamaa' attitudes by some observers. Some Jamists develop an in-group conception that leads them to make invidious distinctions between their spiritual family and all those who do not belong to it. To a degree, this makes certain baba and mama more intolerant and less receptive towards non-Catholics than they otherwise might be; they have a tendency to regard such persons as 'those with pagan practices'. However, the super-Jamaa orientation is even more conducive to baba and mama feeling religiously superior to Catholics who do not belong to their movement. 'In their eyes, we are no longer Christians,' exclaim indignant Catholics who are not Jamists. Some individuals and groups in the Jamaa are indeed convinced that through their participation in the movement they have achieved such a state of purity and clairvoyance that they are no longer capable of sin or in need of sacramental confession.

The super-Jamaa attitude is a complex phenomenon. It reflects the traditional African sense of hierarchy, status, and prestige. It runs counter to the Christian concept of spiritual brotherhood and equality that, in principle, Jamists are supposed to have realized

[1] Letter from Father Frans to Father Jerome, 6 Mar. 1962.

more fully than the 'ordinary' Congolese Christian. But, at the same time, it represents an evolution away from certain black magical notions. For, in traditional Congolese society, striving to surpass others, or even enjoying less adversity and more good fortune than others is considered dangerous. It invites the envy and jealousy of others, feelings that call forth sorcery and witchcraft. Apparently, zealous super-Jamists who see themselves as having spiritually outdistanced those whom they consider 'less Christian and less Catholic' are not afraid of incurring supernatural penalties for this state.

No simple general statement can be made about the impact of the Jamaa on its members' role-set. The balance of changes that the Jamaa effects in its adherents' attitudes, values, and behaviour in the realms of kinship, religion, and magic might be characterized as a shift from tradition to modernity. Yet, in the economic, political, and educational spheres, Jamists are more traditional than other Congolese and less inclined to commit themselves to ideas and forms of action necessary to the development and modernization of the larger society. From an evolutionary point of view, then, the Jamaa is a mixture of 'progressive' and 'regressive' elements. However, if we were to venture an over-all evaluation of the Jamaa's influence on its members, we would characterize it as fundamentally modernizing, on the grounds of the transformations it has effected in two of the primary constitutive elements of primitive and archaic societies: extended kinship and a non-transcendental, magic- and myth-oriented religion.

CHAPTER VII

The Subculture of the Kolwezi Jamaa Clergy

THE impact of charismatic leaders on religious movements is usually accounted for in terms of vague but powerfully compelling 'gifts of grace' that they exhibit. These special qualities, if they are described at all, are generally depicted as highly individual, even unique, personal attributes. More often than not it is implied that such a leader's characteristics are both transcultural and transcendental. In my opinion, this view of the charismatic leader is too ahistorical and asociological. It fails to explain why the 'gifts' of the leader were 'recognized' by those who followed him (her), why the followers were drawn to his (her) person as well as to his (her) message, and why such a leader comes symbolically to represent larger social and cultural processes.

In the case of the Jamaa, the characteristics of Placied Tempels, its charismatic prophet-founder, and his priestly 'lieutenants' cannot be adequately depicted, or their influence fully evaluated without reference both to the social and cultural background they share and to the particular subculture that emerged from their interrelationships. The salient traits that they have in common and with which they infused the Jamaa movement have deep roots in Limburger-Flemish Franciscan culture. As already suggested, some of these traits coincided with attributes of Bantu-African culture; others converged with them. From this point of view, the Jamaa is an emergent product of the blending of two distinctive but not totally dissimilar sets of cultural features.

There are several ways in which those qualities we shall identify as Limburger-Flemish-Franciscan are expressed in the diverse personalities of the priest-leaders of the Jamaa and in the various roles they play in the movement. Through a series of interconnected sociological portraits of these men I will describe how these attributes are woven into their role relations, and suggest how they affected the orientation and atmosphere of the Jamaa.[1]

[1] In order to develop the ideal-typical portraits of the Kolwezi Jamaa priests that I present in this chapter, I have described them and their community as they

In appearance—a self-presentation that he carefully cultivates—
Placied Tempels[1] is the dramatic personification of the old-time
missionary, the Old Testament prophet, and the traditional sorcerer.
His stocky build resembles that of a peasant. But his majestic head,
his hypnotic eyes, his long, flowing white beard, his rich, resonant
voice, and his graceful, evocative gestures are those of a religiously
magnetic leader. He does not have the joyous, frolicsome qualities
of his Order's founder, St. Francis, or his sweet-tempered religious
humility; for all its originality, Placied's spiritual style was more
calculated, more authoritarian, less ingenuous, and more subject
to the streaks of melancholy, suspicion, touchiness, and rage that
characterize many Flemish people. Yet, like St. Francis, he is a
mystic and a man of unusual artistic sensibility, who finds consolation and communion in retreats into nature. His aestheticism has
many facets. In the small group of Jamaa priests most closely
associated with him, Placied has a legendary reputation for gourmet
cooking. He is also known as a connoisseur of music, especially
famous for the valued collection of African songs that he has recorded.
True to his Flemish artistic heritage he finds pleasure in painting.
He played a major role in designing his parish church in Musonoi
and its interior. He gardens with contemplative artistry. He hunts
and fishes with stylized passion. Through these activities he ritually
expresses reverent, harmonious, predatory, and violent aspects of
his relationship to nature, living creatures other than man, and death.
Placied is also a master of epistolary art. He dispatches a constant
flow of long, detailed, highly affective letters, in exquisite penmanship.
Through them he spins a web of words, feelings, images and argu-
ments that bind his followers to his person and message. Letters of
this genre—introspective, emotional, full of word-pictures, emitting
a stirring atmosphere of sensual mysticism—are also continually
written by Placied's Jamaa priests, to each other, as well as to him.
This important mode of communication within the group of charismatic leaders is strongly marked by characteristics of Franciscan
spirituality and life style and by Flemish expressionism.

were up to the late 1960s. In Chapter VIII mention will be made of what has
happened to each of these men since that time.

[1] Although all the persons presented in this chapter are Catholic priests, I
will not refer to them as 'Father'. I have made this decision, not only to avoid the
stylistic awkwardness and sanctimoniousness of constantly citing their clerical
title, but also because in their Jamaa subculture they address each other by their
'religious' name, that is, the first name they assumed on entering religious life.

To some degree, Placied's status as prophet-leader, with all that this involves, creates a certain respectful distance between him and his priestly 'lieutenants'. By and large, however, his relations with them are typical of the intense, intimate style of interaction that characterizes the Flemish-Franciscan subculture in Katanga. In face-to-face encounters as in their correspondence, these men confide to each other their strongest, most private sentiments. Feelings of happiness, pleasure, affection, love, inspiration, refreshment, hopefulness, anxiety, fatigue, discouragement, depression, guilt, despair are so copiously and vividly described to one another that they become a collective experience. The tradition of the Franciscan confessional has left a significant imprint on these exchanges. It is not so much a *mea culpa* attitude that prevails; rather, the ethos is one in which personal and spiritual brotherhood are defined as synonymous with the willingness and ability to reach deep enough into one's life history and unconscious to share the most painful of guilty secrets.[1]

This is not to say that Placied's relationship to the Jamaa priests is saintly and free of tension. On the contrary, he is critical of each one of his colleagues, recurrently expressing disapproval, disappointment, and even disdain for the aspects of their character or activities that he finds objectionable. In his view, Erik, for example, is often too entrepreneurial, Jerome is too much the arrogant and self-proclaiming expert on Luba culture, Bonaventure is too bookishly impressed with formal theology, and Frans too moody and choleric. Placied has elicited almost as much hurt and anger in his group, as devotion and veneration. And despite his insistence on spiritual humility and equality, he has not discouraged his colleagues from viewing him as the singularly gifted, inspired, and mystically endowed leader that he considers himself to be. In this respect, he shows no signs of spiritual self-doubt, and might even be said to exhibit the authoritarian certainty of a prophet who is unwaveringly sure of the religious message he conveys and personifies. In fact, there is a latent grandiosity in the logic of Placied's teachings. Most significant in this regard is the parallel repeatedly drawn between his own encounter with Sister X and the one between Christ and Mary. Unstated but implicit in this comparison is the notion that Placied

[1] This aspect of the Franciscan subculture is a part of the Encounter and Union dimension of the Jamaa. It is difficult to ascertain whether the Franciscans were more influenced by Bantu culture in this regard, or vice versa.

is 'another Christ' in a less exclusively sacramental and symbolic, but more total and literal sense than Catholic theology would hold. It is as if he felt himself to be closer to Christ in person as well as in prayer than the ordinary priest. In a similar way he identifies Sister X with the Virgin Mary.

As noted earlier, although Placied's emphasis on the relationship between Christ and Mary and his own encounter with Sister X go deep into his personality, they are not unique to him. They are a part of the Franciscan-Flemish-Katangese milieu out of which he catalysed the Jamaa. We have already analysed the symbolism of the Virgin in Flanders, and stressed the at once everyday and mystical nature of the sensuality permeating Flemish religious tradition. Placied's view of Mary and her counterpart Sister X is compatible with this tradition. In addition, not only Placied but also his priestly colleagues of Kolwezi have always attached great importance to the meeting of 'feminine' and 'masculine' qualities in religious life. Their conception of God is not of the hyper-virile or of the macho type. In their view, the spiritual qualities of a Flemish Madonna comple-ment those of Christ and blend with them. Thus, they regard love, sensitivity, compassion, tenderness, and the like as attributes heightened in Christ, partly by virtue of His relationship to the Virgin Mary. Even before the Jamaa was born, it would seem, Placied and his colleagues shared the conviction that, in priestly as well as in lay life, the most creative form of spirituality entails deep collabora-tion between men and women. Without fundamentally questioning or altering their vow of celibacy, individually and collectively, these priests have always worked closely with lay religious women[1] and religious Sisters. In addition, several of them affirm that, from the very first, an important aspect of their religious vocation has centred on their association with women, both in the capacity of colleagues and in that of counsellors. Although Placied's encounter with Sister X is perhaps unique in its intensity and its symbolic importance, he is not the only Jamaa priest who has experienced this kind of significant meeting with a woman. At least five other priests have had comparable relationships with women which they have shared with all the Franciscans involved in the Jamaa movement. This process of sharing entails both communal acceptance of the person

[1] The Institute of lay religious women with whom these Jamaa priests have collaborated most significantly is called the Auxiliaires Féminines Internationales (A.F.I.).

who has become a significant other to one of its members, and collective participation in their relationship. The shared encounter is generally not overtly sexual in nature, and the Franciscan–Jamaa participation does not take the form of a gossiping male peer group that derives vicarious or voyeuristic sexual pleasure from the 'exploits' of its members. Rather, the priest–woman relationship tends to be spiritualized; the community regards the woman as a kind of relative, linked to them through the bonds of semi-religious kinship; and spoken and written communications about her are usually phrased in either familial or mystical terms.

Not all the Jamaa priests are equally close to the various spiritual couples. The general pattern is for a particular priest to act as special confidant, sponsor, and protector of the couple in a role that carries both pastoral and familial connotations. He also acts in the capacity of a gatekeeper with the prerogative to admit or exclude others from privileged knowledge of the couple's relationship. In a subculture as verbally and affectively communicative as that of the Jamaa priests, it is significant that these structural aspects of the alliances and the understandings that accompany them are largely unstated and latent in nature. None the less, a diffusely erotic ambience surrounds these relationships. Not only do they partake of what we have called the sensual mysticism of Flanders, they are also quickened by the sublimation of potentially sexual elements in these meetings in depth between men and women, and by their 'guilty secret' nature when seen in the perspective of the traditional orthodox church view of such encounters.

Father Frans, who, for a long time, was considered the most likely charismatic successor to Placied, is a tall, gaunt, almost emaciated man in his late fifties. He is clean-shaven, with thinning, greying, straight dark hair and startlingly blue eyes framed by round, steel-rimmed spectacles. He moves with a spare kind of grace; yet there is something spastic in his quick nervousness, and in various of the expressions that flit across his lean, pale face. Under inner stress, his normally deep, resonant voice takes on a breathless, whispered quality.

Frans is one of the most intelligent, ascetic, and mystical of the Jamaa priests. During the key years of his involvement in the Jamaa (the 1960s) he lived in a simple, shabby but clean and orderly house in the midst of the Union Minière camp (Musonoi), where he was the chief Catholic parish priest. The house was sparsely furnished, but the shelves in the living-room were filled with well-thumbed books on education, spirituality, asceticism, and moral philosophy. On one wall of this room hung a huge, arresting, framed portrait-photograph of Placied, dominated by his leonine head, piercingly prophetic eyes, and flowing white beard. Frans's house was also a repository of Jamaa documents: *mafundisho*, prayers, dreams, and life histories. They were recounted to him by baba and mama, and Frans has recorded and translated many of them. With their knowledge and consent, he has shared these messages with a number of persons who have come to him seeking an understanding of the Jamaa.[1]

Frans's attitude towards the communications he has received and transmitted is more that of an awed, tremulous mystic, at once inspired and troubled by the essence of the Jamaa, than that of an intrigued social scientist, enthusiastically recording his field notes. In a way, he is as much the scribe and evangelist of the Jamaa movement as Tempels himself. Yet, at the same time, he has a fine appreciation of the role that trained anthropologists or sociologists, or talented literary artists like Father Jerome, might play in explaining and evoking the Jamaa. On certain occasions, Frans's talents as a raconteur find expression in stories and anecdotes about the religious insights and experiences of baba and mama. These tales are delivered in an atmosphere of spirituality, mystery, 'Angst', and shy, but robust conviviality, that is not only characteristic of Frans's personality, but also of the Flemish cultural tradition from which he comes.

There is one story from his earlier life that Frans has shared only with those in the Jamaa subculture to whom he feels the closest. It turns on a painful event in his personal life that led to the role he played in helping to create the Jamaa and to his eventual initiation into it. Frans recounted this story to me at the beginning of my first visit to South Katanga to study the Jamaa. Accompanied by Erik, he made an early evening visit to me in my room at the Union Minière Guest House. With the implicit agreement of Frans, Erik also invited Renée Fox (who was at this time scientific adviser to the Centre de Recherches Sociologiques) to be present on this occasion. The fact that she was welcomed by Frans and Erik was very much in keeping with certain premisses and shared intuitions of their subculture. They felt her to be a trustworthy, understanding, and exceptional

[1] I was one of the beneficiaries of Frans's generosity in this respect.

person; a woman who possessed spiritual as well as intellectual gifts; and a Jewess, who was more closely related to Myriam, in both a kinship and mystical sense than they themselves. For these reasons, among others, she was granted more intimate access to their inner world than the priest-colleague from the Centre who made the journey to South Katanga with us. For, although Belgian, Catholic, and a clergyman like themselves, Father Jacques's aristocratic, orthodox and martial kind of piety did not fit the Jamaa priests' subculture. And so, Frans and Erik deliberately arranged their visit with Renée Fox and myself at a time when they knew Jacques would be absent.

The ambience of this visit was extraordinary. Frans, Erik, Renée, and I sat in a dimly lit, shadow-filled room. The curtains were drawn against the evening. In a quavering voice, pitched hardly above a whisper, Frans told his story about a long-ago encounter with a spiritually significant woman. His emotion-laden account re-created for us the fulfilment and religious growth that he and 'the other' had experienced through these meetings, and also their mutual suffering. Somehow, the images and affect evoked by the story made us feel part of a much larger mystery, and also 'one' with each other, in what we later came to realize was the Jamaa way. I had the sense that Renée and I were not only being admitted to an unusually close relationship with Frans, but that we were passing through a rite that inducted us into the Jamaa universe to which he and Erik belonged. Renée had the same experience and understanding of it. From that evening on, we were both given complete entry to the mystic community of the Jamaa priest-leaders.

Frans's capacity for intense feeling is almost convulsive. Periodically, his lean body and sensitive psyche are racked by waves of despair, compassion, remorse, or guilt, and by searing, white-hot bursts of rage. No one has suffered more acutely and visibly than he from the discovery of errors and deviations in the Jamaa, or from the abortive attempts to rectify them. He has been lacerated by his uncontingent loving union with all the baba and mama, on the one hand, and his profound religious distress over their involvement in Jamaa aberrations, on the other. More than once Frans has been brought to the brink of exhausted collapse by his feelings of desolation and responsibility in the face of these developments.

Yet, for all his vulnerable sensitivity, or, perhaps, partly because of it, Frans is an important emotional mainstay for another Jamaa priest, Father Jerome, who is even more touchy and moody than he is. This aspect of their relationship is recurrently expressed in their copious correspondence during the 1960s, when Frans was in Kolwezi and Jerome (except for brief sojourns in Kinshasa and South Katanga) in Belgium. In these letters, Frans shared with Jerome the innermost aspects of his step-by-step initiation into the Jamaa, his joys and discoveries in the movement, and his first apprehensions about its deviations. But he devoted quite as much space and emotion to acclamations of Jerome's social scientific and literary 'genius', and to praises of his writings on Luba culture as well as of the latest novel that Jerome had written. Frans also praised Jerome for his religious sensibilities, and for the brotherhood with which he graced and bolstered Frans's life. And on the many occasions when Jerome expressed fatigue, ennui, or melancholy, Frans offered him thoughtful advise about the rest and recreation that he should take.

Jerome is the anthropologist, novelist, and official genius of the Jamaa priest-leaders. They have a cultic appreciation of his insight into the most profound and recondite aspects of Luba culture, his talent for making it felt through the haunting quality of his writing, and for the skill and courage with which he looks into and communicates himself through his novels.[1] In their view, these abilities, along with his distinctive emotional qualities, are signs of Jerome's extraordinary giftedness.

Jerome is a small man, with straight, thinning black hair, probing black-brown eyes that peer out from behind horn-rimmed glasses, and a swarthy complexion. There is something unaccountably sombre about his ill-pressed, dusty black or charcoal-grey suits, whether dressed in priest's garb or lay clothing. One has the visual impression that Jerome moves in a shadow-coloured world. His is a melancholy, artistic intelligence: genuinely gloomy, but at the same time self-dramatizing; intensely serious, but not totally without elements of spoof. Jerome's temperament is as cherished, and as much a centre of interested concern to Jamaa priests, as are his anthropological and literary writings. His capacity and romantic penchant for dejection, foreboding, suspiciousness, the mysterious and the tragic,

---

[1] Despite Jerome's willingness and, beyond that, his need to share his deepest feelings with his colleagues, and to express them more publicly in his literary works, it is significant that he publishes his novels under a pseudonym. The same is not true of his anthropological publications.

arouse self-recognition, as well as sympathy from fellow Jamaa-priests. His affectivity is not only a theatrical expression of some of their own common, emotional tendencies, but also of characteristic traits in Flemish literature and graphic art. There is also wanderlust in Jerome: the kind of restiveness with the current landscape and the projection of one's yearnings upon it that inspired Breughel to paint mountains on to the flat Belgian countryside. Sensuous elements are persistent in Jerome's works and his person. The mysteries of the dream and reality, birth and death, preoccupy him. And he is prone to the kind of 'Flemish laughter that rings with the gnashing of teeth'.[1]

Jerome's relationship with Frans is his closest bond in the Jamaa priests' circle. He is also strongly linked to Erik, in overlapping though not identical ways. On Jerome's periodic visits to Kolwezi, Erik has been his convivial, generous host, and the person who has most faithfully and empathically listened to his outpourings. Night after night, until two or three in the morning, Jerome and Erik would sit in the living-room of Erik's house and drink a few glasses of whisky together, while Jerome delivered a brilliant monologue about the novel on which he was working; Bantu and Luba culture; English and French schools of anthropology; existential philosophy; his disappointment over the fact that he never had the opportunity to become a professional philosopher; the difficulties of combining priestly, academic, and artistic careers, such as his own; the failure of elders in his Order sufficiently to recognize and esteem his status and accomplishments as social scientist, professor, and novelist; the dangers of psycho-analytic psychiatry, in general, and, in particular, the way that Erik used its insights and techniques in his pastoral work. (It is ironic that Jerome should have discussed this last topic so indignantly with Erik, when all the while he was benefiting from Erik's trained ability to listen and understand.)

Jerome's attitude towards Bonaventure is affectionately patroniz-ing. He views Bonaventure's attempts to theologize on subjects as important to the Jamaa as love, union, and celibacy with the kind of reservations that would ordinarily elicit scorn from him. Instead, he is indulgent with Bonaventure, treating him as an ageing companion (who has never been what Jerome would define as a real intellectual) with whom one should not be unduly critical or combative.

[1] George Hauger, Introduction to *Michel de Ghelderode: 7 Plays*, vol. 2 (New York: Hill and Wang, 1964), p. xi.

Jerome's relationship to Tempels is especially complex and ambivalent. It has also become almost legendary. Jamaa priests often allude to the dramatic falling-out that took place between Jerome and Tempels and have also embroidered a number of tales around this event. For a few years during the earliest phase of Jerome's missionary career he was assigned to an inland parish in a Luba area of North Katanga. There he lived and worked closely with Tempels who was a fellow priest at the mission post. The two men had much in common above and beyond their Franciscanism, mutual work-commitment, and similar social backgrounds. Both were highly intense personalities, as emotional and theatrical as they were intellectual. They shared an at once mystical, artistic, and perverse tendency to disparage all that was 'merely intellectual'. Both were passionately interested and involved in Luba culture. Tempels, the elder of the two, had a headstart over Jerome in this regard, for he had spent many more years among the Luba than Jerome, and had learned both from and about them in the way that he has described in *Bantu Philosophy*. But, because Jerome brought to the situation his anthropological training, his gift for metaphysics, and his novelist's ear and eye, he, too, achieved remarkable knowledge and understanding of the Luba world. Whatever the exact details of the famed confrontation that eventually took place between Tempels and Jerome, we know that it turned on their disagreement over which was the more correct and insightful interpretation of certain aspects of Luba culture, Tempels's or Jerome's. Some degree of unacknowledged rivalry entered into this disagreement, along with the almost inevitable clash of personalities between two men of such intricate and gigantic temperament who worked together this closely. To this day, although Tempels and Jerome have long been reconciled, and their relationship has positive importance for each of them, neither has forgotten the psychic wounds that he feels the other inflicted on him.

In appearance, Bonaventure, the theologian of the Jamaa priest group, reminds one of an old-fashioned school teacher. He is a clean-cut man of medium build, with well-barbered and neatly combed greying hair, steel-rimmed spectacles, and a shyly intelligent manner. Despite his reticence and prime appearance, Bonaventure is also emotional and sentimental.

A classical Franciscan intellectual, Bonaventure has a lifelong interest in the theology of love. He has a fine theological library, and keeps up to date in the field. Although he himself is religiously as well as politically more conservative than fellow Jamaa priests like Tempels, Frans, and Erik, his informed, scholarly searching into the mysteries of love has led him to raise difficult questions about such central issues as the absolute meaning of priestly celibacy.

Bonaventure is an experienced and devoted urban parish priest. His pastoral work has centred on the Union Minière camp where he has been stationed for a good part of his missionary life. There, in a gently authoritarian style—an uneasy mix between his loving intelligence and colonial attitude—he prevails over his parishioners.

Because of his political conservatism and his nervous sensitivity, Bonaventure responded with greater apprehension than other Jamaa priests to the turbulent years in the Congo, just before and after Independence. He alone voiced his concern about the alleged Communism of Patrice Lumumba, for example, and the perilous implications that his take-over of Katanga might have for the country. He was the only Jamaa priest who had the frightening experience of being roughed up by a band of Congolese youths during this period. The incident proved to be far more traumatic to him psychologically than physically, so much so that he spent a full year in Belgium recovering from it. During this time, he read avidly, mainly in theology, spending day after day in the Louvain University library. When the year was over, without rancour or undue anxiety, he gladly returned to the Congo to take up his usual work.

In the eyes of all Jamaa priests, with the possible exception of Tempels and Jerome, Bonaventure's theological knowledge and insight are highly respected. As we have indicated, Jerome is indulgent, but essentially patronizing about Bonaventure's theological pursuits; and Tempels expresses disdain for spiritual understanding that comes primarily from book learning rather than from deep personal experience. Largely because of Bonaventure's selfless response, and despite Tempels's and Jerome's hauteur in this respect, a warm relationship exists among the three men. But the colleage to whom Bonaventure feels closest is Erik. Deeply involved in the white community of Union Minière, Erik threads his way through it without condescension or contempt. He is a man of books, as well as of action, focusing his studies on psychological aspects of some of the theological questions that most engage Bonaventure. He is a skilled and empathic mediator. And he moves with ease in the most mystical milieux of the Jamaa, on the one hand, and the highest managerial settings of Union Minière, on the other. All these qualities draw Bonaventure to him.

At one and the same time, Erik is the psychologist, the entrepreneur, the emissary, and the ecumenicist of the Jamaa priest group. With his deeply tanned and ruggedly handsome face, his thick head of dark hair, his sonorous baritone voice, and his unaffectedly theatrical gift as raconteur, Erik could be type-cast as a cultivated and daring missionary-hero. Although he is neither self-dramatizing nor vain, his presence evokes romantic images about the life of a missionary. Next to Tempels, Erik is the most charismatic of the Jamaa priests. His charisma is more modern and worldly than Tempels's in certain regards, but it is no less sensually mystic. And the word pictures that Erik paints through his story-telling are as vividly folkloric as the images that Tempels creates.

If he were asked directly whether he belonged to the Jamaa, Erik would contend that he is not a member. In the strict sense of ritual initiation into the movement, this is true. Yet, apart from Tempels, no one's identification with the Jamaa is stronger or less wavering than Erik's. And it is he, more than any other Jamaa priest, who has enthusiastically spread the 'good news' of the movement's existence to African, European, and even American circles.

Erik's many-sided role is essential to the internal integration of the Jamaa priest group and to their relationship to social universes outside their own, very special subculture. By virtue of his psychological skills, his capacity to deal with 'spiritual malaise', and his carefully maintained, but convivial air of reserve, Erik is not only a confidant for each of his Jamaa colleagues, but also a mediator whenever difficulties arise between them. He is their liaison with the Belgian management world of Union Minière on which they depend. In an informal sense Erik is chaplain for Union Minière's executives and their families, and their primary spiritual adviser. He constitutes an important link for them with the African community, and a valuable interpreter of it.[1] And he is an attractive and stimulating social companion for many Union Minière couples. He graces their dinner

---

[1] One of the concrete ways in which Erik has served this function is to interpret the Jamaa movement to Union Minière officials who were worried about the impact the Jamaa might have on the attitudes and behaviour of those of their African workers who belonged to it. Erik was both informative and reassuring to Union Minière executives in this regard.

tables; he regales them with choice Belgian and Congolese anecdotes; he discusses business and politics, as well as religion, philosophy, and psychology with them, both with knowledge and with gusto; and he has a way with their children that blends the egalitarianism and joyous innocence of Franciscan tradition. These informal contacts, along with his formal status as Dean (*doyen*) of Kolwezi, give Erik not only entrée to the managers of Union Minière, but also the prerogative to ask them to finance, arrange, or morally support certain things for the priestly community as well as the African lay groups that he represents.

Erik moves with as much ease and conviction in feminine as in masculine circles. In fact, he is the Jamaa priest who most explicitly believes that the work he does for and with women is central to his religious calling. Religious Sisters and lay religious women are among his closest collaborators. He is continually engaged in leading religious retreats for them; and he does a great deal of personal counselling both of lay women and women in religious life. In contrast to the intense, singular, religiously romantic way in which Tempels relates to Sister X, for example, Erik's contact with women is more wide-ranging, less mystical, and more infused with everyday humanity. For this reason, he plays an important role in linking the male community of Jamaa priests interpersonally with numerous women and their various ways of life. These contacts, in turn, both express and enrich the collective appreciation of the feminine principle in religious life that is pivotal in the Jamaa priest subculture.

Erik is at home in a number of other milieux that would be foreign and unsettling to most Belgian missionary priests. He is as comfortable with Americans and Canadians, as he is with Africans and Europeans, and with Protestants, Jews, Freemasons, and 'nonbelievers', as he is with Catholics. In all these circles, he is received cordially and is considered a very intelligent, fascinating, and openminded man, talented and knowledgeable in worldly as well as religious and moral ways. Erik, then, is the most cosmopolitan of the Jamaa priests and thus best equipped to carry out the non-proselytizing ambassadorial role on their behalf that has become uniquely his. In addition, he is the host and the gatekeeper of the Jamaa, receiving people from near and far who have come to learn more about the movement. Erik's own residence in Kolwezi is a true guest-house, constantly filled with visitors of this sort, mingling with the astounding array of other persons who come to his door and partake of his generous hospitality. Erik meets the Jamaa questers, appraises them, provides them with information, and introduces some of them into Jamaa settings to which they would not have been given access without his sponsorship.[1]

Erik's three-month visit to the United States in 1965 was typical of his roles in the Jamaa subculture, but this time, on grander, more ebullient scale. Erik based himself in New York City, and travelled widely in the States and to Montreal. In the course of his trip, he met the most humble parish priests and the most glistening Monsignors. He was introduced into high business circles, to outstanding social scientists in several universities, and to various psychiatric milieux of New York and Boston. He spent more time in the company of American Jews than he did with either Catholics or Protestants. In every setting, women in religious life and laywomen were among his primary contacts. He went to zoos with children he met, rode merry-go-rounds with them, played games with them, and told them stories. Among his more memorable soirées was dinner at the chic Brussels Restaurant in New York City, courtesy of the 'executive suite' of Union Minière representatives in the United States; an equally elegant meal in the Westchester manor house of a top church official; a night of 'rapping' with young people in a Greenwich Village apartment; and a hard-drinking night with the football coach of a Midwestern Catholic University! Erik also made an appearance on TV, and had a letter to the editor printed in the *New York Times*. Wherever he went and whatever he did, he not only deeply impressed people, but he also spoke to them at great length about the Jamaa.

The other man who belongs to the subculture of the Kolwezi Jamaa clergy is the only non-Franciscan among them. This is Benoit, a Benedictine, who was one of the two persons most likely to become Tempels's charismatic successor (the other, as we have indicated, being Frans). In certain respects, it is curious that Benoit is so integrally and focally a part of this Jamaa group. His social origins are different from the others'. He is a member of a French-speaking family from the university town of Louvain, rather than from Flanders or Limburg. He is the son of a physician, and thus of

---

[1] I, myself, was introduced into the Jamaa this way, as was Johannes Fabian. In fact, Fabian first heard of the movement from Erik, when the latter was on an extended visit to the United States in 1965. It was also Erik who invited him to make first-hand contact with the Jamaa.

professional middle-class origins, in contrast to the working-class and petty bourgeois backgrounds of his Franciscan colleagues. The Order and the Abbey that he chose to join are more aristocratic, scholastic, liturgical, work-oriented, and monastic in tradition than are the Franciscans. Yet, although Benoit is a well-adjusted, committed, and respected member of his order, he has certain attitudes and characteristics that align him as much with the Flemish Franciscan traits of the Jamaa as with Benedictinism.

Benoit is smoothly handsome, in a finished *haut bourgeois* way that distinguishes him from his Jamaa colleagues, though, like them, he dresses in the rough, workman's style of the bush priest. He is more reticent and less explosively expressive than the Franciscan Jamists, but he has their eloquence in a quieter, more polished form. He also shares their propensity to establish deep, intimate relations, albeit in a somewhat more private, less collective, way than theirs. Benoit fits the contemplative and yet active masculine world of a Benedictine abbey, but it is as true of him as of the Jamaa Franciscans that women constitute an important part of his religio-personal life. His Jamaa mama and several lay religious women with whom he works, for example, are among his closest companions and confidantes. It is Benoit's sense of mission, however, that most distinguishes him from the majority of his fellow Benedictines, and identifies him with the Franciscan ethos. Benedictine life is traditionally focused on the choir (communal prayer), the library (study of Scripture), and the land (agricultural labour). In Katanga, as elsewhere, this monastic and bucolic emphasis characterizes Benedictine activities. Benoit is one of the few monks who, by choice and conviction, is successfully engaged in urban pastoral work. He is respectful of Benedictine tradition. But he also believes that it is essential for priests to participate in the urban, industrialized aspects of everyday existence in Katanga, rather than withdraw from them, and he feels that this is the most meaningful way to contribute to the lives of the people in the area. He enacts this commitment principally through his role as national chaplain of the Young Christian Workers movement in the Congo. In turn, this role reinforces his bond with the Flemish Franciscan dimensions of the Jamaa; for this movement and its founder, Cardinal Cardijn are very close to Tempels and his colleagues.[1]

[1] There are three other priests who have a significant, but more peripheral relationship to the Kolwezi subculture. First, Monsignor Floribert Cornelis,

These, then, are the six men who (along with certain Congolese baba and mama) make up the charismatic core of the Kolwezi Jamaa. Their entwined sociological portraits suggest how interrelated a prophet-leader like Tempels is with those whom Max Weber would have called his charismatic lieutenants. As the portraits illustrate, such a leader is dependent on his lieutenants, not only for the consolidation of the movement he conceives and founds, but also for its content and ambience. In the case of the Kolwezi Jamaa, leader and lieutenants started with certain cultural and personality traits in common. Thereafter, they collectively experienced and were influenced by the Bantu African universe into which they were transplanted. And out of their complex interactions with each other as well as with Africans, there developed a whole new subculture from which the Jamaa emerged.

Archbishop of Élisabethville, Katanga, like Benoit, is a member of the Benedictine Order, with whom he shares a strong belief in the meaningfulness of urban-industrial pastoral work in a region like Katanga. Cornelis has taken *mafundisho* from a Jamaa couple as a first step towards initiation into the movement. (For a more detailed portrait of Cornelis, see Chapter VIII.)

Second, Xavier, a Jesuit, has a special connection with the Jamaa Franciscans. He is a fully initiated Jamaa member, and a very active priest-leader in the movement. Of good standing in his own Order, some of Xavier's personal talents and traits also fit the Franciscan-infused spirit of Kolwezi. He is an intellectual, joyously mystic and playfully theatrical.

Finally, there is a sense in which I (like Xavier, a Jesuit) have also developed an intimate relationship with the subculture of the Kolwezi Jamaa clergy. This is not just a consequence of my role in the movement as sociologist participant observer; rather, as mentioned in my Introduction to this study, my own West Flemish origins, village, and Christian Workers' Movement background, and my affinity with the Flemish expressionist tradition were decisive in my securing access to the Kolwezi priest group, and, through them, to the Jamaa.

CHAPTER VIII

Reactions of the Institutional Church to the Jamaa

FROM the outset, the Jamaa caused fundamental ideological and structural strains within the Catholic Church. On the one hand, it was viewed as a 'providential' source of religious creativity and renewal. But on the other, many of its charismatic features and its Bantu–Flemish–Franciscan particularities were seen as incompatible with the essential characteristics of an Ecclesia. As such, the Jamaa confronted the institutional Church with a predicament: '... the Jamaa is ... a "double-edged sword": it can do much good, as well as much harm . . .'[1] The issue is that one must be very prudent: not take a stand too soon, neither for, nor against [it], because there is good in it to maintain, less good to correct and "not good" to eradicate.'[2]

As the foregoing suggests, the Church did not respond to the Jamaa in the unitary, resolute, or authoritarian way that stereotypes of the nature of its hierarchy and government might lead one to expect. Eventually, as we shall see, certain bishops did initiate measures to guide, control, form, and, in a few instances, severely curtail the movement. In keeping with the inquisitorial drama conventionally expected from the Roman Curia, at one point the 'case' of Father Tempels and the Jamaa came before the Holy Office.[3] But, by and large, the zigzagging evolution of the Church's

[1] Monsignor Joseph Nkongolo, Pastoral Letter No. 12, 19 Mar. 1965.

[2] Mgr. J. Nkongolo, in a conference to the priests of his diocese during their annual spiritual retreat, held in Bakwanga in July 1963.

The names of bishops, cardinals, and other senior church officials mentioned in this chapter are not pseudonyms. I decided to use their real names for two reasons. First, their official positions make it virtually impossible to disguise their identity. Secondly, most of the materials associated with them that I have incorporated into this chapter are drawn from documents they drafted which are in the public domain.

[3] The Holy Office was the Congregation of the Roman Curia in charge of safeguarding doctrine on faith and morals throughout the entire Catholic world. On 7 Dec. 1965 it was reformed and reorganized by Pope Paul VI, and its name was changed to The Sacred Congregation for the Doctrine of the Faith.

official stand with respect to the movement was accompanied by much searching, debate, dissent, negotiation, and anguish. An analysis of the ways in which the Church responded to the Jamaa, in its various stages of development, provides a new insight into the way that the complex organization of this Ecclesia actually functions.

This chapter spans a period of eleven years: from 1960 (approximately seven years after the inception of the Jamaa), when the movement's so-called 'problems', 'errors', and 'deviations' first became apparent to non-Jamaa priests, to 1971, by which time drastic action had been taken against the Jamaa in several dioceses, and all the Franciscan founder-leaders of the Jamaa had definitively left the Congo. In that period the Congo passed through a number of landmark events that affected the evolution of the Jamaa, and the ways in which the Church dealt with it. They included the aftermath of the tribal conflict of 1959 between Luba and Lulua in Kasai; the advent of Independence in 1960; the Katanga secession of 1960–3; the Congo Rebellion of 1964–5; and the establishment of a one-party State by General Mobutu in 1965, with its ideological emphasis on 'African authenticity'. In the same period, both locally and nationally, the Catholic Church in the Congo underwent a sombre process of self-examination in respect of its missionary achievements, its Africanicity, and its relevance to the social and cultural problems faced by the new nation-state. The influence of Congolese diocesan clergy grew, and more Congolese priests were appointed bishops. These changes in the Congolese Church coincided with the occurrence of the Second Vatican Council (October 1962–December 1965) and were greatly influenced by it. In particular, the Council's emphasis on the spiritual unification of humanity, the role of the Catholic Church in the modern world, the principle of collegiality, the celibacy of the clergy, and the legitimacy of the culturally diverse traditions which the Catholic Church encompasses made a significant impact on the Congolese Church and on its attitudes and behaviour toward the Jamaa.

This chapter is concerned with the various types and phases of response to the Jamaa on the part of the institutional Church during this momentous decade. The concept 'institutional Church' refers to the hierarchy of the Catholic Church: from local parish priest to bishop, to official of the Roman Curia. Although both theologically and sociologically the Catholic laity constitute an integral part of the Church, their reactions to the movement are peripheral to our central theme. We shall concentrate on the ways in which the priestly corps of the Church struggled to come to terms with the Jamaa over the years. Three characteristics of this process are especially notable. We have already alluded to the first of these: the hesitant and non-authoritarian fashion in which the hierarchy dealt with the Jamaa. A second feature was the complex interweaving of many different sorts of informal, as well as formal, modes of response to the Jamaa by an ecclesiastical organization better known for its legalism, bureaucracy, and routinization. Third, the institutional Church's diverse reactions to the movement not only involved priests from every level, but also from an unusually wide range of Orders and congregations.

Church attitudes towards the Jamaa during the years 1960 to 1963 were predominantly favourable, even enthusiastic. By and large, the Jamaa was hailed by most churchmen who came into contact with it, as a 'supernatural' phenomenon, 'born of the Holy Spirit', working in a 'charismatic fashion'. It was welcomed as a 'providential', a 'consoling', and 'inspiring' event, in the midst of the 'critical hours' and 'troubled days' through which the Congo was passing. It was a 'grace' for a parish to have an 'authentic Jamaa', priests testified, for it 'vitalized' and 'animated' clergy and laity alike in a way that they had either 'not known for a long time' or 'ever before'. Jamaa members were lauded for their 'intense piety' and 'zeal'. Their 'fervour', 'élan', 'apostolic charity', and 'Christian tenacity' were considered 'remarkable'. They 'transformed the face of the parish' through their frequent attendance at Mass and participation in communion, their 'sense of prayer', their 'devotion to good works', and by their 'avidity' for 'instructions on how to live a Christian life'. Priests declared that they found Jamaa members 'uplifting' because they 'animated' the parish and eagerly shared certain apostolic responsibilities with them. Beyond that, they enriched the spiritual life of the clergy as well as of the laity through their 'discovery' and 'realization' of a 'more profound love . . . the richness of the love of Christ and the Virgin Mary'. The Jamaa seemed to be an 'authentic Catholic mystery' that bore 'astonishing spiritual fruits'. In its presence, priests became 'better, more saintly'. Attracted above all by the 'example of the Jamists' conjugal life', lay persons were 'engendered' by the Jamaa baba and mama, becoming their 'spiritual children'. In the view of priest commentators, one of the supreme indicators of how 'deeply implanted Christianity [was] in the heads and hearts' of Jamaa members was the way they comported themselves in the 'time of troubles' both in Kasai and Katanga.

[They] succeeded in making the members of different, even enemy tribes live together in a true Christian fraternity . . . At the height of the tribal war between BaLuba and Lulua in Kasai, members of the Jamaa helped each other like brothers . . . In the refugee camp in Élisabethville, they organized big public prayer meetings . . . In Kolwezi, when several agitators wanted to molest a European priest, they formed a human wall, saying, 'If you kill the Father, kill us with him, because the priest and we are one.'

The universalism and love unfalteringly expressed and lived by the baba and mama, even under these adverse circumstances, convinced priests that the Jamaa was a 'rare adaptation of the Christian message to the soul and culture of an evangelized people'. At one and the same time, it was a 'fecund response . . . to the aspirations and mentality of Congolese' and 'authentic Christianity'. Jamists were 'real Christian Africans', who without violating the 'Bantu soul . . . Christianized pagan practices . . . transforming the traditional ways of celebrating births, marriages and deaths'. The Jamaa is 'probably one of the great marvels of the missionary Church of our day', affirmed one priest. This is how most Catholic clergy with any knowledge of the movement felt about it in the interlude of 1960 to 1963. Although after 1963 the problematic aspects of the Jamaa became progressively more apparent to priests and bishops, and their misgivings about it grew, virtually every spoken and written statement that they made about the movement was prefaced by a testimonial to the same forms of 'spiritual richness' and 'extraordinary accomplishments' that they had earlier recognized in the Jamaa.

From the outset of the movement's development, in the early 1950s, Tempels and the first Jamaa priests were aware of the existence of what they called certain 'difficulties' or 'errors' that had 'come to the surface' in the Jamaa. They felt these 'problems' to be an 'understandable', if not inevitable, concomitant of the at once human and transcendental Bantu and Christian encounter that was the essence of the Jamaa. They were confident that through quickened dialogue and deeper union between the baba, mama, and priests, these initial difficulties could be rectified. Tempels wrote: 'Nobody in the Jamaa will be perfect, but at least we will be together, and in union we will know how to correct one another, and in union the priest will be able to be the light inside the Jamaa . . .'[1] In this context, Tempels placed special emphasis on the role that the priest as 'the other Christ', could and should play:

When Christ began his 'jamaa', his community or his church of living stones, each day his disciples displayed erroneous judgements, false attitudes, misunderstandings, faults. Continually, without breaking contact, without ceasing to be jamaa with them, Christ redressed, corrected, taught, enlightened . . . and this first jamaa continued to be a unified group, until the death of Christ, despite these difficulties, faults, errors . . .[2]

Despite Tempels's religious optimism, by 1961 some of his correspondence with clergymen interested in the Jamaa reflected his growing concern about certain of its tendencies. In these letters he expressed disquietude over the almost cultic attitudes on the part of baba and mama toward his person, his utterances, and his leadership:

. . . When one speaks of 'Jamaa', the less one speaks of Father Tempels the better. I say that for the simple reason that the very essence of the Church is to be 'Jamaa'. It is Christ who conceived, wished and commanded it like that. Thus, one should not—if one wishes to remain objective—speak of me. I neither invented nor began the 'Jamaa' . . .[3]

Tempels's disclaimer was not only related to his desire to 'decharismatize'[4] the Jamaa at this stage in its evolution; it was also associated with his desire to check the inclination of some Jamists to feel and behave as if they were members of an exclusive, closed group. These baba and mama were prone to regard 'ordinary' clergy as spiritually inferior to the priests close to their movement, as well as less understanding and trustworthy. Although these Jamists were among the most vigorous members of their parishes as regards external matters, they were reluctant to discuss internal Jamaa matters and experiences with non-Jamaa priests. And more often than not, when they had personal religious problems, they bypassed their local parish priests, travelling considerable distances,

[1] Letter to Abbé Baeyens, a parish priest in Kipushi, written in Kolwezi, 2 Feb. 1961.   [2] Ibid.
[3] Letter to Abbé Louis Gasore, Vicar General of Nyundo (Rwanda), written in Kolwezi, 28 Jan. 1961. An edited version of this letter was printed in *Notre Rencontre* (pp. 27–9) without mention of the fact that it was originally a personal letter.
[4] This is a term I coined; it is not used by Tempels.

if need be, to seek counsel from a Jamaa-priest. This same in-group, 'super-Jamaa', outlook also led such baba and mama to regard non-Jamaa Catholics as less pious and pure and to debar them from participation even in some of their more public religious activities. In at least two of the letters that Tempels wrote to non-Jamaa priests in 1961 he discussed these characteristics of the movement, making it clear that he considered them to be 'difficulties', or, more seriously still, 'errors'.[1]

> Jamaa without priest is not Church; as . . . the priest without union with his people is not Church either . . . This encounter between the priest and his people is a thing that must be born, that must begin in each parish . . . The jamaa of Kipushi will become what the encounter between the bababa and bamama with their parish priest, and the priest with his bababa and bamama become . . . Speak amicably . . . with your people. Speak to them of the spirit of the jamaa, or rather of the spirit of your jamaa in Kipushi. Tell them that a closed jamaa is contrary to the sense of the Church, or of the jamaa as Christ wished it. The jamaa must be open to everyone. Decide together to admit everyone.[2]

1962 was the year that *Notre Rencontre* was published, and that Tempels returned to Belgium for good. The Jamaa spread and grew more widely known. As it did so, its problems as well as its promises and accomplishments began to be apparent to a larger circle of clergy and lay persons. By early 1963, the existence in the movement of what were thought to be doctrinal errors and morally deviant practices disturbed certain non-Jamaa as well as Jamaa priests. So far as their public stance was concerned, Tempels and his priest-followers maintained strict silence regarding any difficulties inside the Jamaa. Their response to any sort of query about the Jamaa was proto-charismatic: 'It is very difficult to explain or understand the Jamaa from the outside. You have to live it, make yourself part of it without reservation . . . It is a kind of life, a mystique about which we do not like to speak . . . The less one speaks of the jamaa, the less one studies it, the less one publishes on it, the better it will go.' What priest-critics were later to call an 'esoteric' attitude of the Jamaa was part of its general attitude. As one critic wrote with mixed irony and indignation:

. . . 'Jamaa-initiates' feel bound to one another by a 'vital, incommunicable' experience which makes them into a sort of spiritual brotherhood

[1] Letters to Abbé Gasore and Abbé Baeyens.
[2] Letter to Abbé Baeyens.

hermetically turned in upon itself, and to which any non-initiate, be he priest or bishop, does not have access . . .[1]

However, by 1963, one of the secondary functions of the mystically exclusive outlook of Jamaa members was to defend the movement against the sort of scrutiny that might lay bare how serious the troublesome aspects of the Jamaa had become.

It was now clear to Tempels and his priest-lieutenants that the errors and deviations were patterned, extensive, recalcitrant, and increasingly organized by a group inside the movement who called themselves 'Katete', and were headed by certain baba. If anything, the errors and deviations were even more pronounced in the Kasai branches of the Jamaa than in Katanga.

Tempels and the Jamaa priests chose to deal with these difficulties in the in-group, informal way that was the hallmark of their charismatic style. Many meetings with each other, and with key baba and mama, were devoted to these problems, as were numerous, long, expressive letters, chiefly from and to Tempels. In effect, what was attempted was a re-socialization of the errant baba and mama through intensive, personal teaching and the use of magnetic suasion and authority. For example, on 2 March 1963 Tempels wrote a long letter to Monsignor Alphonse Ngoie (a Vicar General of the Bakwanga diocese and Jamaa-priest in Ngandajika, Kasai), replying to various questions about the errors and the 'degrees' or 'ways' of the initiation that Ngoie had put to him. Tempels asked Ngoie to share the contents of the letter with another Congolese Jamaa-priest in the area. ('You will need each other to follow "together" the same road of brotherhood, of union . . .') Although Tempels prefaced his remarks with a compassionately resigned statement about the 'inevitability' of the commission of errors by priests as well as a few baba in the movement, his letter was outspokenly critical of four specific errors that 'do not come from the Jamaa spirit'. The first of these was aspiring 'to any type of "superiority"', to want to become a "first baba", a "senior baba", the baba of a whole group . . .'. The second was being 'carried away by egoistic feelings', so that one 'draws the [Jamaa initiate] towards one's self instead of leading him (her) to Christ, to the Virgin'. The third error against which Tempels inveighed was the fact that, 'babas venture

---

[1] Dom Étienne De Schrevel, O.S.B., 'La "Jamaa" au Katanga industriel: Problèmes pratiques de pastorale', mimeographed paper, Jadotville, Paroisse du Sacré-Cœur, Jan. 1965, p. 4.

to lead mamas! With the imminent danger of drawing them to themselves, rather than leading them on the first way to Christ!' 'Let
a baba engender a man child!', Tempels exhorted. 'Let a mama
engender a woman child!' Here, he used Jamaa metaphors to make
oblique but unmistakable reference to the problem of 'carnal union'
between non-spouses. Finally, he referred briefly to another 'possible
error': believing that the Jamaa 'lives in its . . . numerous meetings'
rather than principally through its 'silent contacts of man to man . . .
[and] woman to woman . . . through which we constantly engender
new children in the first way: their encounter with Christ and the
Virgin'. The greater part of Tempels's letter was devoted to a detailed
description of how each phase of the Jamaa's initiation process
ideally ought to unfold. He dwelt on the third and fourth ways with
special concern, apparently because it had been reported to him that
certain baba were excluding the priest from these encounters,
and usurping his role:

> You will now understand that the third and fourth degrees are essen-
> tially the encounter of the baba and mama with the priest, this Other
> Christ. And that it is an unhappy error on the part of one or another
> baba, that he himself can introduce another baba in what he 'calls' the
> third or fourth way! That is suppression of the 'priesthood'. Where then
> will the Jamaa or the Church be? . . .

Tempels opened and closed his letter to Ngoie with the assertion
that neither he himself nor anyone else had '. . . jurisdiction . . .
over the jamaa. In jamaa no one is superior to any other . . . One is
. . . fraternally equal . . .' Nevertheless, in one of his final sentences,
Tempels declared, 'Now, if someone says to You that Father Tempels taught "otherwise"—You will know better.' He thus invoked
his special authority as founder-leader of the Jamaa to countermand
the claims that the 'deviationist' baba and mama were making in
his name.

By the summer of 1963, the problem of errors and deviations
in the Jamaa had become even more pervasive and widely known
to clergy and lay persons outside the movement as well as to its
members. Consequently, when Benoit left the Congo that June
for a vacation in Belgium, he was charged by worried Jamists of
Élisabethville to confer with Tempels about these difficulties and to
ask him how they ought to deal with them. The two men met frequently during the summer to discuss Jamaa matters, and found
themselves in complete agreement on how best to respond to the

deviations. That response took the form of an open latter in Swahili addressed to the 'wababa' and 'wamama' of Katanga, jointly composed by Tempels and Benoit.

Along with your Baba Placide, [the letter began,] we are very troubled about many of the doctrines that are being taught by other babas. I [Benoit] have asked him if all these doctrines are really his. With him, we have drafted this letter, so that you may know truly what doctrine is not his. Also you will be able to put an end to the discussion of the babas who teach errors and who say: our teaching comes from Baba Placide.

The letter listed twelve concrete teachings that certain baba were conveying about Cain and Abel, the angels, Joseph, the Virgin Mary, Jesus, Mary Magdalen, John, the other apostles, the Eucharist, and Pentecost. Benoit and Tempels called each of these notions 'false', 'not from Baba Placide', and 'never taught by [him]'. There are 'other doctrines of this sort', the letter concluded. 'But all of them come from this one idea: that one must unite carnally in order to be truly one! When Baba Placide learnt that these teachings are spread among the babas he was very surprised and extremely saddened in his heart. He wept over his children who want to do wrong to themselves and to other children.' The letter ended with the affirmation that it had been read and signed by Baba Placide 'so that you will know that it comes from me and from him'. It was signed, 'Your poor child, Benoit' and 'Your poor baba, Placide'. A month later, in September 1963, Tempels sent a copy of the letter to Monsignor Ngoie in Ngandajika, encouraging him to circulate it widely among Jamists in the Kasai region:

If You believe that this letter can help your *batatu* and *bamamu*, try to translate this letter or have it translated into Tshiluba! If You think it opportune, You can have it mimeographed and distribute it. I am only trying to help You, and not to impose myself. But since certain *batatu* are spreading errors, citing my name in doing so, perhaps it will help You to send out this letter that carries the name of this unhappy baba Placide.

As this set of exchanges makes clear, by this time, anxiety about the errors and deviations had become more acute among the priest-leaders of the Jamaa as well as its primary teaching baba and mama who were not Katete. Although Tempels and his associates were still unwilling to use other than personal, in-group means to cope with these developments, the founder-leader's authority was now more forcibly invoked. The errors and deviations were explicitly cited, rather than referred to in metaphorical or elliptical terms, and their common essence—the belief that carnal union is a necessary part of spiritual union—plainly stated and refuted. Furthermore, Tempels had evidently come to feel that within the Jamaa discussion of the errors and deviations should no longer be furtive, or confined to a select group of concerned baba, mama, and priests. Rather, recognition that these teachings and practices were incorrect and strongly disapproved by Tempels should be diffused throughout the Jamaa membership in both Katanga and Kasai. The fact that the letter intended for this purpose was written and signed by Benoit and Tempels suggests that at this point in the Jamaa's history, Benoit was the principal candidate for eventual succession to Tempels's role as leader of the whole movement.

Tempels and his Jamaa priest-colleagues would have professed that their intensified efforts to deal with the errors and deviations were not significantly influenced by the disquietude about these aspects of the movement that was increasingly manifest in official Church circles. However, it is unlikely that their lofty disinterestedness and transcendentalism perfectly insulated Jamaa priests from the apprehension expressed by eminent church figures about the 'problems', 'dangers', 'aberrations', 'weaknesses', 'misunderstandings', 'shadows', or 'the less valuable elements' in the movement. Even bishops in the Congo who were sympathetic to the Jamaa, such as Monsignors Nkongolo of Mbuji-Mayi and Cornelis of Élisabethville, felt obliged to issue 'warnings' about the movement to the priests and lay persons in their dioceses. Among the difficulties cited by Cornelis in his Pastoral Letter of 1 September, 1963 were certain 'aberrant doctrines' and dangers of 'heresy', 'syncretism', and 'sensuality'. He and Nkongolo established a few directives concerning the Jamaa. These were designed to keep watch over troublesome aspects of the movement, without 'prematurely . . . taking an [over-all] position' with regard to the Jamaa, 'either for or against', or, in the words of Cornelis, attempting to control it with 'the severe and implacable eye of the inquisitor, the witch-hunter'. Nkongolo assigned to Monsignor Ngoie the task of dealing with all matters relating to Jamaa in his diocese. He also declared that 'only duly authorized persons' would be permitted to teach the *mafundisho*, and that night meetings of the Jamaa were no longer to be permitted. Cornelis's directives included philosophical, intellectual, and mystical considerations, as well as more pragmatic guides for social control.[1] He instructed his priests not to become so deeply involved with Jamaa members that they gave the impression of 'abandoning' their other parishioners. He asked them to 'maintain perfect reserve' with every person with whom they dealt, 'above all with respect to the mamas of the jamaa'. He recommended that experienced priests be admitted to the jamaa, to whom baba and mama would '*spontaneously* [emphasis Cornelis's] submit their teaching, have their theological vocabulary checked, and ask to have the essentials of their taught doctrine recorded in writing, and to be helped to solve concrete problems'. 'Orient the marvellous Christian that you find here and there,' Cornelis exhorted his priests, 'who resembles the Christian of the Middle Ages, in order to integrate him after purification into a liturgical life approved by the hierarchy.' 'Make a serious study of Christian mysticism, in its diverse historical manifestations, as well as the most ancient Fathers of the Church, principally those who expounded the pure doctrine without philosophical or theological superfetations.' In conclusion Cornelis recommended that a 'loving and sympathetic heart' towards the Jamaa be maintained. 'Above all', he wrote, 'let us pray to the Lord to give to everyone, priests and lay persons, the light so necessary to see clearly *together* [emphasis Cornelis's], so that the Jamaa can effectively contribute to the realization of God's redemptive plan.'

Behind these statements by two bishops who were notable for their receptivity to the Jamaa lay more than the need that they both felt for an authoritative pastoral response to the spread of the movement's errors and deviations in their dioceses. The fact that the Jamaa was attracting considerable attention in Rome was the primary external force that put the Congo's bishops under pressure to make some sort of pronouncement on how they viewed and were dealing with the movement. During the last three months of 1962, from 11 October to 8 December more than 2,500 bishops of the Catholic Church convened in Rome to attend the first session of Vatican Council II (the first such Council to be called in over ninety years). This extraordinary gathering of the Catholic Episcopate provided many opportunities for bishops to engage in informal discussion with each other about matters of mutual interest and concern. The Jamaa was one such topic. It both intrigued and

[1] 'Déclaration relative à la Jamaa', Pastoralia no. 12, Archidiocèse d'Élisabethville, 1 Sept. 1963, p. 7 (stencilled document).

troubled a number of bishops that in certain respects this movement appeared to be consonant with the charismatic tradition of Christianity and the vision of Vatican II, while in other respects its mystique not only seemed 'uncontrollable, unverifiable and incomprehensible', but also conducive to grave errors and deviations. In effect, the Jamaa presented the bishops with a vivid, contemporary instance of the inherent strains that exist between charismatic and rational-legal authority in an ecclesia like the Catholic Church, and between its universalistic and culturally specific elements. Bishops from Belgium and those from the Congo and other parts of Central Africa were most likely to talk about the Jamaa. The risks as well as the promises of a rapprochement between 'aspirations of the African soul' and 'authentically Christian values' engaged them all. And the Belgian bishops were also concerned about what consequences might ensue from the fact that Tempels had already taken the first steps towards extending and generalizing the message of the Jamaa by attempting to introduce it into Belgian milieux.

Between the first and second sessions of the Council, in the summer of 1963, the bishops of the Congo formally expressed their collective desire to know more about the Jamaa, 'its nature, origin, development, composition, and consequences'. In July their Permanent Committee ('le Comité Permanent des Ordinaires du Congo') asked the Centre de Recherches Sociologiques, a sociological research bureau attached to the General Secretariat of the Episcopate of the Catholic Church in the Congo to undertake a study of the movement. The spirit in which they made this request was one of anxious inquiry. What they sought was help in deciding how to think of the Jamaa and how to deal with it in their dioceses, as well as how to respond to the questions about the movement being put to them in Rome.

The second session of the Council lasted from 27 September until 4 December 1963. The bishops' preoccupation with the Jamaa had not abated during the nine months between sessions. If anything, their anxiety about the movement had grown. This was one of the reasons why Monsignor Cornelis had felt it important to issue his pastoral letter about the Jamaa on 1 September 1963, several weeks before he returned to Rome for the second session. ('For a while now', this letter began, 'requests for explanations about the Jamaa have been multiplying . . . everyone is questioning himself about it . . .')

One of the major events that contributed to the bishops' increased disquietude about the Jamaa were the repercussions of three visits that two pious French women, Mesdemoiselles M. J. Lebaindre and M. Grandjean made to Tempels at the Franciscan convent in Hasselt on 21, 22, and 29 August 1963. They belonged to a women's sodality, dedicated to the principles and ideals of French Catholic 'integralism'. This is a conservative, fundamentalist movement, socially and politically, as well as religiously, which is concerned primarily with 'the purity of the faith', and is also ethnocentrically Gallic.[1] The spiritual adviser of the group was a priest of like conviction who belonged to the archdiocese of Paris. He played a covert role in influencing the two women's visits to Tempels, their response to their meetings with him, and the actions with regard to Tempels and the Jamaa that they subsequently initiated. Professing a great positive interest in the Jamaa, particularly in the 'mystique of the encounter', they skilfully drew Tempels out, and succeeded in gaining his complete confidence. Not only did he describe to them in detail his encounter with Sister X and the meetings with Christ and the Virgin Mary that flowed from it, but he also entrusted his whole file of personal correspondence to them. They, in turn, made copies of these letters before returning them to Tempels. They incorporated these materials into a document entitled 'The Jamaa', that they drafted, mimeographed, and distributed widely in international church circles. Their report was a detailed denunciation of Tempels and the movement. It placed special emphasis on the evidence these women had been able to gather suggesting that 'total encounter' in the Jamaa meant an 'encounter of the body, as well as of the spirit and the heart'. Between August 1963 and April 1965, Mesdemoiselles Lebaindre and Grandjean made more than a hundred approaches to ecclesiastical authorities, as part of their indefatigable campaign to have official church sanctions taken against Tempels and the movement. Ostensibly, their efforts did not meet with success. They received the following, strongly discouraging response from Cardinal Suenens of Belgium, written on 24 October 1963 from the Council in Rome:

> The Cardinal-Archbishop of Malines–Brussels wishes you to know that he has received your letter. He asks you with insistence no longer to

---

[1] For a scholarly résumé of the origins and characteristics of integralism, see Waldemar Molinski, 'Integralism' in Karl Rahner et al., eds., Sacramentum Mundi, vol. 3 (New York: Herder and Herder, 1969), pp. 151–2.

concern yourselves with the case of Father T. As you have referred it to competent ecclesiastical authorities, they will follow it up in ways that they judge necessary and useful. Thus, you can consider yourselves relieved of all responsibility. Under these circumstances there is no longer any reason to insist on obtaining an audience.[1]

Suenens's icily formal reply not only expressed his own thinly disguised disapproval of the Mesdemoiselles' zeal; it also revealed that, partly as a result of their appeal to 'competent ecclesiastical authorities', the 'case of Father T.' was already being handled by high church officials.

A second event that augmented the bishops' unease about the Jamaa was the distribution in 1963 of Tempels's *Notre Rencontre*, Volume II by Father Maertens, a Flemish Scheutist missionary priest, who directed the Centre d'Études Pastorales in Léopoldville which published the original edition of *Notre Rencontre*. Volume II was another collection of *mafundisho* composed by Tempels that had been issued in August 1962. According to the editor's note that accompanied it, 'the text of this brochure . . . has been mimeographed for the use of only a few persons, from whom it is requested that they communicate their observations . . . corrections . . . or modifications to the editor. It should be noted that for this text, "pro manuscripto", an imprimatur has not yet been given and that the brochure is not for sale to the public.' In all, about one hundred copies of *Notre Rencontre*, Volume II were mimeographed, of which as many as forty were in circulation by 1963, despite Maertens's cautionary statement. These copies were passed on from one person to another in church circles of the Congo, so that a good many more than forty clergymen had occasion to read *Notre Rencontre II*. It was Monsignor Cornelis of Élisabethville who belatedly intervened to prevent any more copies of the manuscript from being distributed. This manuscript was a more hastily composed, personalized, and folkloric interpretation of Christ's life than the first volume of *Notre Rencontre*. It placed even greater emphasis on Christ's humanity, and on his relationships with the Virgin Mary, Mary Magdalen, and John. Furthermore, the way that Tempels described these very human though divine relations in *Notre Rencontre II* was more evocative of the ambiguity and sensuality of his conception of the 'encounter' than his previous writings had been.

[1] Quoted in Peritus (pseudonym), 'L'Église face à la scandaleuse Jamaa', *Le Monde et la vie* (Paris monthly), no. 155 (Apr. 1966), p. 63.

In November 1963 the Holy Office summoned Tempels to Rome to defend himself against a formal accusation of heterodoxy and improper behaviour. Because of his extensive correspondence with Tempels and his important role in the leadership of the Jamaa, Benoit was also implicated in the accusation. Unlike Tempels, however, he did not have to appear before the ecclesiastical court. Tempels was too ill at this time to travel. But at the request of some of the Bishops of the Congo who were attending the second session of the Vatican Council and of four Belgian Bishops (from Antwerp, Brussels, Liège, and Namur), Benoit journeyed to Rome to give a personal account of the Jamaa. One of the chief promoters of Benoit's visit was Monsignor Cornelis who, in his dual capacity as Benoit's Benedictine colleague and his local bishop, was anxious to provide an opportunity for him informally to clear himself with high church officials. Cornelis also hoped that the Jamaa could still be protected against punitive and repressive action by Rome. Benoit's presentation to the Bishops consisted of the following: a historical account of the development of the Jamaa; a synthesis of the doctrine; a testimony to the 'new form of African Christian spirituality' that it represented as well as to the profoundly transforming 'existential experience' that it constituted; an assertion that he was keeping his Bishop informed of the evolution of the Jamaa in his parish; and, finally, the contention that the errors and deviations that admittedly existed in the movement were due to the relative 'newness' of Christianity in a 'pagan milieu', and were specifically 'introduced [to the Jamaa] by former members of the Kitawala, Apostolo and Kimbanguist sects'. The Bishops' response to Benoit's discussion was mixed, but favourable rather than hostile. One bishop asked only that Tempels and Benoit 'stay in Africa with the Jamaa and don't bother us with it in Europe', while others were impressed with the 'possibility that the Holy Spirit speaks through the Jamaa'.

In January 1964 Benoit was permitted to return to the Congo by his superiors at St André, the abbey in Bruges, Belgium, to which he belonged. In their eyes, he was exonerated from all wrong-doing, and he had their permission to continue his work in the Jamaa. There is circumstantial evidence suggesting that Benoit's abbot may have intervened on his behalf in Rome.

Tempels, however, fared quite differently with his superiors. In December 1963 he received a letter from his Provincial which opened with the salutation, 'My poor brother, Father Placide', and proceeded to impose eight sanctions on him, owing to his Jamaa activities both in Europe and in the Congo. Tempels was ordered to live permanently in the Franciscan convent in Hasselt, to which he was to be rather strictly confined. He was not to return to the Congo. His retreats were to be taken in solitude. All the letters he wrote and received were to pass through the hands of his superiors. He was to receive no visits from lay women or religious Sisters. He was no longer to engage in apostolic work that entailed direct personal contact. He was to give no lectures or public presentations of any kind. And his manuscript, *Notre Rencontre II* was not to be published.

In 1964 Tempels appeared before the tribunal in Rome. Only a few details of what transpired are known. Tempels was provided with a lawyer and questioned twice a week over a period of several weeks. Various pieces of data were used as part of the accusatory process, among them the materials provided by the two outraged French women. Written testimonials in defence of Tempels and the Jamaa by priests and lay persons close to the movement were also admitted as evidence. Tempels is said to have experienced great psychic suffering in the face of this inquiry. No official pronouncement was ever issued regarding its outcome. Neither Tempels nor the Jamaa was formally condemned. Instead, the Holy Office made it known to the bishops of the Congo that it was confiding in them the responsibility for 'watching over' the movement and for helping it to maintain a 'healthy orthodoxy'. On 18 June 1965 an article appeared in the Vatican newspaper *Osservatore Romano*[1] which to Rome-watchers carried the coded message that Tempels had been completely absolved by the Holy Office. The article, entitled 'Father Placide Tempels and the Bantu Populations', praised Tempels and his Jamaa for the relevance and profundity of their response to the 'fundamental problem' of the 'adaptation' of Christianity to the 'mentality, psychology and wisdom characteristic of each people'. The article ended on a note of sentimentally effusive praise for Tempels:

In the heart of Africa, where no written document exists, where wisdom is transmitted orally and lives in the daily language of the people, Father Tempels has patiently searched in order to penetrate the psychology of the people, understand their mentality and discover their vibrations, their

---

[1] The article is signed G. C., but the identity of the author is not known.

aspirations towards the common ideas of good, of truth and of love. Upon these ideas, still intact and non-contaminated, he has laboured to graft Christ and his Church.

Even this extravagant, though indirect, message from Rome did not persuade the Franciscan Provincial to relax the sanctions he had imposed upon Tempels. Several of Tempels's Franciscan colleagues attempted to negotiate with the Provincial, but to no avail. The Provincial maintained that he had not received personal or official word from Rome informing him that Tempels had been acquitted. Monsignor Cardijn agreed to look into the situation in Rome on behalf of some of Tempels's supporters, who suspected that the Provincial's position was self-determined rather than decreed by the Holy Office. Cardijn, who had been created a Cardinal in February 1965 and was attending the fourth session of the Vatican Council,[1] first approached Monsignor Pietro Sigismondi. Sigismondi, Assistant Secretary of the Sacred Congregation for the Propagation of the Faith (in effect, the ministry of the Church's Missions), had been Apostolic Delegate and subsequently Papal Nuncio in Léopoldville. It was felt that because of his previous assignment to the Congo and his present office Sigismondi was likely to be well informed about Tempels's case. Sigismondi told Cardijn that, to the best of his knowledge, Tempels had not been censured by the Holy Office. He recommended that Cardijn look further into the matter by consulting Monsignor Angelo Dell'Acqua, Under-Secretary of State of the Vatican. Dell'Acqua, who had served abroad for many years in the Vatican's diplomatic corps and was a guiding administrator in the Second Vatican Council, was considered to be a member of the topmost inner circle of the Church. He was referred to by some as the 'ear of the Pope'. In his turn, Dell'Acqua referred Cardijn to Alfredo Cardinal Ottaviani, Secretary of the Holy Office, the official guardian of the orthodoxy of Catholic doctrine and practice. Ottaviani assured Cardijn that the Holy Office had not condemned Tempels. Then why, Cardijn asked him, was Tempels still subject to a number of sanctions? Ottaviani led him to the reasoned conclusion that these controls emanated from the Franciscan Order, rather than from Vatican authorities.

In fact, Tempels's Provincial had all but revealed this when he offered to drop the measures taken against Tempels if he would

---

[1] The fourth (and last) session of the Second Vatican Council began on 14 Sept. and closed on 8 Dec. 1965.

agree formally to renounce Sister X. The Provincial also indicated that this would be the precondition for his returning to Tempels what he considered to be an incriminating packet of letters. These were letters that Tempels had written to a young girl who belonged to a Catholic group in Antwerp known as Caritas. The members of Caritas prayed together, and also shared their religious reflections and experiences. When the young woman and another girl from the same group visited Tempels and began a steady correspondence with him, Caritas members noted that they became more closed and less communicative in their own religious circle. They attributed this to the negatively charismatic influence that Tempels was exerting upon the girls. Several persons from Caritas went so far as to call on Tempels and ask him to 'release the two girls'. Eventually, one of the girls was persuaded to hand over to the group the letters that she had received from Tempels. These found their way to the Bishop of Antwerp, who, in turn passed them on to Tempels's Provincial. Rather than transmit them to Rome as data relevant to Tempels's trial, the Provincial held on to them, using them to justify the sanctions he had taken against Tempels and as an inducement for him to renounce Sister X. Because Tempels steadfastly refused to 'abandon' any person in this way, and Sister X in particular, the Provincial maintained the sanctions he had imposed. They are in effect to this day. However, Tempels's immediate superior, the head of his convent, has liberally interpreted these measures. Although he is not permitted to engage in apostolic work, Tempels is free to receive visitors, to spend time at relatives' homes, and to correspond with whomsoever he wishes without interception of incoming or outgoing mail by his superior. Tempels's frail health and his age are as much deterrents to his returning to the Congo, as are the Provincial's sanctions.

A few sociological comments are in order on the fact that Tempels and Benoit were asked to account to Rome. This sequence of events reveals how the authority and power structures of the Catholic ecclesia respond to the kinds of phenomena that Tempels and the Jamaa presented. First, it is of some interest that Benoit's involvement in the Jamaa and responsibility for it were of a lesser order than those of its founder-leader, Tempels. It was also attributable to the nature of the relationship between a Benedictine, his monastery, and his abbot. In addition to the vows of chastity, obedience, and poverty, a Benedictine monk also takes a 'vow of stability'. This binds him throughout his life to a particular monastery and its religious community, no matter where in the world he may be assigned to work. The members of a monastery are linked to one another over time and space in a deep familial, as well as spiritual, sense. In the cases of Benoit and Monsignor Cornelis as with all their fellow Benedictines in Katanga, this monastery was St. André in Bruges. The fact that he and Benoit belonged to the same abbey probably reinforced Cornelis's tendency to defend his colleague under his episcopal authority. Moreover, both Cornelis and Benoit were subject to the influence and jurisdiction of the abbot who governed their monastery. An abbot is elected to his office for life. He has strong, and ultimate authority over his monastery. However, his authority is also paternal and beneficent, for it is tempered by the principle of 'discretion' (*discretio*) which is central to the Rule of St. Benedict. This principle is built on two interdependent values: discernment and moderation. Thus, in the cases of Benoit, the Jamaa, and Cornelis, the abbot of St. André acted in accordance with the institutionalized spirit of his office.

The patterns of authority and power that were played out in Franciscan milieux and that affected the fate of Tempels were quite different. The Franciscan Order, of course, was much more fully implicated in the repercussions of the Jamaa's errors and deviations in higher church circles. The movement's founder-leader was a Franciscan as were all but one of the priests associated with its beginnings and, as we have seen, the Jamaa's distinctive subculture was characterized by many (Flemish) Franciscan traits. The General of the Franciscan Order in Rome and the Provincial of the Flemish-Belgian Province had every reason to be as concerned about the implications of the Holy Office's inquiry into the Jamaa for the Order as for the person of Tempels. It was the former that they seemed more intent on protecting. Furthermore, the traditional Franciscan conceptions of the role of Superior and the meaning of the convent differ from those of the Benedictine Order. Franciscans do not take a vow of stability, and the terms of their superiors are relatively short compared to those of abbots. Partly as a consequence, the role of a Franciscan superior *vis-à-vis* his men is not defined in as familial, diffuse, or all-understanding a way. Thus, although there were undoubtedly personal elements in the way that Tempels's Provincial reacted, his response was also conditioned by an institutionalized conception of his office which was unlike that of his closest Benedictine counterpart.

In levying sanctions upon Tempels that were not ordered or even advised by the Vatican, the Franciscan Provincial was also asserting the prerogatives of his office in another regard. In effect, he was affirming his autonomous right to discipline a member of his Order independently of Rome's disposition; at the same time he was contending that without either an official or a personal message from the Holy Office concerning their decision about Tempels, there was no basis for assuming that he had been acquitted by the tribunal. Catholic religious Orders, the Franciscans included, operate under a papal statute, which means that their respective constitutions defining and regulating their distinctive life style have been approved by Rome. However, Rome is not eager to interfere with the way that these constitutions are implemented by the Orders. This is clear from the response of the Vatican officials to the information received from Cardijn regarding the sanctions to which Tempels's Provincial had subjected him. It is of interest that Tempels himself never chose to present his case before the sacred Congregation for Religious in Rome. This provides an appeal system to which all religious priests, Sisters, and Brothers have recourse if they feel they have been unjustly dealt with by a local superior. We do not know to what degree Tempels's failure to avail himself of this mechanism emanated from his latent willingness to submit to the Provincial's rulings or his apprehension over the possibility of having to undergo a second type of Roman trial.

It should be noted that the Franciscan Provincial's power to apply and maintain the sanctions that he took against Tempels was reinforced by the ambiguity with which the highest echelons of the Church handled the 'case' of Tempels. The tribunal before which Tempels came conducted its hearings in secret. The outcome of these hearings was never publicly made known, apart from the 'coded' message that the article in the *Osservatore Romano* contained for 'insiders'. Tempels's Franciscan superiors claimed that they were never officially informed by Rome about its verdict. Thus, an unintended consequence of Rome's secrecy, on the one hand, and its diplomatic reluctance unduly to interfere with the local autonomy of religious superiors, on the other, contributed to the continuation of sanctions inconsistent with the outcome of the Holy Office's inquiry.

By and large, although during the years 1963 to 1966 a number of important confrontations took place between the Church and the Jamaa, the movement was accepted as a promising development, compatible with the most enlightened precepts and goals of Catholic missionary activity. Each time that the Jamaa was vigorously challenged by churchmen, it was always effectively defended by others. For example, 1964 saw the publication of two major articles about the Jamaa by priest-authors, the one eulogistic, the other severely critical.

In a group of articles on the Jamaa that he edited and published, Father O. Gérard, a Scheutist superior in Belgium, hailed the movement as 'a remarkable case of fecund adaptation in Africa'.[1] Admittedly, Gérard went on to say that the Jamaa was susceptible to 'risks and dangers'. Among these were the dangers of 'illuminism', 'a certain eroticism', excessive other-worldliness ('more religious than social'), and a greater emphasis on Bantu philosophy than on 'divine revelation'.[2] But, he continued, 'these few shadows, which for some are reasons for uneasiness and reserve, cannot eclipse the prodigious richness and fecundity of the "Jamaa" . . . The "Jamaa" is probably one of the great marvels of the missionary Church of our day. It constitutes what is perhaps a unique chance for the Church of the Congo and, who knows, of Black Africa.'[3]

In contradistinction to Gérard's laudatory essay and, in certain respects, deliberately opposed to it, was the article on the Jamaa that Father Dominique Nothomb, a Belgian White Father in Rwanda, published in the *Nouvelle Revue théologique*.[4] Despite its innocuous title ('A new form of catechism') and the assertions of appreciation with which the article began and ended, it was a relentless critique of the movement, its 'fragile doctrine', its charismatic nature ('. . . there is no programme, no method, no regulation whatsoever, no organization, no directive coming from above . . .') and of certain 'passages, many alas, . . . in the precious little book', *Notre Rencontre* by Tempels. Nothomb expressed great concern over what he considered Tempels's 'confusion' of 'spiritual paternity' that is 'psychological' in nature, with spiritual paternity that is 'supernatural and Christian'. It is to 'exercise' the latter rather than the former, Nothomb asserted, that the priest 'is sent by Christ and

    [1] O. Gérard, 'Un cas remarquable d'adaptation féconde en Afrique: La "Jamaa"', *Le Christ au monde*, vol. IX, no. 1 (1964), p. 18.
    [2] Ibid., no. 2, pp. 141–2.   [3] Ibid., p. 142.
    [4] Dominique Nothomb, 'Une nouzelle forme de catéchèse', *Nouvelle Revue théologique*, vol. 86, no. 7 (July–Aug. 1964), pp. 725–43.

the Church'. 'Supernatural, Christian, sacerdotal' paternity has two sets of essential characteristics, Nothomb insisted: 'radical discretion and disinterestedness', on the one hand, and a non-egalitarian, non-reciprocal 'universality', on the other. In Nothomb's opinion, the kind of relationship between the Jamaa priest and baba and mama that *Notre Rencontre* advocated 'perverted' these principles. But Nothomb reserved his special indignation for the 'doctrine of total and totally human union' that Tempels set forth. In Nothomb's view, such an attempt of the priest to be 'totally one with his people' was a violation of his 'consecration to God in virginity or celibacy'; for

the consecrated soul must know a certain solitude, a certain affective 'emptiness' . . . Consecration to God in virginity or celibacy consists precisely in keeping intact . . . a certain zone of impenetrable mystery . . . of refusing to entrust . . . this intimate secret to any person whatsoever, in order to offer it to Christ who takes total possession of it . . .

There is still another major theological reason, Nothomb argued, for which the priest's 'encounter' with his people ought not to be 'totally one', in the Jamaa sense of the term.

The priest is a humble minister, a servant of Christ and of men, a poor man himself, wounded by original sin and burdened with faults. He has no right to 'replace' his Lord in the heart of his people nor to impose on them a kind of possessive and proprietary tutelage. He cannot accept that the total love that the Christian owes his Lord be transferred to him . . . He [the priest] must give them something better than himself: the Word of Christ entrusted to the Church, the grace of the sacraments, the consolation of Christian hope, the radiance of Christ's charity . . .[1]

In sum, for Nothomb, the most fundamental and grave 'misunderstanding' in Jamaa doctrine, *Notre Rencontre*, and Tempels's interpretations is that they unduly identify the first and second commandments with one another, that is, the love of God with the love of man.

And so, in various forms during this period of 1963–1966, the debate about the virtues and promises, errors and hazards of the Jamaa proceeded inside the Catholic Church. The source of the difficulties that the movement posed for the doctrine and social organization of the Church was attributed by some to particular characteristics of Bantu culture. For other commentators, such as

[1] D. Nothomb, op. cit., p. 743.

Nothomb, they emanated primarily from the misinterpretations and misunderstandings of Scripture and Catholic doctrine in Tempels's own teachings and writings. In this atmosphere of ambivalence about the Jamaa, favourable attitudes towards the movement predominated sufficiently over negative or apprehensive ones, so that even a Nothomb felt it appropriate to end his critique of the Jamaa in a conciliatory fashion:

> If we have believed it useful, even necessary, to formulate reservations about *Notre Rencontre*, it is with the sole intention of contributing, in a fraternal spirit, to constructive reflection and to an adjustment of doctrine (une mise au point doctrinale) which can only be advantageous to the Jamaa movement and hence, to the Church in the Congo.[1]

In July 1965 the Centre de Recherches Sociologiques issued the final version of the study of the Jamaa, commissioned by the Episcopate of the Catholic Church in the Congo.[2] The report, circulated to all bishops, religious superiors, and Jamaa priests in the Congo, formally crystallized the essentially receptive and permissive stance towards the movement that the Congolese Church took at that time. To some extent, this 'Sociological Analysis of the Jamaa' legitimized such a position, because it carried the authority of a 'serious scientific study', and one that had been commissioned by the Episcopate. The informal transmission of its findings to a wider circle of clergy than those who were official recipients of the report also exerted some measure of social control on those churchmen who were inclined to adopt a more constraining or punitive attitude towards the Jamaa.

'Sociological Analysis of the Jamaa' was based on an earlier document, 'Sociological Notes on the Jamaa', also prepared by myself when director of the Centre de Recherches Sociologiques. These 'Sociological Notes' had been submitted to the Permanent Committee of the Bishops of the Congolese Church in July 1964. Earlier, in April 1964, I had circulated the 'Notes' to the most prominent Jamaa priests who had read them with nervous, critical appreciation. What had worried them most of all was how this report would be viewed by the Congolese Episcopate and eventually by Rome, and with what consequences for the movement. Monsignor

---

[1] D. Nothomb, op. cit., p. 743.
[2] Willy De Craemer, *Analyse sociologique de la Jamaa* (Léopoldville: Centre de Recherches Sociologiques), 1965, 79 pp.

Cornelis and Father Benoit had been the most anxious about how the so-called 'Jamaa paper' would be interpreted and eventually applied by church officials, 'given the mentality of the persons who will read the work'.[1]

... I have set down for you on the enclosed pages the essential comments that I thought had to be made ... I ask you to make strictly personal and private use of them. Under no circumstances do I want my name used in this case. However, I felt I could not pass over certain inaccuracies which might endanger everything, especially given the Roman perspective which you know ...[2]

Both men had written long letters to me congratulating me on my 'illuminating basic research' on the Jamaa, but offering detailed suggestions as to how the final Jamaa report to the bishops might be modified. Mainly, they hoped that the report would not too greatly emphasize several potentially disturbing features of the Jamaa. The ones Cornelis and Benoit cited were: the role that Tempels's encounter with Sister X played in the genesis and content of the movement; the stages of initiation, especially the 'fourth way'; the manner in which Tempels developed certain doctrinal notions in *Notre Rencontre* ('not yet sufficiently elaborated theologically to be subjected to a Roman criticism'); the 'anti-hierarchical character' of the Jamaa; and its other-worldliness or 'break with society'.

Although I took the reactions of Cornelis, Benoit, and other Jamaa priests into serious consideration and though I was sympathetic to their anxieties about provoking the local Episcopate and/or Rome into imposing strict disciplines on the movement, I did not allow the final draft of the report to be unduly influenced by these pressures. The 'Analysis' consisted of five chapters devoted respectively to the history and social composition of the Jamaa, the kind of movement it was, its distinctive initiation and socialization processes, its doctrine, and its dysfunctional as well as functional consequences for its members, their kin, the Catholic Church in the Congo, and for the larger society. Although the 'Analysis' did not pass an over-all judgement on the movement, it did end with a strong,

[1] Personal letter from Mgr. Cornelis to W. De Craemer, 27 Apr. 1964.
[2] Personal letter to W. De Craemer from Father Benoit, 13 July 1964. Benoit's admonition not to cite him in any way was only applicable to the period in the Jamaa's history under discussion, before the case of Tempels and the movement was tried by the Holy Office in Rome.

positive statement about the 'significance and consequences of the Jamaa for the Catholic Church in the Congo':

The . . . Church recognizes the limits and even certain dangers of the Jamaa. [But] it is still more impressed by the creative, spiritual contribution of the Jamaa and by all that it promises for the deep rooting of Christ's message among Catholic Africans in the Congo.[1]

In a sense, this sociological report represented a watershed in the history of the Jamaa's relationship to the official Church. The commissioning of the report by the bishops, the period of research that it entailed, and its final issuance constituted a suspense-ridden interval of 'entente cordiale' between the movement and the Ecclesia in which it originated. From another point of view, however, the spirit of search and beneficence associated with the report lasted no more than a year after it was completed and circulated. Beginning in the spring of 1966, a series of events were set in motion that cumulatively led to the imposition of severe controls on the Jamaa by local church authorities, xenophobically-tinged attacks against the movement by increasingly outspoken African priests, and the forced departure of most of the original Jamaa priests from the movement.

As might have been predicted, it was in the Kasai region of the Congo that the strongest measures were first taken against the Jamaa. The Kasai was the site of the greatest growth of the movement, and of the most widespread and intractable deviations. In a mimeographed letter dated 30 March 1966, and addressed to all the priests under his jurisdiction, Monsignor Bernard Mels, Scheutist Archbishop of Luluabourg, announced the directives that would henceforth apply to the Jamaa. As he explained, in the course of a visit he had just made to most of the mission posts in the diocese, he had become deeply troubled by the fact that 'along with many praises, more or less everywhere, we heard serious criticisms and suspicions [expressed] about the present evolution of the Jamaa'. Mels had reached the conclusion that the doctrinal errors in the movement, its deviations, and its elusiveness were consequences of the Jamaa's development into a 'popular mass movement':

As soon as the number of members became larger, and nuclei developed in sometimes remote localities, it became impossible for Jamaa priests adequately to follow the members and to give them indispensable spiritual

---

[1] Willy De Craemer, *Analyse sociologique de la Jamaa*, p. 79.

direction. The communication of the doctrine and the progressive initiation began to be done by the first 'tatu' and 'mamu', [Tshiluba words for 'baba' and 'mama'] then also by others formed by them, with all the dangers inherent in this system. In effect, persons of good-will are involved, but without theological or scriptural training, often not having the true sense of the Church and not realizing that in matters concerning Catholic doctrine, scriptural interpretation and discipline in the Church, they must refer to priests, non-Jamaa [as well as Jamaa].

In this pastoral letter, the same Monsignor Mels who, after a long visit to Benoit in early 1965 gave his full support to the Jamaa and expressed his unqualified belief in it as a 'truly spiritual Christianity adapted to the Bantu mentality', now took an extremely cautionary position. It was as if his disappointment over the non-realization of some of his original hopes in the Jamaa had joined forces with what he called his 'grave worries' about the movement, in such a way as to make him speak with the voice of a traditionalistic 'defender of the faith'. In his 1966 letter, Mels advocated that the Jamaa be regulated and become more hierarchical; that only a limited number of Jamaa members receive what he called 'advanced training and spiritual guidance'; and that this process 'remain under the vigilance of the authority of the Church which has to be informed objectively and completely in order to be able to watch over its orthodoxy'.

In this same document, Mels issued a series of directives, explicitly designed to effect these goals. He placed his greatest emphasis on the fundamental and many-sided role that Jamaa and non-Jamaa priests alike must play in 'the preservation of the true doctrine of Christ', through a tight control of the movement, its teachings, activities, and membership. He also stressed the importance of strict diocesan jurisdiction over the local Jamaa. Thus, Mels's directives included the prohibition of night-time meetings of the Jamaa, unless they were held 'in a designated place, in agreement with the parish priest, who should have access to them at any time, and . . . be able to participate in them'. Jamaa baba and mama from mission centres and parishes outside the archdiocese of Luluabourg were to be discouraged from organizing meetings or teaching, 'above all, without the consent of local priests'. Local Jamaa priests were to be responsible for 'safeguarding faithfulness to the Jamist ideal'. Each time they delegated this responsibility to a baba, he had to have an 'attestation' to that effect to show to the priests in the parish involved. Jamaa priests of the Luluabourg archdiocese were to be the authorities to whom other Jamists should address themselves 'in order to receive approbation for their progressive initiation' into the movement. Mels stated explicitly that, 'we do not approve the custom of going to other dioceses to receive initiations from priests whom we do not know and who are not mandated by us.' All Jamaa members who had attained a certain 'degree' in the movement should be known as such by their local priests. And it was 'desirable' that Jamaa priests who 'guided certain members in the more advanced aspects of Jamaa spirituality obtain information on . . . at least the apparent value of the candidate' from the priests from his place of residence. Finally, Mels asserted his disapproval of Jamaa groups and meetings organized for young persons: 'The Jamaa is a spirituality for married people . . . The materials treated in Jamaa lessons are not appropriate for the young.'

Mels ended his pastoral letter with an admonition to his clergy to be 'prudent' and 'paternal towards all those among us who sometimes are mistaken albeit in good faith . . . Let us try progressively to lead them back to the right path. We have not come to condemn, but to save and heal.' The contents of this letter, Mels concluded, were to be communicated to the leaders and principal members of the Jamaa in each mission station or parish, as well as to the priests to whom it was addressed. But, Mels stressed, this should be done 'without giving it more publicity than necessary'.

Despite Mels's restraint, his pastoral letter was destined to have a much more widespread impact than he intended or anticipated. Various factors converged to cause this. First, Mels himself was one of the more influential bishops in the Congolese Episcopate. Furthermore, from the inception of Catholic missionary activities in the late nineteenth century up to the time of Mels, the Kasai missions were considered to be models of organizational success, spiritual vitality, and of innovative social action. For these reasons alone, Mels's pastoral stance had important implications for the entire Congolese Church. Although he had counselled discretion, Mels's 'message' travelled rapidly beyond the Luluabourg diocese, via the Jamaa communication network, on the one hand, and that of the national Church, on the other.

The next critical event in what might be called the devolution of relations between the official Church and the Jamaa occurred when a theological study of the movement that had been commissioned by the Episcopate was completed and mimeographed for distribution. This study, entitled *Le Christ parmi les Africains: Essai autour de la spiritualité jamaa*, was written by Godefroid Mukenge, a Congolese Scheutist priest from the Kasai. It appeared in 1968, several years after Mukenge undertook the theological inquiry asked of him. The study's conclusions were highly favourable to the Jamaa.[1] In Mukenge's view, the movement was 'authentically Christian . . .' with a 'truly African countenance', an 'authentically African heart', and some of the 'same synthetic visions' of 'a genuinely evangelical aggiornamento' as contained in the texts of Vatican Council II. Especially notable, Mukenge affirmed, was the fact that the Jamaa, 'in this country of recent Christianity', represented an at once constructive and creative breakthrough of the Congolese Church's long-standing tendency 'mechanically [to] copy . . . Western directives and models'. In his judgement, it also constituted a much-needed exemplification of the 'necessity' and 'urgency' of the fact that 'today, more than ever . . . lay persons must be given the full place which is theirs.' For, Mukenge stated, 'up until now, the apostolate has always been conceived in function of priests, as if only the cleric were the Church.' Arguing on behalf of the Jamaa, Mukenge concluded that:

. . . The spontaneous action and the initiatives of dynamic Christians must be supported, instead of condemning them to silence, based on the conviction that the only valid action is the one that has been mandated by the hierarchy. Pastors should refrain from creating or inciting tension between movements of Western origin, which so far are the only ones to receive official mandate, and movements characterized by a more African sensibility, which emerge through the action of the Holy Spirit . . .

Despite all the work that Mukenge devoted to his theological study of the Jamaa, and the eagerness with which it was awaited by church officials, it was never distributed to the bishops and clergy, as originally intended. Instead, its general circulation was impeded by the bishops from the Kasai region, who neither formally approved the analysis and conclusions presented in the report nor recommended its diffusion. The reasons behind the Kasai bishops' stance are not easy to decipher. By the time that Mukenge's report was completed, the majority of Kasai bishops were Congolese,

[1] The quotations that follow were excerpted from pp. 1–2 and 134–6 of Mukenge's essay.

rather than Belgian, as had formerly been the case. In theory, they ought to have been especially pleased with the emphasis that Mukenge's report placed on two interconnected themes. On the one hand, he stressed how important it was for the Church to become more 'authentically African'; and on the other, he underscored the degree to which the Jamaa exemplified the compatibility between this goal and the deepening of 'authentic Christianity'. However, the Congolese bishops who were educated and socialized in a colonially-oriented, conservative, pre-Vatican Council II conception of the 'Church as Mission' were as apprehensive about the orthodoxy of Mukenge's position, as they were receptive to it. Furthermore, they were concerned about the challenge to their episcopal authority and notion of hierarchy that Mukenge's affirmations about the role of the laity in the Church's 'apostolate' constituted. Assertions such as the following made these bishops uneasy:

> In speaking of the Jamaa in the Congo, we are in the context of a young Church. But the fact that these Christians are young in Christianity, that they are lay persons, and that they are simple people without very advanced religious instruction takes away nothing from the fact that the Holy Spirit, who favours no one in particular, works in them.[1]

In this respect, and in several other regards, the Kasai bishops felt that Mukenge underplayed the development of serious deviations in the Jamaa, as well as the extent to which they originated and were spread among the very kinds of lay persons that his report extolled.[2]

In South Katanga (in the dioceses of Lubumbashi and of Kamina),[3] as in Kasai, the Jamaa began increasingly to fall into disfavour with the official Church. But here the patterns involved were somewhat different, and one of the major net consequences was the deposition of all the Belgian priests who had been charismatic leaders of the movement.

In South Katanga, unlike Kasai, the Jamaa was vigorously supported by local Congolese bishops. In the spring of 1969, for example, Archbishop Eugene Kabanga of Lubumbashi (ex-Élisabeth-

---

[1] Mukenge, *Le Christ parmi les Africains*, p. 2.

[2] It is of some interest to note that Godefroid Mukenge has become bishop of Luisa, in South Kasai. He has been promoted to the ranks of the Episcopate, but to the relatively non-prestigious position of heading a recently created, small, peripheral frontier diocese.

[3] The Kamina diocese includes the city of Kolwezi.

ville) began his initiation into the movement, receiving *mafundisho* twice a week from the same Jamaa couple who had instructed Father Benoit. As a convinced Jamaa member, and one with special authority, Kabanga tried to work from within the movement and to 'purify' it gradually of its errors and deviations. His primary method was thoroughly in keeping with Jamaa norms and with Congolese tradition more generally. He helped to organize a number of meetings in which he tried to act as negotiator between the Katete baba, on the one hand, and the non-deviationist baba and Jamaa priests, on the other. Some of these meetings took place at the Jesuit residence in Lubumbashi, where Father Xavier DeWinter lived with several non-Jamaa colleagues who were sympathetic to the movement and to his involvement in it. Perhaps the most memorable of these meetings was the one that occurred in connection with Palm Sunday 1969. That morning, a completely nude Katete baba appeared in church, and marched in the customary Palm Sunday procession, causing great consternation among laity and clergy alike. In response to this incident, Monsignor Kabanga later summoned the principal Katete baba to the bishop's residence, where he attempted to go through the implications of this occurrence with them. Here, as in all other such meetings with Kabanga, other Jamaa priests, and non-Katete Jamists, the dissident baba proved recalcitrant. They refused to acknowledge any wrong-doing in the Palm Sunday incident, and were unyielding on the more general subject of the errors and deviations into which it was claimed that they and their followers had fallen. Furthermore, in their various meetings with Kabanga, it became apparent that these baba were receiving moral support from a certain type of Congolese priest (a fact to which we shall return).

Like Kabanga, Monsignor Barthélémy Malunga, the Vicar General of the Kamina diocese, also became an initiated Jamaa member. In 1969, he, too, was at work inside the movement, trying to rectify its errors and correct its deviations. Malunga's chief approach was through editing and reorganizing extant *mafundisho*, and composing new ones. He submitted all the *mafundisho* that he revised or wrote to the head baba of the region for his comments and criticisms. The mutually agreed upon *mafundisho* were then taught more widely in local Jamaa circles. Malunga also tried to bring about closer relations between the Jamaa, the Legion of Mary (a pious association of lay Catholics), and other Catholic

Action groups. However, Katete baba and their adherents proved as resistant to Malunga's efforts in Kamina and Kolwezi as to Kabanga's activities in Lubumbashi.

In both milieux, the Katete factions were reinforced in their position by a genre of Congolese priest generally referred to by Congolese lay people as 'un drôle d'abbé' (a queer kind of [diocesan] priest). This sort of man was a curious cross between an old-fashioned, authoritarian priest, a militantly nationalistic Congolese man, and the leader of a traditional African religious movement.[1] Such priests were more numerous and aggressive in urban, industrialized South Katanga, than in the quieter, more rural setting of the Kamina diocese. But in both places their approach to the Jamaa was the same, and their impact equally powerful. In collusion with principal Katete baba, they worked to 'take over' the local Jamaa, to end the charismatic authority of Belgian Jamaa priests in the movement, and to keep them from participating in important Jamaa meetings. The Katete baba and their Congolese priest allies succeeded in doing all this, so that by the summer of 1969, although Father Benoit in Lubumbashi and Father Frans in Kolwezi were not personally disaffected from the movement, they were nevertheless eased out of their positions of legitimate leadership. From this time onwards, none of the original group of Belgian priest-leaders was permitted to have other than a peripheral relationship to the collective activities of the Jamaa.

The years 1969 to 1971 were marked by a series of formal reactions to these Jamaa developments, on the part of four different bishops in South Katanga and in Kasai. The first and most severe of these came from Monsignor Joseph Nkongolo, the Bishop of Mbuji-Mayi, Kasai. In his Pastoral Letter (Number 1), dated 6 February 1969, Nkongolo declared that, 'from this day forward . . . ALL JAMAA ACTIVITY IS SUSPENDED THROUGHOUT THE ENTIRE DIOCESE . . . [capitalization in original text].' Nkongolo recalled that in 1962, he had only authorized the Jamaa 'ad experimentum' (as an experiment). Over the 'seven trial years', he went on to say:

The Jamaa's doctrinal deviations have continued on their course, and do not seem to be amenable to correction, because they are preached

---

[1] This 'drôle d'abbé' pattern extended to Luluabourg, where one such Congolese priest tried to usurp Father Godefroid Mukenge's position in the diocese. Congolese priests who fit this description also 'surfaced' in various regions of the country during the 1964–5 Congo Rebellion.

by persons who, believing themselves to be endowed with special charisma, place themselves above all non-initiates, whether they be priests, or even bishops! The Jamaa is flying into pieces virtually everywhere. There is no ONE JAMAA, but rather VARIOUS JAMAAS, two or three in the same parish, that pull against each other, are cool to one another, and sometimes get into fistfights with each other! . . . The situation is too serious . . . Radical measures are called for . . . Suspension . . . is the only way to put an end to the confusion that prevails in the bosom of the Jamaa, in order to rethink the problem in a calm and clear state of mind . . .

In the interim, Nkongolo appointed a four-man commission of priests 'charged with shedding light on Jamaa spirituality, from a dogmatic, exegetical and moral point of view . . .'. From them was expected a study whose results would help eventually to 're-launch an orthodox Jamaa'. The identities of the members of the commission were kept secret, and all those interested in providing them with relevant information were encouraged to do so through the impersonal medium of the secretariat of the bishopric.

The next major stand taken by a bishop against the progression of deviations in the Jamaa and the seeming incorrigibility of the Katete factions came from the Luluabourg diocese in Kasai. (A Congolese priest, Monsignor Martin-Leonard Bakole, had succeeded Monsignor Mels as archbishop of this see.) In his Pastoral Letter (Number 8), of 19 October 1970, Bakole set forth what he termed his 'exact position . . . on the Jamaa and its future'. His statement about the Jamaa and the constraints on the movement that it imposed were considerably milder than those issued by Nkongolo. He was also more inclined than Nkongolo to work from within the movement, relying heavily on the major non-Katete baba of the region.

After briefly reviewing some of the early contributions that the Jamaa had made to 'the harmony of the Christian family' as well as to 'positive charity in the difficult moments that the country has known', Bakole turned to the 'abuses . . . deviations . . . and aberrations . . . that very quickly found their way into [the movement]'. These have developed 'to such a point', he declared, 'that at the present time, it is only from this negative perspective that one knows the Jamaa . . . Almost everywhere, the Jamaa seems to have transgressed its principles . . .' Bakole, like Nkongolo, appointed a committee to make a study of 'doctrinal points' in the Jamaa. To this committee, which he called a 'Council of Sages', he nominated the principal baba-founders of the Jamaa in the diocese, his Vicar

General Monsignor Kapanga, and also the same Father Mukenge (now Rector of the Major Seminary), who had made the theological study of the Jamaa commissioned but never circulated by the Episcopate. To Mukenge and Kapanga, Bakole entrusted the task of 'controlling and guiding' the Council's work so that it would be done 'in conformity with the theology of the magisterium [ordinary teaching] in the Catholic Church and the authentic Gospel of Christ'. From this council, Bakole expected 'a sure criterion to distinguish the leopards from the lambs' in the Jamaa. While their study was still in progress, the only important prohibition to which Bakole subjected the movement was that of forbidding the conferring of the 'third way' on anyone in the diocese.

The most poignant pronouncement on the Jamaa came from Monsignor Eugene Kabanga, Archbishop of Lubumbashi, on 30 October 1970, eleven days after Bakole's pastoral letter appeared. Kabanga reluctantly admitted the failure of all his efforts as a Jamaa member to re-socialize the Katete groups in the movement. His new position was enunciated through an intermediary. The letter on the Jamaa that he released on 30 October was signed by his Vicar General, Monsignor André Muanza, whom he authorized to speak in his name. The letter was addressed to all the priests of the Lubumbashi archdiocese and copies 'for information' were sent to every bishop in whose territory the Jamaa existed.

The Kabanga–Muanza letter made a much stronger affirmation than either Bakole or Nkongolo of 'all the good that has been realized by the Jamaa'. In fact, it went so far as to say that:

> The religious deepening it creates, the authentic charity it develops, the Christian sense of family it helps discover, all that is a certain sign of the supernatural influence that guides it. This movement which is manifestly born of the action of the Holy Spirit in our Christendom enriches it to such a degree that it is our heartfelt desire to support it so that it can realize all the spiritual good of which it is the bearer.

However, the letter conceded, this same inspired movement had developed doctrinal errors and moral deviations of sufficient gravity 'seriously [to] alter . . . the sense of the Church'. Kabanga's deep personal chagrin over the futility of his own efforts to 'purify' the Jamaa from within showed in his letter:

> . . . Certain members of the Jamaa have claimed and still claim to receive their message from God alone and deny the apostolic authority exercised by the Bishop and his emissaries. The episcopal authority has been

very patient for a long time, always hoping that the dissidents, moved by Christ's grace, would come to understand their errors and return to better dispositions. The situation has not improved. Therefore we can no longer postpone taking measures so that the Jamaa will be purified of its harmful elements, and will put the charismas that God has conferred upon it at the service of the Church . . .

For these reasons, the letter went on to say, the Archbishop of Lubumbashi had decided that, until further notice, all activities of the Jamaa were suspended, especially meetings to initiate new members into the third way. Kabanga qualified his stand by permitting several kinds of Jamaa meetings to continue. Meetings called by the priest of the parish to which a local Jamaa belongs were to be allowed. At these, *mafundisho* could be given either by the priest himself or by a lay person whom he designated. Gatherings of Jamaa members for funerals and mourning rites, as well as for the rendering of mutual aid, were also approved.

Like Nkongolo and Bakole, Kabanga established local procedures for reappraising the Jamaa. He did this with the continuing hope both that the movement could be helped to 'rediscover its original inspiration' and that he himself could arrive at enlightened policy decisions regarding the Jamaa. Rather than appoint a study commission or a committee of sages, Kabanga put a particular Congolese diocesan priest, Abbé Tharcisse Isimba, in charge of 'the problem of the Jamaa'. Isimba was empowered to make contact with all priests in parishes where a Jamaa existed, and to call parish and interparish Jamaa meetings either for the transmission of religious teachings, or for the collection of information. Eventually, he was to present a report to Kabanga, who would then 'take whatever decisions were appropriate to restore the Jamaa to full activity in the archdiocese'.

In the autumn of 1971 a fourth bishop of the Catholic Church in the Congo took action against the Jamaa. Monsignor Victor Keuppens, Bishop of Kamina, issued a letter making public his official 'condemnation' of the Jamaa in his diocese (of which Kolwezi was a part). This action dealt a particularly hard blow to the movement, not only because some of the measures imposed were more severe than those enforced by Nkongolo, Bakole, and Kabanga, but also because their symbolic import was very great; for Kolwezi was the site of the Jamaa's charismatic beginnings.

Earlier in 1971, when the Kamina diocese was split into two parts,

Keuppens had become bishop of the new Kolwezi diocese (while Monsignor Malunga was named bishop of the reorganized Kamina diocese). Keuppens's appointment and his move to Kolwezi seem to have brought him into closer contact with certain parish priests in that area who were worried about the Jamaa. They had grown increasingly distraught over what they felt was the uncontrolled spread of Jamaa deviations, and their own loss of ecclesiastical authority in the face of them. Keuppens, himself a Franciscan, was now directly influenced by several fellow Franciscans in Kolwezi whose pastoral outlook was quite different from that held by Jamaa priests like Tempels, Frans, Erik, and Jerome. In effect, it was the 'routinized' version of Franciscan tradition which came to predominate. This aspect emphasized organizational efficiency, priestly authority, and the virtue of obedience, rather than the affectivity, joyous mysticism, and loving union with all living creatures expressed by St. Francis.

Keuppens's letter condemning the Jamaa and prohibiting virtually all its activities deeply shocked Father Frans. Although he had known that an episcopal pronouncement on the Jamaa was forthcoming, his earlier discussions and negotiations with the bishop had led him to believe that it would be a moderate statement. Instead, Keuppens's letter was drastically disapproving.

Keuppens had moved by degrees toward this extreme position throughout 1971. At first he merely set certain conditions on Jamaa meetings, such as ruling that they could be held in parish halls, but not in private homes unless a local parish priest was present. After a number of months, in response to persisting Katete practices, and the mounting indignation of non-Jamaa priests, Keuppens took a second, more serious, step. He announced that any Jamaa member who did not immediately cease to practise the deviations, or who participated in them in any way, would be denied the Church's sacraments. Before any Jamist engaged in these practices could be fully reinstated in the Church, he or she would have to express repentance for past misdeeds by making an individual confession to the parish priest. Not long after this announcement a dramatic test case arose in the diocese. A Jamaa mama died, and was refused a church burial by her parish priest. Grief-stricken and angered by the occurrence, Father Frans committed a twofold act of religious defiance. He not only disobeyed his bishop by providing the mama in question with a religious burial service, but he crossed over juridical church boundaries to do so. He performed funeral rites in a parish where he had no legal right to do so: in the parish to which she belonged, rather than the one of which he was a pastor.

The Keuppens's letter of autumn 1971, then, constituted a third step in a progression of acts to curtail and reform the Kolwezi Jamaa. After it appeared, a group of local Jamaa members, who continued their meetings without approval, were denied communion. They responded by walking out of their parish church. A chain reaction of Jamaa protests was thereby ignited. As an expression of their solidarity with the reprimanded group, Jamaa members in several other parishes ceased attending Mass. Since Jamaa baba and mama were the most devout members of every Kolwezi parish, the churches were soon emptied.

These occurrences did not make Keuppens retract his decisions. But it is significant to note that at a provincial meeting of the Katanga bishops held in Lubumbashi at the end of 1971, Keuppens's policy was not adopted more generally. Although his condemnation of the Jamaa was discussed and considered in the end, the bishops decided against a joint statement. It seems likely that Monsignors Malunga and Kabanga played significant roles in preventing a collective condemnation of the Jamaa throughout Katanga. It was left to each bishop to determine how he would deal with the movement in his own diocese.

By 1971, then, although no provincial, national or supra-national church action had been taken against the Jamaa, the movement was subject to a wide range of formal regulations, restrictions, and penalties in the key dioceses of Kasai and Katanga. Furthermore, a number of its original priest-leaders had permanently left the Congo. Tempels, of course, was still confined to the Franciscan convent in Hasselt. The stresses and strains of this last phase of Jamaa history proved too much for Frans, who suffered a breakdown and had to return to Belgium. The nationalization of Union Minière, as well as the increased Africanization of the Congolese Church, diminished and made obsolete the very special pastoral roles that Erik had formerly played. Gradually he came to see that because he was locally associated with a now disparaged era in Katanga, Union Minière, and the Jamaa, there was no meaningful role he could play. After a period of work in Kinshasa at the secretariat of the Episcopate of the Congolese Catholic Church, he too left for Belgium. Elderly, tired, physically ailing Bonaventure also retired to Belgium. Jerome had become a professor of anthropology in a North American university. He continued to spend every summer in Belgium, and to teach and write out of his expert knowledge of Luba culture. I myself, now a member of the sociology faculty of a Canadian university, was writing my doctoral dissertation on the Jamaa. I commuted each summer to the Congo, to keep abreast of developments in the society, and to continue my research activities there. Benoit and Xavier were the only two of the first Jamaa-priests who still lived and worked all year long in the Congo. But, as indicated earlier, they had been pushed to the periphery of the movement's activities by Katete groups and by the intervention of a few Congolese diocesan priests. And so, Tempels, Frans, Erik, Bonaventure, Jerome, myself, Benoit, and Xavier were dispersed and disbanded. Yet, we retained our belief in the 'original inspiration' of the Jamaa, our common mystical memories, and an abiding sense of the deep and complex ways in which we were irrevocably linked to each other.[1]

Local Congolese clergymen who felt that the official Church had failed to bring its full force to bear on disciplining the Jamaa continued to be heard. One of the most vociferous was Abbé Placide Mukendi, of Mbuji-Mayi. Mukendi published a long, accusatory article entitled, 'La Jamaa et son avenir' [The Jamaa and its Future], in the March 1971 issue of the *Revue du clergé africain*,[2] a journal of long-standing reputation and influence in church circles throughout Central Africa. In addition to his own observations, Mukendi cited as primary sources 'information' and 'documentation' provided

---

[1] The exodus of some Jamaa priests from the Congo, and the increasing marginality of others, is part of a larger social process currently under way in Zairois (Congolese) society. Both in Catholic and Protestant Church milieux, Independence has not only led to a greater preponderance of African clergy, but also to a diminution and a certain devaluation of the missionary role. Historically, it has always been part of missionary ideology that an ultimate goal of the missions was to train qualified indigenous personnel to replace the foreign cadres. However, the transition now taking place is not without strain for foreign missionaries, whose anticipatory socialization only partially prepared them for their displacement. This transition is made all the more difficult by some of the anti-mission, anti-foreign propaganda surrounding it, by the difficulty of finding meaningful roles to play in the missionaries' home countries, and by what appears to be the closing down of missionary activities in other world areas as well.

[2] Placide Mukendi, 'La Jamaa et son avenir', *Revue du clergé africain*, Vol. XXVI, no. 2 (Mar. 1971), pp. 142–68.

by 'priest-colleagues', and also by the French women, Mesdemoiselles Lebaindre and Grandjean, who had earlier denounced
Tempels. Mukendi blamed the errors and deviations of the Jamaa
on Tempels's own writings and teachings, particularly his concept of
encounter. Mukendi cited this as 'the cause of most of the troubles
in the Jamaa'. He inveighed against the 'fanaticism' of Jamaa members who seemed to think that Tempels's teachings are 'more evangelical than the doctrine of the Church'. And he was particularly
vitriolic about the fact that 'certain wicked tongues go so far as
to attribute [the errors and deviations] to Blacks who wanted to
Africanize the Christian religion! They thereby assume that the
original Jamaa was completely pure, completely immaculate.'
In Mukendi's opinion, 'the purification of the Jamaa is . . . impossible', so that the only appropriate solution was to 'strike it once
and for all . . . from the list of Catholic movements'. This, ideally,
should be done through a common accord of church officials on all
levels of the hierarchy: from the Provincial Conferences of the
Bishops of Katanga and Kasai to the Plenary Assembly of the entire
Episcopate of the Congo, to the authorities in Rome. Mukendi's
article ended with a renewed attack on the 'great defenders of the
Jamaa in the very bosom of the Church' and a reaffirmation of his
own orthodox faith:

> They [the Jamaa defenders] include bishops, priests, religious, sisters
> and even lay persons capable of deploying—as they have always done up
> until now—all their diplomacy to defend [the Jamaa]. It is even reported
> that a Franciscan has said that the Order will defend the Reverend Father
> Tempels to the end! Is it the Reverend Father Tempels or Christ whom the
> Church must follow? . . .[1]

> Believing ourselves to be acquitted of our duty with respect to the People
> of God, we now only have to thank all those who helped us . . . realize
> this modest work . . .
> It is up to those who are in charge of leading the People of God to
> find what they *must* [emphasis Mukendi's] do for the greatest glory of God
> and for the greatest good of the faithful.[2]

At the end of 1971, the 'visible', non-Katete Jamaa continued
faithfully within the limits set by the bishops of Katanga and Kasai,
acting independently of one another. It was a more prudent, repe-
titious, and conventional Jamaa than the one that existed in the

[1] P. Mukendi, op. cit., p. 166.   [2] Ibid., p. 168.

1950s and '60s. The Katete faction continued to function, unpersuaded and seemingly undiminished by all the formal and informal attempts of the official Church to bring it back into line. But now, partly as a consequence of these efforts, the Katete-Jamaa had gone underground, where it was no longer possible for the Catholic Church of the Congo directly to observe or influence it.

CHAPTER IX

Social and Cultural Significance
of the Jamaa

ONE of the most distinctive characteristics of the Jamaa is its transformative power. The changes that it effects in the Bantu beliefs, attitudes, and behaviour patterns of its African membership are more profound and lasting than those brought about by most other Central African religious movements. Although the Jamaa builds on the earlier conversion of its baba and mama to Catholicism, the impact of the movement goes deeper than earlier relationships with the Church that these men and women are likely to have had. It is not only African lay members who have been significantly changed by their participation in the Jamaa, but also the group of European priests who helped to found and shape the movement. Like the baba and mama, they have recurrently testified that involvement in the Jamaa constitutes one of the most important religious and personal experiences of their lives.

The capacity of the Jamaa to transmute the attitudes and behaviour of its members has implications that extend beyond the empirical parameters of this particular movement. The Jamaa seems to have properties that enable it to change basic cultural and even personality patterns to a greater degree than most social environments and structures do. Thus, studying the Jamaa allows us to identify social arrangements that are conducive to breakthroughs in what Talcott Parsons has called the pattern-maintenance characteristics of culture and personality.

The general sociological significance of the Jamaa lies not only in its bearing on the dynamics of cultural and psychic change; the movement also reveals what aspects of Bantu, Flemish-Belgian, and Catholic culture are the most persistent. For, even in the face of the Jamaa's powerfully transformative qualities, certain culture patterns that its members brought to the movement have been particularly steadfast. An examination of the Jamaa thus sheds light on some of the origins and modalities of non-change as well as change.

The most fundamental change that the Jamaa has wrought in its African members is diminution of the high level of existential anxiety and distrust transmitted to them through the apprehensive world-view of their traditional culture. Looked at from this vantage point, initiation into the movement requires and develops the capacity to relate to others and to open one's self up to them with growing confidence, love, and faith. Ideally, this continually expanding circle of others begins with the husband–wife relationship, advances to encounter and union with Christ and Mary, comes to include the priest as 'the other Christ' and representative of the Church, and moves outward from there to encompass other relatives, Jamaa baba and mama and their spiritual children, and even strangers. The ideology, sequence of rituals, and patterned mystical religious experiences that the Jamaa provides seem to be effective in inducting members into an outlook characterized by increased personal, interpersonal, and cosmic trust and security. Closely associated with the development of a less dreading and vigilant perspective is the evolution from particularism towards universalism that Jamaa members also undergo. With these shifts in their relationship to their own inner thoughts and feelings and to those of significant others, Jamaa members become less fearful of the metaphysical forces unleashed by conscious or unconscious human interventions. This, in turn, reduces their need to have offensive or defensive recourse to traditional magic in order to protect themselves and their kin against adversity.

Jamaa priests as well as lay members grow in trust, capacity to love, and universalism. The priests also develop deeper, less apprehensive contact with their own unconscious thoughts, feelings, and dreams. Their participation in the movement progressively frees them from fears about strong emotions, self-divulgence, and affectionate closeness to others which their religious training and vows had previously instilled in them. Their sense of solidarity with lay people and Africans increases, as does their sense of unity with one another. Furthermore, the Jamaa strengthens their commitment to Catholicism and enriches their cultic observance in ways that expand rather than contract their view of other religions and persuasions.

Another basic change that the Jamaa produces in its baba and mama is in attitudes towards work and towards the allocation and meaning of money and material possessions. The distinctive elements in the Jamist attitude to work are subtle. The profound religiosity of the baba and mama does not express itself in the fervent sense of vocation or calling that, for example, characterizes the Protestant ethic. For, in the Jamaa value system, work is not as important as spiritual activities concerned with encounter and union between husband and wife. It is this relationship and the effort to perfect it that constitute the cornerstone of the movement. The oneness of husband and wife is considered to be the indispensable precondition for establishing the kind of personal relationship with Christ and Mary from which all transformative effects of the Jamaa are believed to flow.

Although the Jamaa's emphasis on mystical encounter reduces work to a lower level of importance, it does not lead the baba and mama to neglect their work or disparage the importance of doing it well. On the contrary, at Union Minière, for instance, Jamaa men are known to be exemplary employees. They work conscientiously, with notable skill and pride in accomplishment, and their absentee rate is low. Jamaa women tend to be diligent housekeepers, maintaining a more orderly and well-tended home than many non-Jamaa women.

The excellence in work that Jamaa members display seems to be a consequence of the security and solidarity they achieve through the movement rather than of a religious belief in the inherent sacredness of work or in its ultimate meaning. The reduction of anxiety and distrust that the Jamaa effects, along with the increased sense of oneness that it builds, seem to enhance the ability of the baba and mama to do their assigned work with competence, composure, and satisfaction. This is all the more remarkable when one considers how much of their psychic energy is invested in the explicitly religious activities of the movement. Only those relatively few members of the Jamaa who are primary school teachers (*moniteurs*) are subject to conflicts between their occupational and religious obligations that have deleterious consequences for their work (as indicated in Chapter VI).

The attitude towards work that characterizes the baba and mama has its counterpart in the subculture of Jamaa priests. The Flemish, Franciscan-Catholic, working-class tradition in which these priests originate is one that trained them to value work positively and to perform it vigorously, methodically, and well. Although in this tradition work is considered a major focus of human existence, it is not approached with pious solemnity or mystically glorified. It is carried out in an intensive way, galvanized by a matter-of-fact, though religiously derived, conviction that well-performed work is meaningful and good. The Jamaa priests brought this outlook on work into the movement. It has been strengthened by the ways in which their participation in the Jamaa has enhanced the sense of creativity and significance that they derive from their work as priest-missionaries. In turn, the revitalized relationship to their work that the Jamaa priests enjoy contributes to the quiet, steady way in which the baba and mama go about their daily tasks.

The Jamaa also exerts a distinctive influence on its members' conceptions of money and material possessions. Jamaa families take fastidious care of their homes and their personal belongings. They regard the willingness of husbands and wives to collaborate in the planning and administration of the family budget as symbolic of the open, egalitarian, trusting relationship between husband and wife that should develop through participation in the Jamaa. They also consider it important to contribute money, as well as goods and services, to ceremonial and mutual-aid activities associated with the movement. Yet, the over-all Jamaa attitude towards money and possessions is detached and disinterested. Baba and mama attach greater importance to spiritual than to material attainments, and they do not value money and possessions as ends in themselves. Such attitudes are markedly different from those held by non-Jamaa men and women of similar backgrounds. Congolese who do not belong to the movement are more inclined to covet and accumulate money and possessions, and to seek higher status and more power through them. Involvement in the Jamaa has modified the outlook of baba and mama on material things so that it resembles the pragmatic idealism with which Jamaa priests fulfill their vow of poverty. Money and goods are not rejected with other-worldly absolutism. Rather, they are regarded and used in ways that symbolize or help to attain the spiritual values and goals of the movement. Thus, the particular type of Catholicism with which African Jamaa members have had the closest contact has significantly altered their economic orientation. In addition, traditional African gift-exchange patterns have influenced the Jamaa propensity to share freely their worldly goods with members of the large, extended kinship system that the Jamaa constitutes.

We have seen that the Jamaa has a latent, constraining influence on its members' participation in both the educational and political sectors of Congolese society. Here, the other-worldly tendencies of the movement are the most salient. Jamaa educational and political perspectives originated in some of the mystical preaching of Tempels that were incorporated into the *mafundisho*. They have been reinforced by the quietly indignant way in which Jamaa members have reacted to the moral deportment of the educated élite in Congolese society, and to the divisiveness, violence, and corruption that marked Congolese political life in the early years of Independence. Thus Jamaa withdrawal from the political sphere and its playing-down of formal education contain elements of religiously based passive protest. These attitudes towards education and the polity sharply distinguish Jamaa from non-Jamaa Congolese: ambition, and zeal to obtain as much schooling and as much political interest as possible are two of the most prominent characteristics of present-day Congolese social life.

In active and passive, manifest and latent ways the Jamaa has affected the attitudes and behaviour of its members in the major institutional spheres of their society. The Jamaa has transformed critical aspects of its African members' traditional outlook on kinship, economy, polity, and education, as well as religion and magic. The testimonials, dreams, and expressive behaviour of the baba and mama indicate that these changes are not superficial, but involve deep layers of their personalities.

Jamaa priests have been as profoundly influenced by their involvement in the movement as lay members. Their commitment to Christianity is deepened, revitalized, and made more personal. Their conception of the Catholic Church and their relationship to it take on new existential and human significance. And they achieve a greater degree of synthesis between Bantu African and Belgian Catholic cultures than they have previously known. All this is accompanied by the kinds of emotion, both painful and exhilarating, and of religious experience which suggest that the Jamaa brings about personality changes in its priest members as well as in its baba and mama.

Certain features of the Jamaa and of the setting in which it has developed contribute to the movement's powerful capacity to change its members' beliefs, attitudes, and behaviour. To begin with, the Jamaa has sustained much of the emotional, charismatic atmosphere that characterized its early days. Furthermore, the Jamaa's doctrinal and ritualistic emphasis on union involves its members in a continuing series of encounter group experiences. The high value placed on feeling in both Bantu culture and Franciscan culture adds to the emotional quality of the Jamaa's ambience. The climate that is thus created facilitates the conversion of beliefs and attitudes.

The impact of the Jamaa on its African members is increased by their traditional 'other-orientation'. Their sense of identity is more communal and less individualistic than that of persons socialized in a modern Western society. As we have seen, the Bantu cosmic view in which the baba and mama were raised stresses the power that the thoughts and feelings of significant others have over the events that befall them. This belief develops a high level of sensitivity to what other people think and feel, and of concern about living up to their expectations. The interaction between this traditional disposition and the face-to-face, small-group affectivity of the Jamaa helps to effect radical changes in African members' beliefs, attitudes, and behaviour.

The various ways in which Bantu African and Flemish Franciscan cultural traditions parallel each other enhance the Jamaa's capacity to alter the outlook of its priest as well as its lay members. To a degree that was not anticipated either by the priests or by the baba and mama, each of these groups brought to the movement a heritage that emphasized feeling, expressive symbolism, sensual mysticism, kinship-like conceptions of solidarity, and the spiritual meaning of encounter and union. Thus, in the Jamaa subculture these traditions meet and reinforce each other, eliciting from its members a sense of mutual recognition. In turn, this recognition is experienced as a sign of confirmation. Jamaa priests, baba and mama, all feel that the convergence of their Christianity and Africanicity is not only morally desirable, but also 'providential'.

Finally, the time and place in which the movement is set have influenced its transformative potential. We have already indicated that certain characteristics of the Jamaa grew out of the responses of its members to the turbulence and anomie of the post-Independence years. In these respects, the general social, economic, and political conditions of the country and of Katanga province have been precipitating factors in the formation of Jamaa ideology and its capacity to change attitudes. The urban-industrial milieu created by Union Minière's presence in Katanga has had a similar effect. Most Jamists are migrants from the Kasai hinterland. They have been attracted to South Katanga because of the work opportunities provided by the mining company and its subsidiaries. The lives established by these baba and mama are more physically and sociologically separated from their extended kinship system than those of any other comparably large group of Congolese. This displacement and distancing have sufficiently freed Jamists from their villages and clans to make them receptive to the new Jamaa 'way'.

The general climate of the Catholic Church in the Congo has also played a significant role in priming its members for the changes that the Jamaa has been able to effect. Although the movement began in the 'golden age' of colonialism in the Congo, it took root and grew during a period when the Catholic Church, like other non-indigenous institutions, was beginning to feel uneasiness and doubt about its role and policies in an African society. This malaise was heightened by the advent of Independence. The more local questioning in which the Congolese Church was engaged was amplified by Vatican Council II. On a world-wide level, the Council worked towards a reformulation of the Church's conception of the meaning of 'Mission' in modern times, and of the relationship between the universal Church and its particular forms of incarnation in different cultural traditions. Both the end of the colonial period and the *aggiornamento* of Vatican Council II helped to instill in Jamaa priests the motivation to search for a better understanding of both Christianity and Africanicity.

The transformative powers of the Jamaa notwithstanding, certain Bantu elements persist in the mentality of the movement's African membership. These are among the most deep-rooted and tenacious components of Bantu culture and social structure. We have shown that the Jamaa's system of beliefs and rites and the quality of interpersonal relations that it engenders reduce the anxiety and distrust inherent to the Bantu cosmic view. Yet, as Jamaa members' life histories and dreams reveal, their involvement in the movement does not totally or permanently dispel their apprehension about the harm that can be inflicted on them by humanly directed supernatural forces. Thus, the baba and mama maintain a certain vigilance and are periodically subject to attacks of spiritual anxiety, particularly those caused by their belief in the dangerous workings of dead ancestors.

The overweening importance of kinship in Bantu life is still visible in the movement's self-conception and in the relationships that the members establish with Christ and Mary as well as with one another. Jamaa means family, and there is a real sense in which the entire movement can be seen as a spiritualized kinship network that extends from the husband–wife relationship to Christ and the Virgin. All the relationships in the movement are copies of the kinship model, as the terms of address baba, mama, and *mwana* (child) indicate. There are, however, two significant ways in which the Jamaa has refocused traditional kinship patterns. It gives predominance to the conjugal family unit, especially the husband–wife relationship, and it redefines the bases of kinship so as to include spiritual as well as biological kin.

Despite the universalistic tendency in the Jamaa to broaden the conception of kinship beyond one's own family, clan, and tribe, traditional forms of particularism persist in the movement. Tribalism has not completely vanished, and there is still a recognized need to preach against it, manifest in Jamaa parables and *mafundisho*. It could even be claimed that the movement has generated a new form of tribalism of its own: the 'super-Jamaa' sense of identity and solidarity, and conviction of superiority to all non-Jamists.

A persistent question about the movement raised by social scientists and interested onlookers as well as by Catholic clergy and church officials is: How Catholic is the Jamaa? An obvious cause for this question is the deviations that are so troubling to church authorities and to many members of the movement. Although these deviations have attracted a great deal of attention, they are not as problematic either doctrinally or ideologically, as some other Jamaa tendencies. For the deviations are clearly not consonant with Catholic belief and practice; they are unambiguously rooted in Bantu culture; and they can be diagnosed as structured departures from approved cultural patterns in that tradition.

There are other Jamaa patterns that pose more subtle problems about the conformity of the movement with established Catholic doctrine and praxis. One of the most conspicuous of these is the emphasis that the Jamaa places on loving one's fellow woman as well as fellow man, and on the religious significance of human encounters between lay persons and priests. In the African and Franciscan setting in which the Jamaa has unfolded, this encounter-in-love has an erotic dimension even when marital fidelity and celibacy are perfectly maintained. A haunting preoccupation of those who belong to the Jamaa or know it well is whether this sensuality is truly spiritual, reconcilable with mystical Catholic traditions, compatible with priestly celibacy, and acceptable within the framework of orthodoxy. No easy answer has been found. Resolving it is made difficult by the supreme importance of love in the Christian message, the acknowledged interrelationship between the love of God and the love of man as stated in the first and second commandments, and by the official Church's acceptance of sensual mysticism as integral to the Franciscan charisma and to the lives of many canonized saints.

Finally, there is a pattern in the Jamaa belief system that implicitly challenges the foundation of Christianity and its Old Testament origins. This is the virtual absence of God the Father in the movement's teachings. He is all but eclipsed by the Christ-and-Mary couple. It is curious that the Catholic Church has failed to take notice of the extent to which Jamaa conceptions of Christ and Mary dominate in this respect. The overshadowing of God the Father to this degree by His Son and the Virgin Mother is contrary to biblical tradition. It symbolically weakens Christianity's ultimate religious reference to a Yahweh-like supreme authority and, by according almost co-equal status to Christ and Mary, it elevates the feminine principle in Catholicism to one of parity with its traditionally predominant masculinity.

Many of the ways in which the official Church has responded to the Jamaa do not conform either to common assumptions about how this Ecclesia is structured and functions, or to conceptions in social organizational theory about the essential properties of such a highly formal, rational, centralized, and authoritarian bureaucracy. However routinized, in Weberian terms, the Church may be, it remains committed to its charismatic origins and traditions. Some of the structural strains involved in combining charismatic with rational-legal values and norms are visible in the Church's manner of dealing with the Jamaa. Church authorities felt that their offices as well as their faith obliged them to exert some disciplinary control over the movement, particularly with respect to its deviations. At the same time, most church authorities have exhibited a great deal of sociological ambivalence about intervening in this way. Both in public and in private, they have prefaced almost all their written and spoken commentary on the Jamaa with praise for the charismatic inspiration and renewal that the movement represents. These statements are genuine expressions of their collective belief in the importance of the charismatic dimension in religious life, and in its more than human source. They also contain the shared recognition that, however threatening it may be to established ways and vested interests, even as powerfully entrenched and orthodox an organization as the Catholic Church must continually undergo some degree of renovation and adaptation if it is to remain credible as well as viable.

In its reactions to the Jamaa the Church has not exhibited the unwavering certainty about its doctrinal position or its organizational policy that stereotype views about this kind of bureaucracy would lead one to expect. On every level of the organization discussion, debate, soul-searching, and vacillation have occurred. This has been as characteristic of the highest church authorities as of other echelons. Furthermore, this very study is both an expression and a consequence of the systematic doubting and searching in which the Church has been engaged. Thus, the means that the Church has used to achieve greater enlightenment about the Jamaa have included social scientific research, as well as prayer and the gathering of personal opinions from laity and clergy alike.

In its deliberations about the movement, the Church has proved to be less monolithic than even knowledgeable observers generally suppose. There is a real structural and moral sense in which, as the saying goes, 'all roads lead to Rome'. The Church is a pyramid with the Roman institution of the papacy at the top. And the ultimate authority on matters of faith and morals resides in this office in collaboration with the *collegium* of bishops. The summoning of Tempels before the Holy Office is a classic example of the exercise of this massively centralized and hierarchical authority and power by the Roman Curia. However, it was an exceptional occurrence in the history of the way the Church has dealt with the Jamaa, and the ultimate jurisdiction over Tempels's fate has come to rest in the religious superior of the province of his Order rather than in papal or episcopal officeholders. The picture of the way in which the Catholic Church operates that has emerged from this study is of a hierarchy that nevertheless contains and accommodates a series of collectivities which have carefully circumscribed but considerable discretion and autonomy. This feature of the Church has been dramatically illustrated by the interaction between Rome and the Franciscan Order over the case of Tempels and by Rome's recurrent insistence on the fact that the local bishops rather than the Curia should take responsibility for handling and trying to resolve the problems of the Jamaa.

In the case of the Jamaa, as with numerous other church matters, the establishment in the early 1960s of National Episcopal Conferences has reinforced this tendency to delegate certain functions with accompanying authority to specialized centres within the Ecclesia. In fact, the National Secretariat of the Congo's Bishops Conference played a critical role in persuading local bishops in Katanga and Kasai to assume responsibility for the Jamaa rather than refer it to Rome as they were predisposed to do. Thus, instead of decreasing local responsibility, as organizational theory might have predicted, the addition of a new bureaucratic layer to the structure of the Church has enhanced it.

It has become apparent that, like any other social organization, the Church relies heavily on informal as well as formal mechanisms of communication and social control. What is particularly striking here is the degree to which the Church uses structured ambiguity to impose discipline and implement policy. To this day, for example, it is not clear exactly what decision the Holy Office reached in the case of Tempels, or whether they subsequently altered it. We have only elaborately evasive oral statements made by senior church officials and a cryptic message in the Vatican newspaper about Tempels's status. This ambiguity made it possible for disciplinary action to be taken against him and to be maintained in such a way that it cannot be directly attributed to the Roman Curia. Whether such sociological ambiguity and the consequences that ensue from it are deliberately engineered or unintended is an unresolved issue.

Bibliography

ANON. 'Le Père Placide Tempels s'explique.' *La Voix de Saint Antoine*, no. 6 (Sept. 1967), 5–14.

BANQUE NATIONALE DU CONGO. *Rapport annuel 1967*. Kinshasa, 1968.

BARRETT, DAVID B. *Schism and Renewal in Africa*. Nairobi: Oxford University Press, 1968.

BOONE, OLGA. *Carte ethnique du Congo: Quart Sud-Est*. Tervuren: Musée Royal de l'Afrique Centrale, 1961.

BRAEKMAN, E. M. *Histoire du protestantisme au Congo*. Brussels: Éditions de la Librairie des Éclaireurs Unionistes, 1961.

BRASS, WILLIAM, et al. *The Demography of Tropical Africa*. Princeton, N.J.: Princeton University Press, 1968.

Centre de Recherche et d'Information Socio-Politiques. *Morphologie des groupes financiers*. Brussels: CRISP, 2nd edition, 1966.

CHARLES, PIERRE. 'Note relative à l'ouvrage du R.P. Tempels, intitulé 'La Philosophie bantoue''.' *Bulletin des Séances*, Institut Royal Colonial Belge, no. 2 (1946), 524–32.

DE CRAEMER, WILLY. *Analyse sociologique de la Jamaa*. Léopoldville: Centre de Recherches Sociologiques, 1965.

—— and FOX, RENÉE C. *The Emerging Physician*. Stanford: The Hoover Institution, 1967.

—— 'The Jamaa Movement in the Katanga and Kasai Regions of the Congo.' *Review of Religious Research*, 10, no. 1 (Fall 1968), 11–23.

—— VANSINA, JAN, and FOX, RENÉE C., 'Religious Movements in Central Africa: A Theoretical Study.' *Comparative Studies in Society and History*, 18, no. 4 (Oct. 1976), 458–75.

DENIS, JACQUES. 'Élisabethville: matériaux pour une étude de la population africaine.' *Bulletin trimestriel du Centre d'Étude des Problèmes Sociaux Indigènes*, no. 34 (1956), 137–95.

DE WAELE, FRANK, 'La catéchèse dans les Jamaas à Léopoldville.' Kinshasa, 1965. Unpublished manuscript.

DOUGLAS, MARY. *Purity and Danger*. New York: Frederick A. Praeger, 1966.

FABIAN, JOHANNES. 'Dream and charisma: "Theories of dreams" in the Jamaa movement (Congo).' *Anthropos*, 61 (1966), 544–60.

—— *Jamaa: A Charismatic Movement in Katanga*. Evanston, Ill.: Northwestern University Press, 1971.

FORTES, MEYER, and DIETERLEN, GERMAINE, eds. *African Systems of Thought*. London: Oxford University Press, 1965.

Fox, Renée C. 'The Intelligence Behind the Mask.' Unpublished paper, 1968.

—— De Craemer, Willy, and Ribeaucourt, Jean-Marie. ' "The Second Independence": A Case Study of the Kwilu Rebellion in the Congo.' *Comparative Studies in Society and History*, 8, no. 1 (Oct. 1965), 78–109.

Gérard, O. 'Un cas remarquable d'adaptation féconde en Afrique: La "Jamaa".' *Le Christ au monde*, IX, no. 1 (1964), 18–36; no. 2 (1964), 129–42.

Gérard-Libois, Jules. *Katanga Secession*, trans. Rebecca Young. Madison: The University of Wisconsin Press, 1966.

Goffman, Erving. *Asylums: Essays on the Social Situation of Mental Patients and Other Inmates*. Garden City, N.Y.: Doubleday Anchor Books, 1961.

Hauger, George. *Michel de Ghelderode: 7 Plays*. New York: Hill and Wang, 1964.

Hodgkin, Thomas. *Nationalism in Colonial Africa*. London: F. Muller, 1956.

Horton, Robin. 'African Traditional Thought and Western Science.' *Africa*, 37, no. 2 (Apr. 1967), 50–71; no. 3 (May 1967), 155–87.

Janssen, Th. M. 'Religious encounter and the "Jamaa".' *The Heythrop Journal*, VIII, no. 2 (Apr. 1967), 129–51.

Lou, Dom. *Souvenirs et Pensées*. Bruges: Desclée De Brouwer, 1945. (Trans. Michael Derrick, *Ways of Confucius and of Christ*, London: Burns & Oates, 1948.)

MacGaffey, Wyatt. 'Religious Movement in Zaïre.' *African Studies Review*, XIV, no. 3 (Dec. 1971), 517–19.

Mauss, Marcel. *The Gift*, trans. J. Cunnison. Glencoe, Ill.: Free Press, 1954.

Ministère des Colonies. *Plan décennal pour le développement économique et social du Congo Belge*. Brussels: Les Éditions De Visscher, 1949.

Molinski, Waldemar. 'Integralism.' *Sacramentum Mundi: An Encyclopedia of Theology*, ed. Karl Rahner et al. New York: Herder and Herder, 1969, III, 151–2.

Mottoulle, L. *Politique sociale de l'Union Minière du Haut-Katanga pour sa main-d'œuvre indigène et ses résultats au cours de vingt années d'application*. Brussels: Institut Royal Colonial Belge, 1946.

Mukendi, Placide. 'La Jamaa et son avenir.' *Revue du clergé africain*, XXVI, no. 2 (Mar. 1971), 142–68.

Mukenge, Godefroid. *Le Christ parmi les Africains: Essai autour de la spiritualité Jamaa*. Luluabourg, 1968.

Mukenge, Léonard. 'Croyances religieuses et structures socio-familiales en société luba: "Buena Muntu", "Bakishi", "Milambu".' *Cahiers économiques et sociaux*, V, no. 1 (Mar. 1967), 3–94.

188 BIBLIOGRAPHY

MULAGO, VINCENT, and THEUWS, T. *Autour du mouvement de la 'Jamaa'.* Léopoldville: Centre d'Études Pastorales, 1960.

NEUT, ÉDOUARD. *Jean Jacques Lou: Dom Lou.* Brussels: Éditions Synthèses, nos. 192–3, 1962.

NOTHOMB, DOMINIQUE. 'Une nouvelle forme de catéchèse.' *Nouvelle Revue théologique*, 86, no. 7 (July–Aug. 1964), 725–43.

O'BRIEN, CONOR CRUISE. *To Katanga and Back: A U.N. Case History.* New York: Grosset and Dunlap, 1962.

PARSONS, ANNE. *Belief, Magic and Anomie.* New York: The Free Press, 1969.

PARSONS, TALCOTT. 'Christianity', *International Encyclopedia of the Social Sciences*, ed. David L. Sills (1968), 2, 425–47.

—— 'On the Concept of Value-Commitments.' *Sociological Inquiry*, 38, no. 2 (Spring 1968), 135–60.

—— and PLATT, GERALD M. 'Some Considerations on the American Academic Profession.' *Minerva*, VI, no. 4 (Summer 1968), 497–523.

PERITUS, 'L'Église face à la scandaleuse Jamaa.' *Le Monde et la vie*, no. 155 (Apr. 1966), 24–5, 62–3.

PIROTTE, JEAN. 'Une expérience chrétienne au Congo.' *Neue Zeitschrift für Missionswissenschaft*, XXIV, no. 4 (1968), 282–92.

POSSOZ, E. *Éléments de droit coutumier nègre.* Élisabethville: Lovania, 1943.

—— 'Études claniques.' *Revue juridique du Congo*, 41ᵉ, no. spécial (1964), 215–33.

ROBERT, MAURICE. *Contribution à la géographie du Katanga.* Brussels: Institut Royal Colonial Belge, 1954.

RUBBENS, ANTOINE, ed. *Dettes de guerre.* Élisabethville: Éditions de l'Essor du Congo, 1945.

RYCKMANS, PIERRE. *La Politique coloniale.* Brussels: Éditions Rex, 1934.

—— *Étapes et Jalons.* Brussels: Ferdinand Larcier, 1946.

—— *Dominer pour servir.* Brussels: Édition Universelle, 1948.

SOHIER, A. *Le Mariage en droit coutumier congolais.* Brussels: Institut Royal Colonial Belge, Mémoires, XI, no. 3, 1943.

—— 'La politique d'intégration.' *Zaïre*, V, no. 9 (Nov. 1951), 899–928.

SOMERS, E. 'Causerie sur la Jamaa.' *Revue du clergé africain*, XXI (Nov. 1966), 571–81.

TANNER, R. E. S. 'The Jamaa Movement in the Congo: A Sociological Comment on Some Religious Interpretations.' *The Heythrop Journal*, IX, no. 2 (Apr. 1968), 164–78.

TAYLOR, JOHN V. *The Primal Vision.* London: S.C.M. Press, 1965.

TEMPELS, PLACIDE. *Catéchèse bantoue.* Bruges: Abbaye de St André, 1948.

—— *La Philosophie bantoue*, trans. A. Rubbens. Paris: Présence africaine, 1961.

—— *Notre Rencontre*. Léopoldville: Centre d'Études Pastorales, 1962.

—— 'Le Renouveau communautaire.' Unpublished paper, 1967.

THEUWS, T. 'Philosophie bantoue et philosophie occidentale.' *Civilisations*, 1, no. 3 (1951), 54–63.

—— 'Le réel dans la conception luba.' *Zaïre*, XV, no. 1 (1961), 3–49.

—— *De Luba mens*. Tervuren: Musée Royal de l'Afrique Centrale, 1962.

—— 'Le Styx ambigu.' *Bulletin trimestriel du Centre d'Étude des Problèmes Sociaux Indigènes*, no. 81 (1968), 3–33.

TIMMERMANS, FELIX. *The Christ Child in Flanders*. Chicago: Henry Regnery, 1961.

TURNER, VICTOR W. 'Symbols in African Ritual.' *Science*, 179 (16 Mar. 1973), 1100–5.

Union Minière du Haut-Katanga. *Union Minière du Haut-Katanga: 1906–1956*. Brussels: L. Cuypers, 1956.

—— *Monographie 1958*. Brussels: Éditions IVAC, 1958.

VANHOVE, J. 'L'œuvre d'éducation au Congo Belge et au Ruanda-Urundi.' *Encyclopédie du Congo Belge*. Brussels: Éditions Bieleveld, 1953, III. 749–89.

VANSINA, JAN. *Introduction à l'ethnographie du Congo*. Brussels: Éditions Universitaires du Congo, 1965.

—— *Kingdoms of the Savanna*. Madison: University of Wisconsin Press, 1966.

—— 'Religions et sociétés en Afrique Centrale.' *Cahiers des Religions Africaines*, 2, no. 3 (Jan. 1968), 95–107.

VAN WING, JOSEPH. 'Quelques aspects de la situation sociale des indigènes au Kasai et au Katanga.' *Bulletin des Séances*. Institut Royal Colonial Belge, no. 1 (1948), 111–35.

—— *Études Bakongo*. Brussels: Desclée De Brouwer, 1959, 2nd edn.

WETTER, FRIEDRICH. 'Franciscan Theology', in *Sacramentum Mundi: An Encyclopedia of Theology*, ed. Karl Rahner *et al*. New York: Herder and Herder, 1968, II. 346–9.

YOUNG, CRAWFORD. *Politics in the Congo*. Princeton, N.J.: Princeton University Press, 1965.

Index

Abel, 77–9, 144
Adam, 59, 77, 79. *See also* original sin
adaptation, concept of, 18 f., 22 f., 151
Analyse sociologique de la Jamaa, 7 f., 158–60
André, Baba, 110 f.

baba and mama, 6, 9, 48, 50 f., 60, 67 f., 71–4, 87, 89, 115, 118, 138, 141–5, 171, 175 f., 178 f., 181; relationship with one another, 58 f., 103–5, 107–9, 111, 115; relationship with priests, 63–5, 75, 86, 139, 146
Bakole, Martin-Leonard, 167–9
Bantu: beliefs and cultural traditions, 24, 27–9, 84–9, 94, 97, 100–2, 108, 114, 116–8, 176, 180–2; taboos, 80. *See also* kinship
baptism, 17 f., 61
Barrett, David, 1
Bonaventure, Father, 122, 128–31, 172

Cain, 77–9, 144
Cardijn, Joseph Cardinal, 31 f., 35, 134, 152, 155
Centre de Recherches Sociologiques, 3–6, 8, 147, 158
Charles, Pierre, 32
colonial administration, 16, 23, 46
Conakat, 46
Congolese Rebellion, 8, 93, 137
Cornelis, Floribert, 134 n., 145–7, 149 f., 154, 159

Damien, Father, 112 f.
Dell'Acqua, Angelo, 152
Dellepiane, Monsignor, 29 f.
De Winter, Xavier, 56, 135 n., 165, 172
Diop, Alioune, 26 f.
dreams, 85, 89, 93–7, 110 f.

encounter, concept of, 58 f., 62–4, 68 f., 71 f., 74, 87, 105 f., 111, 118, 124, 149, 173, 180, 182
Erik, Father, 122, 125 f., 128, 130–3, 171 f.

Eve, 59, 77–9. *See also* original sin
évolués, 22, 44

Fabian, Johannes, 2 f., 133 n.
fecundity, concept of, 22, 36, 38, 59, 73, 77, 79, 84, 87–9, 103
Flemish cultural tradition, 83 f., 85, 128, 177 f., 180
Fox, Renée C., 125 f.
Franciscan theology, 81 f.
Frans, Father, 34, 71, 75, 122, 124–7, 133, 166, 170 f.

Gérard, O., 156
gift-exchange, 25 f., 111, 178
Grandjean, M., 148 f., 151, 173

H., Abbé, 12 f.
Hemptinne, Félix de, 17, 29–31
Hodgkin, Thomas, 15
Holy Office, 136, 150–2, 154 f., 184 f.

Isimba, Tharcisse, 169

Jacques, Father, 126
Jamaa: attitude toward education, 113–15, 117, 178 f.; belief system, 57–65, 88 f., 181; economic attitudes and behaviour, 109–12, 178; deviations, 4, 6–8, 47, 66, 75–81, 85, 126 f., 137, 139–46, 150, 154, 156, 164–8, 170, 173, 182 (*see also* Katete); forms of address, 12, 182; impact on personality of members, 115 f., 179; impact on world-view of members, 116–19; initiation into, 5, 58 f., 66–75, 86, 89, 143, 159, 169; meetings, 50 f., 169; occupational stratification of members, 10, 49 f.; parent–child relationship, 108 f.; political attitudes of members, 112 f., 178 f.; rites, 57, 66–75, 80 f., 84–6, 89, 181; spirituality, 7 f., 114; symbolism, 82–103. *See also* baba and mama, *mafundisho*, and priests
Jerome, Father, 122, 125, 127–30, 172